A Natural History of the Romance Novel

A Natural History of the

Romance
Novel

PAMELA REGIS

University of Pennsylvania Press, Philadelphia

10 9 8 7 6 5 4 3 2 1

Published by
University of Pennsylvania Press
Philadelphia, Pennsylvania 19104-4011

Library of Congress Cataloging-in-Publication Data
Regis, Pamela.
   A natural history of the romance novel / Pamela Regis.
      p.   cm.
   Includes biliographical references and index.
   ISBN 0-8122-3303-4 (cloth : alk. paper)
      1. Love stories, English—History and criticism. 2. Love stories, American—History
and criticism. I. Title.
PR830.L69R445   2003
823'.08509—dc21   2002045412

For Edward

CONTENTS

Beth went out with Eric last night (as you may or may not know). I'm REALLY ANGRY (not at her, but at him) but of course he's not here and she is. I hate everything. I'm holding my breath.

—Handwritten on the flyleaf of a library copy
of *Pride and Prejudice*

PREFACE

The Most Popular, Least Respected
Literary Genre

This book defines the modern romance novel written in English and traces its development from 1740 through the 1990s. The definition and literary history of the romance novel will provide critics with a clearer understanding of the genre's nature and scope. They will also form the basis for a counterargument to the widespread disdain for and condemnation of this literary genre.

It is a commonplace in works about the romance novel to point to the genre's popularity. In the last year of the twentieth century, 55.9 percent of mass-market and trade paperbacks sold in North America were romance novels (Romance Writers of America, *Website*). In 1996 the genre generated approximately one billion dollars in sales of 182 million books. More than two thousand titles were released that year (Romance Writers of America, *Welcome*). These are astonishing figures. No other popular form—not mysteries, Westerns, science fiction, fantasy, thrillers, horror, or spy novels—is as popular. Nor is so-called "literary" fiction. Nor is nonfiction. Romances are the most popular books in the United States.

Popularity, however, does not mean acceptance. Writers of romance novels appear regularly on the *New York Times Book Review*'s Best Sellers List. During ten weeks in late 1997 Johanna Lindsey, Kaye Gibbons, Julie Garwood, Sandra Brown, Nora Roberts, Catherine Colter, Judith McNaught, and Jude Deveraux all made the list. During that same ten weeks the *Review* ran its crime column several times, in which Marilyn Stasio reviewed a short stack of mysteries; and once Gerald Jonas provided a similar service for science fiction. Yet the romance novel went unreviewed, despite its strong presence on the list, despite its dominance in the bookstores.

The newspaper of record simply reflects the usual lack of respect accorded to this genre in the larger culture. Women admit that they cover a romance novel if they are going to be reading in public—on an airplane or subway. They would not feel the need if the book were, say, a mystery.

There is also a widespread assumption that these books are easy to write. Any number of people have smilingly said to me that they are considering writing a romance novel. They often claim that they will do so—presumably from beginning to end—over the Christmas holidays. (I smile back, and tell them that they certainly should not let anything stand in their way.) Any novel that apparently can be produced this quickly fails to earn respect. Appearances, of course, are deceptive. It takes most romance writers just under a year to write a book (Romance Writers of America, *Website*).

This lack of respect results, in part, from a lack of understanding, both of the heroine herself and of the genre in which she appears. The heroine appeals largely to a female audience. The romance is the most female of popular genres. Nearly all of the writers and readers are women. Men have traditionally controlled which books get reviewed, and the effort that they must make to read across the gender barrier is very great. Women read across this barrier much more readily, the practice having been acquired early on in their reading lives. Jane Tompkins notes that in our culture "stories about men . . . function as stories about all people," so "women learn at an early age to identify with male heroes" (*West of Everything* 17). Many men lack this experience of reading across gender lines. Thus, romance novels resonate less readily with them. One male friend to whom I occasionally give romance novels usually cannot finish them because he claims that "nothing is happening." I typically finish the science fiction that he gives to me. I learned as an adolescent to identify with the heroes of science fiction novels. He had no corresponding practice with the heroines of romance novels. Our experience, I suspect, is not unique. It is difficult to understand a kind of literature that you do not read (although undergraduates attempt this feat in colleges everywhere).

Even female readers who (presumably) can identify with the heroine misunderstand the romance novel because they suffer from a flawed conception of what a romance novel is, or from a partial knowledge of the genre's history. As we shall see in Part I, the literary critics who level the most serious charges against the genre are women. Some of these critics make statements about "the romance" in such a way that the entire genre is characterized—negatively—by its association with a few texts that a critic mistakes as representative. Their conception of the range of the romance novel, of the true boundaries of the genre, is inadequate in that they mistake a part—a few texts—for the whole—for the entire genre. Other critics speak from an incomplete knowledge of the form itself. They focus on the ending to the exclusion of all other narrative events present in the romance novel.

In Part I of the text that follows, I review the critical response to the romance novel, focusing on the negative assessments, and especially on the argument that accuses the form of the romance novel itself of enslaving its readers. I then defend the form against these charges. In Part II, I define the romance novel and analyze its essential component parts. The definition lays out the set of narrative elements without which the work is not a romance novel of any kind. Identifying these essential elements—the core romance novel if you will—takes us to the heart of the genre; it permits us to understand a romance novel in terms of its key elements. From this understanding emerges a picture of the ideas that inform this most common of literary plots. From this definition we understand, too, how the novels work, how they achieve their effects upon readers. In Part III, I offer a partial remedy for critical ignorance of the genre's scope. Here I provide the first chronological look at the romance novel written in English from the explosive success of Samuel Richardson's *Pamela*, published in 1740, to E. M. Forster's *Room with a View* (1908). Part IV explores the genre's history in the twentieth century.

What emerges from this exploration are the virtues of the romance novel heretofore largely hidden from both mainstream literary culture and from most critics. The genre is not silly and empty-headed, as mainstream literary culture would have it. Quite the contrary—the romance novel contains serious ideas. The genre is not about women's bondage, as the literary critics would have it. The romance novel is, to the contrary, about women's freedom. The genre is popular because it conveys the pain, uplift, and joy that freedom brings.

PART I

CRITICS AND THE ROMANCE NOVEL

THE ROMANCE NOVEL AND WOMEN'S BONDAGE

More than any other literary genre, the romance novel has been misunderstood by mainstream literary culture—book review editors, reviewers themselves, writers and readers of other genres, and, especially, literary critics. Deborah Kaye Chappel has characterized critical response to the romance novel as a "dogged insistence on containment and reduction" (5). Even the most cursory survey of criticism of this genre yields a ringing condemnation of it: critical characterization of the romance novel is overwhelmingly negative. The titles alone of critical works on the genre attest to widely based censure. Romance novels are badly written: consult Rachel Anderson's *The Purple Heart Throbs: The Sub-literature of Love.* These novels are schlock: Julia Bettinotti and Pascale Noizet title their book *Guimauves et fleurs d'oranger* (Insipid novels and orange blossoms). They are capitalist tools: read Paul Grescoe's *Merchants of Venus: Inside Harlequin and the Empire of Romance.* While a reader's rejection of the romance novel merely reflects her taste, a critic's published rejection is supposed to be the result of analysis based on clear reasoning and sufficient evidence. The critic's condemnation, especially when it is shared by a number of other critics, stands as a plausible evaluation of the genre unless it is answered.

Critical rejection of the romance novel emanated from the wave of feminism that arose in the 1960s. Germaine Greer, one of the leaders of that movement, inaugurated the modern criticism of the romance novel in 1970, striking a theme that becomes a commonplace in subsequent criticism—that of the romance novel as an enslaver of women: "The traits invented for [the hero in romance novels] have been invented by women cherishing the chains of their bondage. . . . Such . . . creatures [heroes of this type] do not exist, but very young women in the astigmatism of sexual fantasy are apt to recognize them where they do not exist" (176). Earlier criticism of the romance novel had also found the genre lacking, but fell short of attacking it as an enslaver. In *Pamela's Daughters,* Robert Palfrey Utter and Gwendolyn Bridges Needham mix objective literary historical research with a dismissive tone as they survey heroines from the eighteenth century to the twentieth. At no point, however, do they accuse the novels of enslaving the reader. Greer is the first to accuse the romance novel of putting the reader in bondage, and her charge echoes through subsequent critical condemnations.

Critics line up to condemn Harlequin Romances, a series of short romance novels issued monthly. Like other novels marketed as easily recognizable brands, they are known as "categories." Their popularity surged in the 1970s, and they have remained a vigorous part of the market, often serving as a training ground for writers who go on to write longer, more complex books. Of these shorter books, Tania Modleski concluded in her 1982 study, "The heroine of the novels can achieve happiness only by undergoing a complex process of self-subversion, during which she sacrifices her aggressive instincts . . . and—nearly—her life" (*Loving with a Vengeance* 37). For Modleski, the heroine's bondage (and presumably the reader's as well) is self-imposed. Leslie W. Rabine claims: "[Harlequins] work to recuperate women's subversive fantasies into structures of patriarchal power" (188). Here the chains of the reader's mental bondage are forged by the male-dominated society. Keya Ganguly sees the reader's bondage as political. For her, certain themes in romance novels "bolster the New Right's colonizing of 'family' values and the reactionary articulation of morality as inhering in monogamy, motherhood and heterosexuality." Thus these novels reflect the "heterosexist family ideology of our culture" (144). Looking again at Harlequins, Susan Ostrov Weisser sees the bondage operating on an interpersonal level: "The good heroine and her wonderful/terrible rival push or clash against one another but never talk to each other about their situation with anything like interest or curiosity, never work together to accomplish a goal, never imagine for each other the possibility of a female-female relation outside a narrative centered on a man as the coveted prize" (278). These critics would have it that Harlequins reinforce what Greer called "bondage" on any number of levels.

Other critics, when they shift their sights to romance novels other than Harlequins, still condemn the genre. Kay Mussell finds a reinforcement of the traditional feminine role: "[T]he essential assumptions of romance formulas—belief in the primacy of love in a woman's life, female passivity in romantic relationships, support for monogamy in marriage, reinforcement of domestic values—have not faded." For her, these novels fail "to elaborate mature and triumphant models for female life beyond marriage, motherhood, and femininity"(Fantasy 189). For Jan Cohn, "[t]he deep flaw of romance fiction . . . lies in the ultimate failure of romance to provide, even in fantasy, a satisfying answer to the problem of women's powerlessness" (176). For Jeanne Dubino, readers of these books use them to fill an emptiness in their lives: "Not finding what they want in 'real' life, millions of women turn to romances in a vicarious attempt to compensate for the lack of attention and validation they get in their own lives" (107). Anne Cranny-Francis, interested in the feminist use of a variety of popular literary forms, explains why the romance novel is the most difficult genre to turn to feminist ends: "Romantic fiction . . . encodes the most coherent inflection of the discourses of gender, class and race constitutive of the contemporary social order; it encodes the bourgeois fairy-tale" (192). In their claims that romance novels are directed at female "passivity" (Mussell) and "powerlessness" (Cohn), that they "compensate" for the deficiencies of real life (Dubino), or that they "encode the bourgeois fairy-tale" (Cranny-Francis), these critics reduce romance readers to a state of childlike helplessness, and the novels themselves to the sort of books that such children read. These critics of the romance novel would have it that Greer's "bondage" is, for romance heroines and readers, manifested by a (reading) life shaped by infantile fairy tales.

Some of the charges critics make against the romance novel are based on faulty reasoning. Many critics who conclude that the romance novel enslaves its readers are guilty of hasty generalization. Their evidence is scant given the breadth of the conclusions they offer. Consider three prominent studies of romance novels published in the 1980s. Mariam Darce Frenier in *Good-Bye Heathcliff* read category romances published from 1979 through 1987 to chart the changing power of the romance heroine and to discover what this change might "tell us . . . about white American women's fear or acceptance of feminism and feminists" (4). Radway in *Reading the Romance*, the single most influential work on the romance novel, examined a lone group of romance readers who favored one subgenre of the romance novel—the sensual long historical—yet she drew broad conclusions about "the romance-reading process" on that basis alone (215). Modleski in *Loving with a Vengeance* read Harlequins (along with gothics and soap operas) and on that evidence drew sweeping conclusions about what constitutes "narrative pleasure for women" (32).

Each of these three critics examines a narrow segment of the late twentieth-century romance novel market to draw her conclusions. Frenier reads only category romances published during a nine-year period. Radway is widely quoted as the expert on romance novels, yet her book focuses on one narrow segment of the twentieth-century market, the sensual long historical, and then she examines only twenty of those titles identified as "ideal" by the group of readers she chose to study. Modleski's examination is limited to Harlequins; she cites just nine of them. Yet these critics make conclusions about the romance genre as a whole or about an unacceptably broad section of it. Frenier speaks of the "newer romance" in her conclusion (105). Radway's conclusion, like her title, specifies "the" romance (215). Although Modleski confines her conclusions to the Harlequins she has read, other critics make the leap to "the romance" as a whole when they use her conclusions. These authors of three of the founding texts in the criticism of the romance novel all generalize hastily.

The error continues, as two more recent articles from the next generation of critics of the romance novel demonstrate. Ganguly, exploring the politics of "resistant readings of hegemonic texts," cites just seven Harlequins, which she describes as "typical romance novels" and from which she draws sweeping conclusions (143). Weisser, exploring the "bitch" figure in Harlequins, cites only two romances, yet she makes claims about "the plot of *the* Harlequin novel" (278, emphasis added). The practice of these critics reflects the widespread assumption that a very small sample of contemporary works can yield conclusions applicable to a whole range of romance novels. The 1992 reprinting of a chapter from Modleski's *Loving with a Vengeance* implies, as well, that generalizations made about the older books still apply to recent ones. Hasty generalization has become something of a habit among critics of the romance novel.

Out of this error arises condemnation. Critics mistake the romance novel's effects because they do not know, precisely, what a romance novel is. They equate the genre as a whole with a formula (a subset of the larger genre) or they identify it in terms of incidental elements, such as the sex scenes (which are widespread but not essential in a romance novel). This impoverished view of the genre results, in part, from a narrow acquaintance with it: critics misunderstand the extent and significance of the genre's literary history. They generalize hastily from a small group of texts to the genre as a whole.

In a genre as old, as flexible, and as ill defined as the romance novel, it is, perhaps, understandable that many critics would mistake a few texts as representative of the whole. The repeated commission of this simple logical error is a barometer of critics' disdain for their subject matter, but the romance is not the first form to be disdained and misunderstood by critics. Indeed, the novel itself suffered this dismissive attitude for most of the two centuries of its popularity.

If this error—hasty generalization—were the only problem with criticism of the romance novel, the corrective would be a more comprehensive examination of carefully chosen representatives of the genre. Indeed, I undertake this examination in Parts III and IV. But the critics make a second mistake: they attack the romance novel for its happy ending in marriage. This claim is not a product of hasty generalization because the happy ending in marriage (or in betrothal, the promise of marriage) is a formal feature of every romance novel. If the genre really deserves the respect of critics, and I think it does, then this attack must be examined and answered.

2

In Defense of the Romance Novel

Romance novels end happily. Readers insist on it. The happy ending is the one formal feature of the romance novel that virtually everyone can identify. This element is not limited to a narrow range of texts: a marriage—promised or actually dramatized—ends every romance novel. Ironically, it is this universal feature of the romance novel that elicits the fiercest condemnation from its critics. The marriage, they claim, enslaves the heroine, and, by extension, the reader. In this argument the heroine's quest—which is to say her adventures, vicissitudes, or the events that she confronts in the course of the narrative—is at odds with the novel's ending, namely, the heroine's union with the hero. This view is widespread among critics, and in Part III we will see versions of it applied to texts such as *Pamela* and *Jane Eyre* from commentators as different as Terry Eagleton and Wayne Booth. Here I wish to explore the argument in principle—in its most general version, which damns all romance novels because they are romance novels.

Rachael Blau DuPlessis, writing about nineteenth-century novels, offers the best statement of the argument criticizing the ending in marriage. Janice Radway applies this argument to the twentieth-century popular, mass-market romance novel. DuPlessis explains the effect of the romance novel's ending in marriage: "As a narrative pattern, the romance plot muffles the main female character, represses quest . . . [and] incorporates individuals within couples as a sign of their personal and narrative success. The romance plot separates love and quest . . . is based on extremes of sexual difference, and evokes an aura around the couple itself" (5). DuPlessis claims that quest and love within these books are in conflict. She asserts that the marriage plot "with difficulty revokes" the quest portion of the narrative: "the female characters are human subjects at loose in the world, ready for decision, growth, self-definition, community, insight. In the novels that end in marriage . . . there is a contradiction between two middle-class ideas—gendered feminine, the sanctified home, and gendered human, the liberal bourgeois ideology of the self-interested choice of the individual agent" (14). To accomplish the marriage that is the goal of the marriage plot, the female protagonist chooses the "gendered feminine," the role of wife in the marriage. For her, quest is over.

Radway's observations of the "social and material situation within which romance reading occurs" echo DuPlessis's descriptions of the nineteenth-century romance. Like DuPlessis, Radway finds the ending of romance novels troublesome. For her the "ending of the romance undercuts the realism of its novelistic rendering of an individual woman's story" and so "reaffirms its founding culture's belief that women are valuable not for their unique personal qualities but for their biological sameness and their ability to perform that essential role of maintaining and reconstituting others" (208).

Both of these critics find that what DuPlessis calls "quest" and what Radway calls the heroines' "idiosyncratic histories" are destroyed by the ending (Radway 209). In this view, the ending in effect cancels out the narrative that has gone before, at least the elements of the narrative that depict a heroine as quester, as the participant in and creator of her unique history. Both the heroine and readers of such books are bound by them into marriage.

These two major charges made against the romance novel are accepted by the critical community at large. Critics claim that the romance novel

- extinguishes its own heroine, confining her within a story that ignores the full range of her concerns and abilities ("muffles the main female character") and denies her independent goal-oriented action outside of love and marriage ("quest," "idiosyncratic histories")
- binds readers in their marriages or encourages them to get married: it equates marriage with success and glorifies sexual difference.

In this view the romance novel straightjackets the heroine by making marriage the barometer of her success. Its ending destroys the independent, questing woman depicted in the rest of the story. In depicting a heroine thus destroyed, the romance novel sends a message to readers that independent, questing women are actually better off destroyed. When the novel destroys its heroine, it urges its readers to become imprisoned—it urges them to marry—or it locks them ever more securely in the prison of the marriage they are already in.

Because this charge claims that the form of the romance novel genre—its ending in marriage—extinguishes the heroine and binds the reader, every romance novel by virtue of its being a romance novel has these powers to extinguish and bind. If this argument is right, *Pride and Prejudice,* for instance, an acknowledged work of genius, must, because it is a romance novel, extinguish Elizabeth Bennet and bind its readers. I intend the whole of the present work to stand as a refutation of this claim. Here I would like to outline the general shape of that refutation.

My response to critics is, in part, that this complaint about the ending of the romance novel is more nearly a complaint about ending itself than a complaint about a given kind of ending. Narratives end. Ulysses returns to Ithaca. Tennyson finds the pathos in that return: "How dull it is to pause, to make an end" ("Ulysses," line 22). The *Odyssey*'s reader is nonetheless glad to see the hero return home to Penelope. Homer's reader rejoices that clever Ulysses has evaded and outsmarted the various creatures, gods, and natural disasters that for ten years have impeded his return from Troy. So, too, do readers of romance novels rejoice when the heroine evades and outsmarts the people and events in the novel that are in the way of her marriage and when, like Ulysses, she cheats fate and is free to choose the hero. At the end of the *Odyssey* we hear no more of Ulysses. His quest is over. So, too, is a romance heroine's quest at the end of a romance novel. But just as Ulysses is not "extinguished," neither is the romance heroine. Her narrative, like that of Ulysses, has simply ended.

Romance writers look at the conclusion of the heroine's quest and see victory. Linda Barlow and Jayne Ann Krentz assert, "[A]s the romance novel ends . . . [t]he heroine's quest is won" (20). In the last chapter of *Pride and Prejudice,* Darcy's sister notes with some alarm Elizabeth's "lively, sportive manner of talking to her brother" (345). Elizabeth Bennet has not been extinguished, despite her becoming Mrs. Darcy. In *Pamela* the eponymous heroine must confront the members of her husband's community, which has become Pamela's community as well, who disapprove of her marriage. This she does with energy and audacity to the applause of her new husband

and the horror of the old society that her marriage rousts from its staid assumptions about who should marry whom. Far from being extinguished, Pamela becomes more powerful and active after her marriage. Novels end, including romance novels. We imagine that heroines go on, even if we do not see them do so.

Part of the claim about the extinguished heroine is that, whatever the nature of the ending—defeat or victory for the heroine—the romance novel ignores the full range of the heroine's concerns and abilities. Yet this claim, like the complaint about the "extinguished" heroine, might be made about almost any protagonist of almost any genre. If *Pride and Prejudice* alludes to, but does not explore in detail, Elizabeth's intellectual development through her reading and study of music, then *Moby-Dick* alludes to, but does not explore in detail, Ahab's life on shore, where his sea-going skills, much in evidence in the novel, would be eclipsed by whatever landsman's abilities he may or may not have possessed. Art is selective. No protagonist is presented as fully as she or he might be. True, some romance novels once depicted women who did little except wait to be married. This has never been the usual sort of romance heroine, and by the early 1980s, almost all romance novels, no matter how modest, depicted women who had active careers, and who kept them after they married. Heroines in even the most modest popular romance novels are social workers, linguists, journalists, caterers, entrepreneurs, public relations people, horse trainers, ranchers, screenwriters, veterinarians, teachers, detectives, and so on.

Critics claim that in equating marriage with success for the heroine, the romance novel reconciles readers, who are overwhelmingly women, to marriage which keeps women subservient. And it is not just the plot of the romance novel, but its form that reconciles women to marriage. This is a very strong statement of this genre's power to compel its readers. This claim has two versions—one quite sweeping, the other more circumspect, but ultimately more damaging.

First, the sweeping claim. In her conclusions, Radway spells out what the romance novel ought to be doing instead of "reaffirm[ing] its founding culture's belief that women are valuable . . . for their biological sameness and their ability to perform that essential role of maintaining and reconstituting others" (208). Romance reading, Radway opines, "gives the reader a strategy for making her present situation more comfortable without substantive reordering of its structure *rather than a comprehensive program for reorganizing her life in such a way that all needs might be met*" (215, emphasis added). This statement rests on the assumption that literature can provide a "comprehensive program for reorganizing" the life of the reader. To take this assumption literally, we must imagine a novel providing, through its form or through its content, a "program" for reorganizing readers' lives. Has any book ever done this? Certain novels of ideas come to mind as possible candidates. *Uncle Tom's Cabin* contributed mightily to the abolition of slavery. *1984* remains a strong argument against totalitarianism. Certain books with charismatic protagonists inspire readers to pursue certain professions. Harper Lee's *To Kill a Mockingbird* has sent some of its readers to law school. James Herriot's *All Creatures Great and Small* has undoubtedly inspired some of its readers to become veterinarians. Any number of books motivate readers to become teachers. But none of these books can be said to lay out a comprehensive program.

Radway's criticism of the romance novel is a criticism of its form: the ending is the culprit. Can the form of a novel accomplish, or, as Radway claims, thwart, a "comprehensive program for reorganizing" the reader's life? Of course not. Literary forms do not have this power. Readers are free to ignore, skip, stop, disbelieve, dislike, reject, and otherwise read quite independently of the form. Readers of a given genre often read with another genre in mind. Female readers have done this for generations. For example, many have read science fiction with romance novel conventions in mind, attending hard to the romantic subplot and skimming the adventure or journey that provides the primary structure of the book. Some men begin to read romance novels and abandon them, claiming that "nothing is happening." They have a different set of generic expectations in mind. True, form shapes reading. It creates a certain set of expectations in a reader who is in tune with the form. But because readers are free, form cannot compel the aesthetic, intellectual, or psychological belief in those expectations. Thus, the strongest version of the claim that these books are powerful enough to relegate women to patriarchy and marriage is simply not true.

This leaves the second, more circumspect claim about the romance novel binding its readers. To restate this claim: Even if the form itself cannot compel readers, even if literature, including the romance novel, cannot provide a comprehensive plan for life itself, books do influence their readers. Reading about a heroine getting married in book after book must surely reinforce patriarchy and strengthen an institution—marriage—that damages many women trapped in it. This claim rests on the assumption that because marriage is the ending of these romance novels, it is its governing element.

It is not. Romance novelist Suzanne Simmons Guntrum asks, "[W]hy read a novel when we already know how it is going to end?" and answers, "because it is the process, not the conclusion, that we are reading for" (153). What Guntrum calls the "process" is contained in one of the eight essential elements of the romance novel, the barrier. This element, along with a second narrative element called "the point of ritual death," provides the best defense against the claim that the marriage is the most important element of the book, the element that fixes the book's meaning on a reader.

Here I must anticipate my argument in Part II of this study to present, in brief, my definition and analysis of the romance novel's form. First, the definition: The romance novel is a work of prose fiction that tells the story of the courtship and betrothal of one or more heroines. All romance novels contain eight narrative elements: a *definition of society*, always corrupt, that the romance novel will reform; the *meeting* between the heroine and hero; an account of their *attraction* for each other; the *barrier* between them; the *point of ritual death*; the *recognition* that fells the barrier; the *declaration* of heroine and hero that they love each other; and their *betrothal*. I will consider each of these narrative elements separately in Part II and offer examples to illustrate them. My argument here will focus on the barrier and point of ritual death, two narrative elements that are far more important than the ending in determining a romance novel's meaning.

The "barrier" is the conflict in a romance novel; it is anything that keeps the union of heroine and hero from taking place. The "point of ritual death" is that moment in a romance novel when the union of heroine and hero seems completely impossible. It is marked by death or its simulacrum (for example fainting or illness); by the risk of death; or by any number of images or events that suggest death, however metaphorically (for example, darkness, sadness, despair, or winter).

The ending in marriage so objectionable to critics is more accurately a betrothal (an actual marriage is an option in the romance novel). It results from the surmounting of a barrier. Seeing the barrier overcome is for many readers and writers the focus of the book. A blinkered look at the form's ending might suggest a single issue for the romance novel, but the barrier's flexibility and ubiquity force a wider view. The barrier can raise virtually any issue the writer chooses. A writer might create a series of funny miscommunications as a barrier between heroine and hero and the result is a "screwball" relationship between a woman and a man who would declare their love for each other if only each could understand what the other was saying. At issue is the difficulty and importance of communication. Another writer might create a heroine who is the daughter of alcoholic parents for whom the barrier is her belief that the hero's courtship will return her to a family in which the adults do not fulfill their obligations. The result is a dark romance novel in which the heroine perceives the hero's declaration of love as a threat. At issue is the difficulty in breaking old family patterns and of distinguishing love from unhealthy demands. If the novel is a romance novel, however, these barriers will fall. The screwball heroine and hero will finally understand each other; the daughter of alcoholics will finally realize that the family the hero promises is different from the family her parents made. Any issue (from incest and spouse abuse to not putting the top back on the toothpaste) and everything in between (from interpersonal issues to world politics) can be depicted in the barrier. In overcoming the barrier, the heroine moves from a state of bondage or constraint to a state of freedom. The heroine is not extinguished and the reader is not bound. Quite the contrary. The heroine is freed and the reader rejoices.

The point of ritual death provides a similar set of possibilities for meaning in the romance novel form. This element marks the moment when no happy resolution of the narrative seems possible. The heroine herself is threatened, either directly or indirectly, actually or symbolically. Her escape from ritual death involves an overthrow of the most fundamental sort. It is death itself that is being vanquished, and life itself that the heroine will win. Ritual death in the screwball romance novel could take any number of forms. In keeping with the light tone of the work, the heroine could be laid up with a cold after being drenched in an unexpected downpour, her illness a simulacrum of death. All of the resources of slapstick are available to suggest death at that moment when the betrothal of the heroine and hero seems least likely. Ritual death in the darker romance novel, in which the heroine is the child of alcoholics, might take the form of a friend becoming destructively drunk. To darken the mood more, the friend might be a recovering alcoholic. To further darken the mood, the friend might die. Again, this marks the point at which the union of heroine and hero seems impossible. In both cases, the heroine symbolically overcomes death.

The heroine of the romance novel, then, undergoes two great liberations. She overcomes the barrier and is freed from all encumbrances to her union with the hero. She cheats ritual death, symbolically or actually, and is freed to live. Her freedom is a large part of what readers celebrate at the end of the romance. Her choice to marry the hero is just one manifestation of her freedom. This state of freedom is the opposite of the bondage that feminists claim is the result of reading romance novels—both for heroine and reader. Here is the reason that readers react to the happy ending with enthusiasm—with joy. Each of the other elements of the romance novel offers other delights to the reader, but the barrier and point of ritual death answer the critics' chief complaint most directly: heroines are not extinguished, they are freed. Readers are not bound by the form; they rejoice because they are in love with freedom.

Romance novels are a subgenre of comedy. The freedom of the comic heroine, which is to say the heroine of the romance novel, differs from that of the comic hero. For comic heroes, freedom seems nearly absolute. Often they are princes or nobles. The new society that is inaugurated by their union with the heroine will perpetuate the state as well as humanity. If the traditional blocking character in comedy, an opposing father (or *senex*) is also the king, the marriage of the hero, his son, heralds the ascension of the next generation to rule. The ending of a comedy that focuses on the hero promises not only a marriage and children, but the hero's coronation and heirs. The freedom won for the comic hero is total.

For comic heroines, including the heroine of the romance novel, the freedom at the end of the book is often provisional. Like the comic hero, the heroine is freed from ritual death: her life is restored to her, symbolically or actually. Like the hero, the heroine is freed from the barriers to her union with the hero. Unlike the hero, the heroine's relationship to society and, in many cases, to the state, is not that of a prince or ruler who will lead that state, but that of a woman whose freedom is constrained by that state. The heroine's freedom in the form of her life, her liberty, or her property may be in doubt not only in the original society that promotes the barrier, but also in the new society at the end of the work. Nonetheless, the heroine's freedom, however provisional, is a victory. She is freed from the immediate encumbrances that prevent her union with the hero. When the heroine achieves freedom, she chooses the hero. The happy ending celebrates this.

In the remainder of this study I explore in detail issues dealt with briefly in this defense—the form of the romance novel, including its definition and an analysis of that definition. I also present a history of the romance novel written in English from the eighteenth century, when the form was all but synonymous with the English novel, up to the year 2000, when the genre constituted a large percentage of the fiction sold and read in the English-speaking world.

PART II

❧

THE ROMANCE NOVEL
DEFINED

3

THE DEFINITION

*A romance novel is a work of prose fiction that tells the story of
the courtship and betrothal of one or more heroines.*

As this definition is neither widely known nor accepted, it
requires no little defense as well as some teasing out of distinctions between the term put forward here, "romance novel,"
and terms in widespread use, such as "romance" and "novel." I
begin with the broadest term, "romance."

The term "romance" is confusingly inclusive, meaning one
thing in a survey of medieval literature, and another, not
entirely distinct, in a contemporary bookstore. Ask at a bookstore for a copy of the *Morte Darthur* and the clerk will take you
to the "literature" section; a glance at the book's introduction
will inform you that Malory's prose account of King Arthur is
called a "romance." Ask for a romance and the clerk will take
you to the (generally) large section of the store stocked with
Harlequins, Silhouettes and single-title releases by writers such
as Nora Roberts, Amanda Quick, and Janet Dailey. Can Malory's *Morte Darthur* and Quick's *Deception* both be romances?
They can be and are, but only *Deception* is also a romance novel
as I am defining the term here.

Robert Ellrich hazards a definition of the old, encompassing
term "romance": "the story of individual human beings pursuing their precarious existence within the circumscription of
social, moral, and various other this-worldly problems. . . . the
romance . . . means to show the reader what steps must be taken
in order to reach a desired goal, represented often though not
always in the guise of a spouse" (274–75). A bookstore clerk

acting on a request for this sort of book could plausibly lead a customer to most of the fiction (and all of the self-help books) in the store.

"Romance" in this its broadest sense begins at least as early as the Greeks. Margaret Anne Doody describes texts as old as the fourth century B.C. that tell a story of passionate love, separation, and triumph (6). Jean Radford notes that this larger sense of romance includes "Greek 'romances,' medieval romance, Gothic bourgeois romances of the 1840s, late nineteenth century women's romances and mass-produced romance fiction now" (8). Northrop Frye explains, "In the Greek romance we find stories of mysterious birth, oracular prophecies about the future contortions of the plot, foster parents, adventures which involve capture by pirates, narrow escapes from death, recognition of the true identity of the hero and his eventual marriage with the heroine." The conventions of the romance are very stable; the basic story, Frye notes, has not changed in the centuries that followed its advent in ancient times (*Secular* 4). For Frye, the essence of romance is the "idealized world" it embodies in its texts (*Anatomy* 367). All popular genres—mysteries, thrillers, horror, science fiction, and, of course, the romance novel itself—are romances in this broader sense. It is this larger group of texts that Radford refers to when she defines the romance as "a non-mimetic prose narrative focusing on emotion" (8). Combining these definitions we have the romance presenting an ideal world, whose representation takes considerable liberties with verisimilitude (mimesis) and focuses on emotion. Describing not the text but "the reader, the writer, and their experience," Kathleen Gilles Seidel claims that "fantasy is the most important element in the appeal of popular fiction" (159). In Seidel's account of readers and authors, the idealized world, the non-mimetic representation, combined with the focus on emotion, become "fantasy." These definitions of romance in the largest sense focus on what is depicted—an idealized world—and how—non-mimetically—and on that depiction's status in the minds of authors and readers—fantasy. This ancient, ideal, non-mimetic fantasy world can be represented in verse, either dramatic or narrative, or in prose. It includes a huge variety of texts including most of the popular works ever written. But it groups together rather than distinguishing Quick's *Deception* and Stephen King's *Dead Zone.*

If "romance" presents one set of confusions to the romance novel's definition, then "novel," that relatively new form that now dominates literature, confuses in a different way. Is a novel a romance or are the two forms distinct? This question has preoccupied critics since the English novel began its advance toward literary preeminence. The term "novel," came into use in the late seventeenth century. The next century saw the burgeoning of the novel's popularity, and by 1785 Clara Reeve in her *Progress of Romance* felt a need to distinguish the older form, romance, from the upstart novel. She defined the novel as "a picture of real life and manners, and of the times in which it was written," whereas the romance "in lofty and elevated language, describes what has never happened nor is likely to" (111). This is the "ideal, non-mimetic, fantasy" world that we have seen in later definitions of the romance. Reeve's definition of romance is taken up by Sir Walter Scott and Nathaniel Hawthorne (among others) in the nineteenth century, and Joseph Conrad in the twentieth. Deborah Ross claims that this novel/romance distinction has been manipulated to argue that women always write the wrong sort of books—"novelists" such as Henry Fielding could scorn "romancers" such as Eliza Haywood. Then, years later, when the aesthetic wheel had turned, "romancer" Sir Walter Scott scorned "novelist" Jane Austen (2–5). This slippery distinction, which Ellrich has called "critically distortive and ideologically pernicious," is of little help in defining the romance novel (277). Doody collapses the distinction as well, by applying the newer term "novel" to the ancient texts she studies: "the Novel as a form of literature in the West has a continuous history of about two thousand years" (1). The distinction hangs on "mimesis," but when, in a given work, mimesis shades off into the ideal of fantasy without actually becoming supernatural, whether or not the work is mimetic is a matter of some judgment, and the assigning of one or the other term—romance or novel—becomes invidious. For example, romancers Hawthorne and Melville used the distinction to assume the aesthetic high ground; they looked down upon the mere "novelists" in the area below. This distinction tells us little, however, about the texts that either camp writes, including romance novels.

When critics consider "romance" and "novel" together, that is when they narrow their scrutiny to prose fiction love stories, they begin to focus on the elements most associated with the popular romance novel: love and the happy ending. In his brief glance at the romance novel, which he calls "the romance," John Cawelti offers this definition of the genre in its popular incarnation: "The crucial defining characteristic of romance is not that it stars a female but that its organizing action is the development of a love relationship, usually between a man and a woman. . . . The moral fantasy of the romance is that of love triumphant and permanent, overcoming all obstacles and difficulties" (*Adventure* 41–42). Kay Mussell offers *Pamela* as an early example of the romance novel and notes that "the central plot device of vicissitudes and trials giving way to a happy marriage is standard for such books" (*Women's Gothic* 3). She notes that all romance novels "focus on love, courtship, and marriage" (*Fantasy* 29). Radway polls the "Smithton" readers who respond that "a happy ending" and "a slowly but consistently developing love between hero and heroine" are the two most important "ingredients" in a romance novel. These readers also "project themselves into the story," they "become the heroine" (67). Deborah Chappel identifies the "basic structural definition" of the romance novel: "the central conflict is always about the love relationship between the hero and heroine and the hero and heroine always end up together" (7–8). These definitions have in common, first, love between a heroine and hero; second, the triumphant, permanent, happy ending, usually in marriage; and finally, discounted by Cawelti but emphasized by the readers Radway studied, the importance of the heroine.

Recall my definition: *A romance novel is a work of prose fiction that tells the story of the courtship and betrothal of one or more heroines.* This definition focuses on the narrative essentials of the romance novel—those events, including the happy ending, without which there is an incomplete rendering of the genre. In naming the narrative elements of "courtship" and "betrothal" and in emphasizing the heroine, this definition departs from earlier efforts to define the romance novel. "Courtship" and "betrothal" translate the love and happy ending elements of these earlier critics' definitions into narrative events. Heroines and heroes in love conduct a courtship—that is the action in the novel that expresses the love noted by all of the critics. Courting couples become betrothed—that is the action that leads to the universally endorsed happy ending. The wedding itself is often omitted, but it is always promised in a betrothal. This shift from a statement of theme ("love relationship") to a designation of narrative elements makes the identification of romance novels straightforward. If the narrative elements are present, a given work is a romance novel.

The shift to narrative elements also invites an "opening out" of the one-sentence definition of the romance novel by identifying the common elements of the romance. This identification, in turn, invites analysis, permitting, as it does, a comparison of works across time and space and directing the focus of that comparison to the meaning of the action that makes a romance novel a *romance* novel. Such comparative analysis of plot elements has focused heretofore almost entirely on sex scenes, which are optional or accidental occurrences in the romance novel. See the early analysis of such scenes in Germaine Greer (179–83) and in Ann Barr Snitow who argues that such scenes are pornography (151–60). Carol Thurston provides the most extended examinination of such scenes in *The Romance Revolution: Erotic Novels for Women and the Quest for a New Sexual Identity.* A larger narrative surrounds such scenes and precedes the highly scrutinized ending. Analyzing the essential elements of this narrative will yield a far more balanced, significant view of the romance novel. This opening out will also explain the final element of the proposed definition: its focus on the heroine.

A WORD ABOUT FORMULA

The term "formula" is often confused with "genre," and this confusion is particularly widespread in critical work on the romance novel. "Formula" denotes a subset of a genre. It is narrower than a genre. The elements of the genre are all present in the formula, but their range of possible embodiment has been constricted.

The connotations of "formula" are quite negative. The term implies hack-work, subliterature, and imagination reduced to a mechanism for creating "product." An indication of how loaded this term is can be gathered from the sentence, *"Pride and Prejudice* is a work of formula fiction." In some meanings attached to the term by critics of the romance novel this sentence is denotatively accurate, no matter how connotatively absurd. The term "formula" has its place. It is not, however, a synonym for genre, which is a less loaded, more accurate term for the romance novel.

The romance novel has often been described as being written according to a formula. When, for example, Gabriele Linke states "category romances are based on variations of the same narrative archetype—the romance formula" (197), she follows the lead of John Cawelti, who inaugurated the contemporary discussion of the genres of popular fiction and who used the word "formula" to denote these genres. Cawelti was interested in a variety of "popular" forms and devoted very little space to the romance novel. This use of the term obscures the relationship between popular titles and canonical works that no one regards as "formula" fiction, but that, in fact, share what Linke calls a "narrative archetype." It also highlights the inessential "accidents" of the formula and obscures the underlying essential elements of the genre. This emphasis on accident invites criticism that misses the point of the romance novel.

A second source for the "formula" designation is tipsheets—the descriptions of publishers' separate lines issued to guide writers. Modleski cites tipsheets in her discussion of the "formula" in Harlequin romances (35–36). These guidelines do indeed specify the requirements of a given formula, which makes works written to these specifications formula fiction. But the issue is complex. Not all writers of category fiction use the guidelines. Nora Roberts, one of the most successful writers of Silhouette romances in a variety of that Silhouette's lines, does not (Mussell, "Interview with Roberts" 162). The current Silhouette "Editorial Guidelines" never offers a description of the larger genre, the romance novel, itself. Instead, it lists descriptions such as the following:

SILHOUETTE YOURS TRULY. 50,000 words . . .
Category romance, very contemporary, fast-paced, fun, flirtatious, entertaining, upbeat and sexy. Real-life hero and heroine meet directly or indirectly through a form of written communication. Let romantic conflict build to a satisfying happy ending. Marriage not required.

This tipsheet does define a formula within the larger genre to which such a book would also belong—the romance novel. A Silhouette Yours Truly must include a meeting of heroine and hero which takes place via written communication. This is just one possible fulfillment of a narrative element that every romance novel contains—the meeting of heroine and hero. It seems reasonable to speak of formulas within the romance novel genre. They provide a description of what Nora Roberts calls the "culture" of each series (Mussell, "Interview with Roberts" 162). Of course, the formula still satisfies the requirements of the genre as a whole: it is a wholly contained subset of that larger genre.

If "formula" is sometimes substituted for "genre," the reverse also happens. What is actually a formula, a subset of a larger genre, is mistaken for that larger genre, and conclusions based on a narrow set of texts are indiscriminately applied to the larger genre. Radway makes this error. Like all formulas, hers is too narrow to define the genre as a whole. Like many, it leads to destructive conclusions about the larger genre when its strictures are applied beyond the narrow list of texts to which it applies.

Radway lists the "thirteen logically related functions" that account for the heroine's "transformation" in the romances designated as ideal in her 1980 survey of a group of romance readers. The first function she lists in "the narrative structure of the ideal romance" is "the heroine's social identity is destroyed" (134). Radway's description of the ideal romance is formulaic rather than generic because it expresses only one possible fulfillment of the genre's initial action—the disordering of the old society that will be replaced at the novel's end by a new society, represented by the union of heroine and hero. Narrower than genres, formulas describe a possible (and perhaps widespread) embodiment of a given element of a literary type rather than describing all possible embodiments of that element. The test is simple: if we can name any romance novel that does not begin with the destruction of the heroine's social identity, then Radway's description is formulaic, not generic. *Pride and Prejudice* is such a book; it does not begin with the destruction of Elizabeth Bennet's social identity. (Elizabeth's social identity is threatened by Lydia's elopement, but this event does not occur at the beginning of the novel, and does not, ultimately, result in that identity's "destruction.") Radway's description, then, is a formula, a subset of the genre. Yet her conclusions concern the genre as a whole. To cite one instance of many, she claims: *"the romance* continues to justify the social placement of women that has led to the very discontent that is the source of their desire to read romances" (217, emphasis added).

4

THE DEFINITION EXPANDED

Thus far interpretation of the romance novel has focused heavily on the ending in part because the other essential narrative elements of the form have remained unidentified. A romance novel—a work of prose fiction that tells the story of the courtship and betrothal of one or more heroines—requires certain narrative events. They are essential, for without them the work is not a *romance* novel. In this chapter I expand my basic definition to identify and define the eight essential narrative elements of the romance novel as well as the three incidental elements that sometimes occur and are typical of the romance novel, if not essential to it. In identifying these narrative elements I provide critics with an expanded vocabulary for discussing the romance novel. I hope, too, that identifying the essential elements will direct discussion of the genre to its core and permit critics to view distracting particulars—such as the sex scenes—in the context of the genre's essential elements—those that establish a given work of prose fiction as a romance novel.

I have chosen to illustrate each element with episodes from *Pride and Prejudice* (1813), which fulfills the requirements of the basic definition: it is a work of prose fiction, and it tells the story of the courtship and betrothal of one or more heroines—of Elizabeth Bennet, in depth; of her sister Jane Bennet, in outline; of another sister, Lydia Bennet, and of Elizabeth's friend Charlotte Lucas, in fragments. It is probably the best-known canonical romance novel. Its familiarity to many readers will aid in understanding the elements I identify. Its masterpiece status will help lay to rest the notion that all romance novels are hack-work. To counter the opposite idea—that contemporary romance novels must be mere corruptions of the great works of the past such as *Pride and Prejudice*—in a final section I analyze a contemporary romance novel, Kathleen Gilles Seidel's *Again* (1994), to demonstrate the continuity of the form and its vitality in the hands of a popular novelist.

The essential narrative elements of the romance novel derive in part from the larger genre to which it belongs. Just as narrow romance formulas are subsets of the more extensive romance novel, the romance novel itself is a subset of both comedy and of romance in its larger sense (as we saw earlier). The boundary between these quite extensive genres—between comedy and romance—is not sharply drawn. Rather, Northrop Frye tells us, "comedy blends insensibly into romance" (*Anatomy* 162). The romance novel is located in this area of overlap between comedy and romance in the larger sense. Here the sublime absurdity of comedy is not completely pure, and the ideal fantasy of romance in the larger sense has not completely faded. In drama and film a genre has been named using these two sweeping terms: Shakespeare's *As You Like It* is a "romantic comedy," as is George Stevens's *Woman of the Year.* Frye links the romance's plot to comedy's: "A romance is normally comic, in the sense that usually the heroine's wiles are successful and the story ends with marriage or some kind of deliverance" (*Secular* 92). The essential elements of the romance novel's plot can best be identified and analyzed through the set of narrative events linked to comedy's ending in marriage with suitable changes made to account for the heroine's central role in the romance novel.

The writers of Greek New Comedy, a form that emerged three hundred years before Christ, established the pattern of comedy, which the romance novel would modify some twenty-one centuries later. For most of this time comedy's protagonists have been male. "What normally happens," Frye tells us, "is that a young man wants a young woman, that his desire is resisted by some opposition, usually paternal, and that near the end of the play some twist in the plot enables the hero to have his will." The context of comedy, its setting, is society. Comedy's "movement . . . is usually . . . from one kind of society to another" (*Anatomy* 163). This, then, is the usual sequence that the reader encounters—an old society (which is often corrupt, decadent, weak, or superannuated), a hero, his intended, paternal opposition to his intended becoming his wife, a removal of that opposition, the hero's triumphal betrothal, and a wedding symbolizing a new, vital society.

Although the heroine is essential to the sort of comedy Frye is delineating, she is not the focus. She is, after all, the object of the hero's desires, not the one desiring. The romance novel puts the heroine at the center of the book, at least coequal with the hero, or occupying more of the spotlight than he does. Her desires are central.

What are the consequences of this shift to a female protagonist? The typical conflict in comedy between the hero and his father, in which the father as *senex iratus* (angry old man) blocks his son's attachment to the heroine, and, in some instances, pursues the heroine himself, loses its psychological force. The primal conflict between father and the protagonist, his son, in competition for the same woman changes beyond recognition if that protagonist is a female. In the romance novel, the protagonist, who is the heroine, and her same-sex parent, her mother, are rarely in competition for the same man. Such situations do exist; however, in most romance novels the comedic conflict shifts from the parent-child rivalry of the *senex* and hero to a heroine who is without parents (they are dead as in *Jane Eyre*) or practically so (they are absent from the scene as in *Pamela* or ineffective as in *Pride and Prejudice*) and who must struggle against other impediments to achieve union with the hero. Male comedic protagonists, who typically enjoy full freedom outside of their families, must overcome their fathers. Female comedic protagonists—the heroines of romance novels included— must overcome the laws, dangers, and limitations imposed upon them by the state, the church, or society, including the family (Jane Eyre had no immediate family; Pamela Andrews and Elizabeth Bennet had useless families). For most of the history of the romance novel, these restrictions were placed upon the heroine simply because she was female. The romance novel's focus on the heroine, then, is a focus on women's problems.

Another consequence of a female protagonist hinges upon the freedom that characterizes the final society in comedy. Frye tells us, "The society emerging at the conclusion of comedy represents . . . a kind of moral norm, or pragmatically free society. Its ideals are seldom defined or formulated. . . .We are simply given to understand that the newly-married couple will live happily ever after, or that at any rate they will get along in a relatively . . . clear-sighted manner" (*Anatomy* 169). This creation of a couple that gets along clear sightedly is the goal of most romance novels. Accomplishing this "pragmatic freedom" is, Frye claims, "a movement from illusion to reality . . . [h]ence the importance of the theme of creating and dispelling illusion in comedy: the illusions caused by disguise, obsession, hypocrisy, or unknown parentage" (170). Like her male counterpart, the female protagonist achieves freedom at the end of the work. Unlike him, she does not so much throw off the threat of an overbearing parent in competition for the same goal as she rejects various encumbrances imposed by the old society to arrive at a place where society stops hindering her. Her movement in the romance is from a state of unfreedom to one of freedom. This freedom is limited—"pragmatic" as Frye would have it. For a heroine, especially, it is not absolute. It is freedom, nonetheless.

THE EIGHT ESSENTIAL ELEMENTS OF THE ROMANCE NOVEL

Eight narrative events take a heroine in a romance novel from encumbered to free. In one or more scenes, romance novels always depict the following: the initial state of society in which heroine and hero must court, the meeting between heroine and hero, the barrier to the union of heroine and hero, the attraction between the heroine and hero, the declaration of love between heroine and hero, the point of ritual death, the recognition by heroine and hero of the means to overcome the barrier, and the betrothal. These elements are essential.

In addition, the romance novel may include scenes depicting a scapegoat exiled, bad characters converted to goodness, and the wedding, dance, or fete that traditionally ends the comedy. These elements are accidental—optional—although they occur often enough to be characteristic of the romance novel.

Elements both essential and accidental can appear in any order. The wedding between heroine and hero, for example, can occur before any of the other elements. In this case the resulting marriage of convenience must overcome barriers to become a true marriage. Elements can also be doubled and even tripled in the same scene or action; that is, a single action can accomplish the narrative purpose of two or more elements. Declaration and betrothal, for instance, often occur together, as heroine and hero declare their love and propose in the same scene. A single element can also occur more than once. For example, a novel can depict more than one proposal between the same heroine and hero. In addition, any element can be diminished, so that it is merely reported after it happens "off"; that is, a writer, without dramatizing a certain element, without representing it with action and dialogue, can, in the voice of the narrator or one of the characters, let the reader know that it has happened. Conversely, any element can be expanded to any length and dramatized in detail with action and dialogue, thus becoming a governing element of the novel. This flexibility is as evident in romance novels, which are often accused of being all the same, as it is in any other genre. Indeed, looking at the embodiment of any given element in any given romance novel can be key to understanding what is at stake in that novel.

Society Defined

Near the beginning of the novel, the society that the heroine and hero will confront in their courtship is defined for the reader. This society is in some way flawed; it may be incomplete, superannuated, or corrupt. It always oppresses the heroine and hero. Sometimes, as in some Harlequins and Silhouettes, this society is barely sketched—the heroine and hero may be the only representatives of it that we see. In Victorian novels it can be a large community or even an entire nation. In historical romance novels the society is carefully drawn and its unfamiliar principles explained.

In *Pride and Prejudice*, Austen sketches this society in her first chapter in which Mrs. Bennet tells her husband that Darcy and Bingley, the novel's heroes, have moved into a neighboring estate. Mrs. Bennet's talk of Bingley's income and her report of the preemptive visit of Sir William and Lady Lucas, the other leading family in the neighborhood, to the rich young bachelors is the primary vehicle for the reader's construction of the initial condition of society in this novel. As much as Mrs. Bennet discloses in her short conversation with her husband, a great deal of the information needed to complete this picture of late eighteenth-century country life would have been in the mind of Austen's contemporary reader. The scene or scenes defining the society establishes the status quo which the heroine and hero must confront in their attempt to court and marry and which, by their union, they symbolically remake.

The Meeting

Usually near the beginning of the novel, but also sometimes presented in flashback, the heroine and hero meet for the first time. Some hint of the conflict to come is often introduced. In *Pride and Prejudice*, Elizabeth and Darcy, as well as Jane and Bingley, meet at the ball at Meryton. Bingley dances every dance. In the gathered society of his new neighborhood his actions bespeak friendliness, and dancing itself is a symbol of harmony. Darcy's behavior bespeaks unfriendliness and his refusal to dance with anyone except the ladies of his own party is a symbol of disharmony. He makes this discord personal when Elizabeth overhears him saying of her, "She is tolerable; but not handsome enough to tempt me" (9). Thus begins the conflict between Elizabeth and Darcy, the barrier to their eventual betrothal.

The Barrier

A series of scenes often scattered throughout the novel establishes for the reader the reasons that this heroine and hero cannot marry. The romance novel's conflict often consists entirely of this barrier between the heroine and hero. The elements of the barrier can be external, a circumstance that exists outside of a heroine or a hero's mind, or internal, a circumstance that comes from within either or both.

External barriers include elements of the setting, especially the society in power at the beginning of the work, as well as the heroine or hero's family, the economic situation of either or both halves of the couple, and coincidence. Setting includes geography—physical separation is sometimes part of the barrier—as well as society and its rules. In older comedies the *senex* often embodies these strictures in his opposition to the match between heroine and hero. Economics includes the income that the heroine and hero can bring to a potential union as well as their prospects for future prosperity. Coincidence includes events, such as a natural disaster, over which the heroine and hero have no control that impede their union. Elements of internal barriers include the attitudes, temperament, values, and beliefs held by heroine and hero that prevent the union. Many recent romance novels have barriers that are entirely internal—they grow out of the psychology or subjective state of the heroine and hero.

The barrier drives the romance novel. It is spread throughout most instances of this literary type, and it encompasses a wide variety of issues. Through this element a writer can examine any situation within the heroine's mind or in the world itself. Literally any psychological vice, virtue, or problem, any circumstance of life, whether economic, geographical, or familial can be made a part of the barrier and investigated at whatever length the writer sees fit. At stake in the romance novel, then, is more than the marriage.

In *Pride and Prejudice* there are four barriers between the four bridegrooms and brides to be: simple ones between Charlotte and Mr. Collins, between Lydia and Wickham, and between Jane and Bingley, as well as a far more complex one between Elizabeth and Darcy. Multiple heroines mean multiple barriers which the writer can array so as to intersect, comment on each other, echo, contradict, and so on. The barriers between all four couples in *Pride and Prejudice* will later be examined at length (chapter 8), but here a sketch of the barrier between Elizabeth and Darcy will illustrate the concept.

Most of the usual external barriers function at one time or another in their courtship. The society in power at the beginning of the book, best represented by Darcy's aunt, Lady Catherine de Bourgh, tries to impede the union; she expresses that society's objection to the lowness of Elizabeth's family. Mr. and Mrs. Bennet each act as barrier at one time or another: Mrs. Bennet by her offensive, overbearing fatuousness; Mr. Bennet through his inability to prevent Lydia from bringing scandal down upon the entire family. Money is a consideration. Darcy's £10,000 per year is two hundred times greater than Elizabeth's income from the settlement that she could bring to the union—interest of about £50 per year. There is a false heroine, Caroline Bingley, and a false hero as well, Wickham. Caroline, by seeming to be attached to Darcy, and Wickham by actually attaching himself to Elizabeth, impede the union between heroine and hero. The internal barrier elements are named in the title, of course—Darcy's pride and Elizabeth's prejudice prevent them from seeing each other clearly. Overcoming these internal barriers helps to brush aside the external ones. In many romances, *Pride and Prejudice* among them, components of the barrier are in virtually every scene until the heroine and hero are betrothed.

Removal of the barrier usually involves the heroine's freedom from societal, civic, or even religious strictures that prevented the union between her and the hero. This release is an important source of the happiness in the romance novel's happy ending. The barrier's fall is a liberation for the heroine. It is a moment of rejoicing for the reader, whose response to the heroine's freedom is joy.

The Attraction

A scene or series of scenes scattered throughout the novel establishes for the reader the reason that this couple must marry. The attraction keeps the heroine and hero involved long enough to surmount the barrier. Attraction can be based on a combination of sexual chemistry, friendship, shared goals or feelings, society's expectations, and economic issues. In modern works, these separate motives get lumped together under the rubric "love." Some romance novels interrogate this notion of love, others simply assume it.

In *Pride and Prejudice* we have four instances of attraction. Charlotte and

Mr. Collins, for whom even the temperate term "attraction" is almost too warm, are drawn together because he is an eligible man with connections and economic prospects enough for a rapidly aging near spinster, and she is a suitable wife for a clergyman whose conscience can be at rest after he proposes out of duty to Elizabeth, his distant cousin. Lydia and Wickham are sexually attracted; they actually live together without marrying. They have little else to keep them together, and, despite their marriage, they eventually drift apart. Jane and Bingley each possess a good-natured disposition. In addition, Jane is a great beauty and Bingley is sexually attracted to her. Bingley is also wealthy, although not as rich as his friend Darcy. Elizabeth and Darcy come to share a friendship, a crisis (leading to shared goals and feelings), and sexual attraction (and for Elizabeth, of course, there is the fact that Darcy is one of the richest men in England). The money works ironically—it is not enough of an inducement for Elizabeth the first time Darcy proposes, but the reader is glad it is there the second time he offers his hand, and she accepts him.

The Declaration

The scene or scenes in which the hero declares his love for the heroine, and the heroine her love for the hero, can occur anywhere in the narrative. Their variable placement helps create the variety of plots within the set of possibilities open to the romance novel. Move the declaration scene up, coincident with the meeting scene, and the novel presents a love-at-first-sight situation. Love at first sight is common in hero-centered comedy, where the heroine does not need to be wooed, merely wrested free from societal (especially parental) strictures that prevent the hero from marrying her immediately. Move the declaration to the very end of the novel, and the heroine and hero declare their love for each other after the novel's barrier has been surmounted; often enough, the barrier was their inability or unwillingness to declare for each other, and the declaration scene marks the end of this barrier. With the heroine in the center of the narrative, it usually becomes a story about the courtship, about the choice of a spouse, with the heroine's declaration scene placed correspondingly late. Often, too, there is a separate declaration scene for the hero and the heroine.

Pride and Prejudice provides an instance of this splitting of the declaration. Darcy declares for Elizabeth in the middle of the novel: "In vain have I struggled. It will not do. My feelings will not be repressed. You must allow me to tell you how ardently I admire and love you" (189). Elizabeth declares for Darcy at the end of the novel: "Elizabeth . . . gave him to understand, that her sentiments had undergone so material a change, since the period to which he alluded, as to make her receive with gratitude and pleasure, his present assurances" (366). *Pride and Prejudice* rejects the love at first sight convention, presenting instead the slow development of love and regard between heroine and hero.

Point of Ritual Death

The point of ritual death marks the moment in the narrative when the union between heroine and hero, the hoped-for resolution, seems absolutely impossible, when it seems that the barrier will remain, more substantial than ever. The happy ending is most in jeopardy at this point. In coining the phrase "point of ritual death," Frye has noted how often, "comic stories . . . seem to approach a potentially tragic crisis near the end" (*Anatomy* 179).

The heroine is often the target of ritual death, and beneath her very real trials in the narrative is the myth of death and rebirth, which echoes, however remotely, the myth of Persephone. In brief, Persephone, a virgin, is loved by Hades, who abducts her and carries her off to his underworld kingdom of death to be his wife. Her mother, Demeter, goddess of corn and hence of agricultural bounty, searches for her, leaving the earth barren. Persephone is returned to her mother, and fruitfulness is restored to the earth (Hayes 195–200). Just as Persephone must escape the kingdom of death to restore fruitfulness, increase, and fecundity to the entire earth, the romance novel heroine must escape her "death" to live to see her betrothal and the promise of children that it brings. When the romance novel heroine was depicted as a virgin (as she was for most of the genre's history), this restoration of fecundity was made all the more poignant.

Frye notes that this rescue of the heroine from the underworld is sometimes "vestigial, not an element of the plot but a mere change of tone" (*Anatomy* 179). Often enough death itself, or an event equated with death, threatens or actually transpires at this point when the barrier seems insurmountable. The death is, however, ritual. The heroine does not die. She is freed from its presence, and this freedom is the mythic counterpart of the freedom that results from the lifting of the barrier. The reader's response, again, is joy. The reader rejoices in this escape, however symbolic, however merely hinted at.

In *Pride and Prejudice* the point of ritual death is Lydia's elopement with Wickham. From the perspective of the developing relationship between Elizabeth and Darcy, Lydia's timing is perfectly wrong. Austen, writing in

Elizabeth's point of view, tells us, "[N]ever had she so honestly felt that she could have loved [Darcy], as now, when all love must be vain" (278). Lydia's elopement is spoken of by family members in terms that could be used to refer either to a dead sister or to one who is cohabiting with a man who is not her husband. Ever-hopeful Jane asks, "[C]an I suppose her so lost to everything?" (275). The blunter sister, Elizabeth, says, "[S]he is lost forever" (277). During the long search for the fugitive couple, Mr. Collins writes a letter of condolence to his cousin, Mr. Bennet, which puts Lydia's elopement in grim perspective: "The death of your daughter would have been a blessing in comparison of this" (296–97). Lydia's elopement is spoken of as if it were a death. Elizabeth suffers at the same time a social death, which puts in place an apparently unbridgeable gulf between her and Darcy.

No one actually dies. Lydia is dead to her family—lost like Persephone, willingly abducted by the one truly evil character in the novel. Reaching back as it does to the mythic foundations of narrative, the point of ritual death can evoke a complex response from the reader. Yet the point of ritual death always functions comprehensibly within the narrative. An unsophisticated, inexperienced reader responds to the peril of the situation, or to the darkened mood, even if the mythopoeic meanings do not resonate for her. A more sophisticated reader, or a reader more experienced in reading romance novels, responds to the peril, the mood, and to the repetition of the imagery of death.

The Recognition

In a scene or scenes the author represents the new information that will overcome the barrier. In older comedies, where the opposition to the marriage is paternal, the hero is often recognized—that is, revealed to be of noble parentage—and so worthy to marry the heroine. Sometimes the heroine's true lineage is revealed, or, as in some of Shakespeare's comedies, the heroine's true gender emerges from beneath the man's clothes she has been wearing. In either case the protagonist is recognized for who he or she truly is, and this recognition fells the barrier and permits the betrothal to go forward.

In romance novels, the heroine is at the center of the recognition scene, where any number of things can be "recognized." If the barrier has been external, these impediments are removed or disregarded. Far more common in contemporary romance novels is an interior barrier, in which case the recognition scene consists of the heroine understanding her own psyche better. In the course of the book she has learned to know herself and to distinguish sound perceptions from unsound. She sees the hero clearly and realizes her love for him. Both what is recognized and when it is recognized vary enormously. In an upbeat, rapidly paced book, the recognition scene may be in the last few pages and lead directly to the ending. In a bittersweet, slower-paced book the recognition scene may be quite early, and the barrier, which eventually falls, does not do so quickly.

In *Pride and Prejudice* Elizabeth's recognition of her own prejudice is paralleled by Darcy's tempering of his own pride. This recognition happens over a series of scenes, beginning near the center of the book. After Elizabeth has read Darcy's long letter explaining his actions towards Wickham, we learn that Elizabeth's views have changed not only regarding Darcy, but regarding herself as well. Elizabeth says to herself, "I have courted prepossession [prejudice] and ignorance, and driven reason away. . . . Till this moment, I never knew myself" (208). Elizabeth's revaluation of Darcy means a simultaneous self-revaluation. At the conclusion of Lydia's marriage contract with Wickham, when it becomes clear that Elizabeth's sister and Darcy's enemy will, indeed, be married, Elizabeth thinks again of Darcy, knowing that a match with him is impossible given the "gulf impassable between them" that Lydia's marriage to Wickham represents. "She began now to comprehend that he was exactly the man, who, in disposition and talents, would most suit her. His understanding and temper . . . would have answered all her wishes. It was an union that must have been to the advantage of both; by her ease and liveliness, his mind might have been softened, his manners improved, and from his judgment, information, and knowledge of the world, she must have received benefit of greater importance" (312). The internal barrier—Elizabeth's prejudice against Darcy— has fallen. She had been disguised from herself, prevented from knowing her own mind. Elizabeth recognizes that Darcy has told the truth about Wickham, that he has engineered Wickham's marriage to Lydia, and that she loves him. The heroine is free of the barrier; it falls before her newly recognized state of mind; she is released to act on her love for the hero.

The Betrothal

In a scene or scenes the hero asks the heroine to marry him and she accepts; or the heroine asks the hero, and he accepts. In romance novels from the last quarter of the twentieth century marriage is not necessary as long as it is clear that heroine and hero will end up together. If the betrothal is split into a proposal scene and an acceptance scene, the novel's focus often turns inward, to confront the internal barrier that prevents the proposal scene from also being an acceptance scene.

Such is the case with *Pride and Prejudice*. Darcy proposes twice. Midway through the book, disastrously, just after declaring himself, he asks for Elizabeth's hand in such a way that she angrily turns him down. In the clearest fantasy element in the novel, Darcy, one of the richest men in England, whose self-absorption and ideas of his own importance have been a life-long fixture of his thinking, asks again at the end of the work. Elizabeth's self-examination has led her to understand him, and she accepts. Together the proposal and the acceptance constitute a betrothal. The heroine's freedom to accept the hero's proposal has been granted her both by her escape from ritual death (a mythical escape) and by her defeat of the barrier (a realistic escape).

THREE ACCIDENTAL ELEMENTS CHARACTERISTIC OF THE ROMANCE NOVEL

These eight essential narrative events provide a romance novel with its basic structure. Without these, the work is not a romance novel. Three other narrative events are frequent but not essential in romance novels: the wedding, dance, or fete; the exile of a scapegoat character; and the conversion of a bad or evil character.

Wedding, Dance, or Fete

In a scene or scenes the promised wedding is depicted, or some other celebration of the new community is staged, such as a dance or a fete. The emphasis here is on inclusion, and this scene is promised in every romance, even if it is not dramatized. Society has reconstituted itself around the new couple(s) and the community comes together to celebrate this. For the heroine, this society represents a place to exercise her newly acquired freedom from ritual death and from the barrier, however compromised that freedom might be by the very society she joins with in celebration.

In *Pride and Prejudice* we get a mere mention of Elizabeth and Jane's wedding: "Happy for all her maternal feelings was the day on which Mrs. Bennet got rid of her two most deserving daughters" (385). The last chapter, however, includes an account of Mr. and Mrs. Fitzwilliam Darcy's circle, offering a portrait of the new society that is the final outcome of the romance novel.

Scapegoat Exiled

In a scene or scenes a representative of wrongheadedness in the romance novel, a character who, wittingly or not, prevents the heroine and hero from marrying, is ejected from the new society formed by their union. In *Pride and Prejudice*, there is no thoroughgoing scapegoat. Wickham is the nearest possibility, but his exile is only partial. "Though Darcy could never receive *him* at Pemberley, yet, for Elizabeth's sake, he assisted him farther in his profession. . . . with the Bingleys they [Wickham and Lydia] . . . frequently staid" (387).

The Bad Converted

In a scene or scenes, we see one or more opponents of the marriage converted to an acceptance of it and incorporated into the society formed by the union at the end of the novel. In *Pride and Prejudice*, Lady Catherine, acting like a scapegoat, at first exiles herself, "all intercourse [between Lady Catherine and the Darcys] was at an end." Elizabeth heals the breach, and Lady Catherine "condescended to wait on them at Pemberley" (388). Aldous Huxley and Jane Murfin, writing the screenplay of the 1940 MGM film version of *Pride and Prejudice*, turn the indignant, disapproving Lady Catherine of the novel into an affectionate (if crusty) guardian to her nephew, Darcy. She not only approves of but also brokers the marriage between him and Elizabeth. In the romance novel, with its emphasis on inclusion, the bad can become good with comparative ease.

THE STRUCTURE OF KATHLEEN GILLES SEIDEL'S *AGAIN*

To demonstrate that the form of the contemporary romance novel is not simply a corruption of timeless masterpieces such as *Pride and Prejudice*, I offer an analysis of Kathleen Gilles Seidel's *Again* (1994). As a student of narrative form—Seidel wrote a dissertation on how novels end—she manipulates these elements more consciously than many authors. Still, her books are commercial. Her presses—Harlequin, Pocket, NAL/Oynx—publish many romance writers with no claim to writing "literary fiction." Seidel incorporates the eight essential elements of romance, and two of the three incidental ones, in a manner so masterful that it leaves no doubt as to the vitality of the form in contemporary hands.

In *Again,* heroine Jenny Cotton is the creator and writer of a soap opera set in the period of the English Regency (1811–20) called *My Lady's Chamber.* The soap opera provides a plot within the novel's plot, and Seidel uses the soap plot to mirror, sometimes ironically, the action in the contemporary plot. Not surprisingly, she also doubles many of the elements of the romance novel in the soap's plot line.

The society defined in this novel is presented in the personal histories of the heroine and hero, and in the interactions of the group of people who work on the soap. By way of ironic contrast, the society is also defined by the social strictures of the society of the English Regency—the divisions and limitations imposed by that period's rigid class structure.

The heroine's childhood was motherless, and her father, who had traveled as a professional billiards player, ran a pool hall in the Midwest town where Jenny grew up. On the school bus one morning she met the "other man," (the false hero) Brian, a fatherless child of an alcoholic. They left their Midwestern hometown after high school: he to act, she to write. At the book's opening they have been a couple for fourteen years and are living together, unmarried. Childhood society in her hometown, revolving around girls and their mothers, made the motherless Jenny feel marginal. As an adult, she has turned her workplace into her only society, where she has become absolutely essential—too essential—the only problem solver. Even Brian, her boyfriend and housemate, works for her as an actor on the soap. At the beginning of this novel, in the initial set of conditions that help to define society, this heroine creates her own society in order to have any place in society at all.

Hero Alec Cameron is a new actor appearing on Jenny's soap opera. The hero's society is also in part a heritage of his childhood. In his home in Nova Scotia, his family had to confront and surmount the grief of losing one of his sisters to leukemia. Later his first marriage, to an emotionally needy wife, fails. His experience with women is of "the slowly dying younger sister, the high-strung, fragile wife" (353). The hero's society is less flawed than the heroine's. He has not had to create his society. Within his society, however, his most important relationships were with two women (his sister and his ex-wife) who made demands upon him which he could not meet. The hero needs to expand his society to include relationships with women whose demands he can meet. Jenny needs a different society altogether, one that has a place for her that she does not have to create and sustain single-handedly. It is the work of this novel to forge that new society.

The meeting between heroine and hero takes place at the studio where the soap opera is taped. When the false hero says to the heroine, by way of introducing the real hero, "Jenny, meet our new duke," the dual temporal settings on which this book operates—Regency and contemporary—are introduced (20). Jenny has hired Alec to play the duke of Lydgate, a character which Jenny has created and whose story she writes. The meeting reinforces the theme of the disordered society that this comedy must put right: Jenny has created the reason for Alec's entrance into her society and the society itself that he enters. The false hero introduces change when he presents Alec to his significant other; he will act as a change agent at another crucial point as well. The meeting between heroine and hero contains, in embryo, the entire action of the book.

We read an account of the meeting between the heroine and the false hero, Brian, told in flashback. They met on the bus on the way to high school in their small Oklahoma town the first day of their sophomore year. Later, we are asked to consider the idea of meetings when Jenny walks down the hero's street in Manhattan and identifies it as a perfect New York street, the kind that got used in movies that were romantic comedies, movies where the characters "met cute" (330). Significantly, there are no meetings represented in the soap opera plot. The soap plot in this novel, like real soap plots, is open ended, episodic. Alec is new to the show, but his character is not—another actor had originated the role of the duke of Lydgate.

The attraction that the false hero, Brian, feels for Jenny is his response to her freedom. He longs to be free from his past—his alcoholic father and controlling mother—and she represents this to him. Alec, the hero, finds her fresh and uncomplicated, he is "enchanted" by her capacity to have fun (21). His attraction is also physical; there is sexual chemistry between them. Above all, he is attracted to her imagination.

Jenny's attraction to Brian had been gratitude that someone had noticed her, despite her tomboy, outsider status in her hometown. She had assumed that their lack of sexual spark was her fault. By contrast, Jenny's attraction to Alec is sexual, and she also responds to his goodness, his concern for others, his desire to be responsible for everyone all the time. She rescues him from the excesses of this impulse, but responds to it nonetheless. Jenny's waning attraction to Brian is registered in the soap plot. The characters Lady Varley and Lord Courtland are supposed to have loved each other from childhood (just like Jenny and Brian) and are supposed to have a love that stands in contrast to "the other characters' flighty passions or rigid coolness;" they go three months without expressing that love (145).

Her attraction to Alec is registered when Jenny introduces a new female character, who is fun-loving and breezy (like Jenny's best self) and is attracted to a character who is like Alec's best self—gallant, protective, but not overwhelmed by the responsibility to fix everything for everybody all the time. In the contemporary plot, Jenny's shifting attraction to Brian wanes and her attraction to Alec intensifies.

The barrier is doubled because the heroine is involved with two men. She lives with Brian. They are acknowledged as a couple by everyone, yet their relationship has not progressed to the expected and required outcome of the romance: it has not progressed to betrothal. The barrier between Jenny and Brian is, paradoxically, the freedom that Brian would have to give up if he were to marry her. He is self-centered in his demands for freedom. This self-centeredness is reflected in his unwillingness to help buy the house that he and Jenny had been looking for. She buys it herself, alone, but he moves into it with her. Alec helps illuminate this barrier in his interpretation of his character in the soap, the duke of Lydgate. Alec plays this character based on Brian as if his attitude is the same as Brian's toward everything: "I'm all that matters" (111).

The barrier between Jenny and the hero Alec is, for half of the book, Brian, the other man, to whom Jenny has promised to be true. Then, inexplicably, Brian marries another woman and that barrier is removed, at least in the sense that Brian is no longer available to be Jenny's husband. However, the emotional backwash from this betrayal of Jenny lingers, and Jenny must deal with the feeling that she had failed as a woman in keeping Brian. This is made more difficult by Brian's choice of a wife—a young actress whose foremost asset is her extremely sexy body. Brian was a primarily external barrier—Alec could not express his attraction for Jenny while Brian was around. This barrier element also has internal consequences in Jenny's psyche. He has reinforced her feelings of inadequacy as a woman. When Brian is no longer a part of the barrier, the focus shifts to the soap opera itself, to her involvement with it, to her having made it her life. Alec explains to her, "You get everything you need from it. I can't compete with that" (335). This is his analysis of the barrier. She immediately understands that this analysis is incomplete, but it is some time before she can articulate how. Alec believes, falsely, that in order to get love, he needs to continue behaving the way he always has, the way his family and his first wife expected him to: he must help people. But Jenny doesn't need help. So, he concludes, she cannot love him. This is wrong. The identification of this barrier, which Jenny makes with the aid of the story she has been writing for the soap frees Alec to move beyond it.

Jenny's barrier must fall as well. Brian is gone. She exorcises his demon by understanding and identifying with her long-dead mother, who possessed a powerful imagination and who bequeathed it to the heroine. She might not be as sexy as Brian's new wife (no one is as sexy as Brian's new wife), but she has power—her imagination—and it is feminine power because it has come from her own mother. Acting through this power, Jenny convinces Alec that he should not equate giving love with helping her, and the barrier is finally down.

The barrier, then, in this romance, is more than the obstacles to marriage that the hero and heroine must overcome. It includes the larger ideas that this romance interrogates—the effects of one's family of origin on one's adult behavior, the nature of the romantic choices a given person makes, and the way emotional problems can be solved. As in many contemporary novels, the final barrier here, the one that seems insuperable, is self-knowledge.

The point of ritual death occurs when Alec simply does not show up for work one day. In an inversion of the mythic pattern whereby the heroine, or someone who represents her, disappears into the underworld, Alec simply removes himself from the world of the heroine. This, too, resonates much more strongly in the emotional world of the book than in the workaday world. Jenny simply writes him out of the taping for a few days, but his emotional behavior is the real issue: "Alec had been angry for a moment, for one flashing, red-hot moment, he had been angry at Jenny. He wasn't angry anymore. And it was a form of death" (345). The union between Jenny and Alec seems impossible.

The declaration in this novel is fragmented into four parts as heroine and hero each declare their love for the other, first to her- or himself, and then to their beloved. Alec declares his love for Jenny to himself very early, but cannot act on the knowledge because she is still Brian's partner. Jenny declares her love for Alec to herself very late. In the time between these two declarations the barrier, with all of its emotional complexity, plays itself out. Alec's declaration to her is unstated, but communicated all the same. He begins to tell her, "Surely you've realized—" but she stops him, "Alec . . . I don't know anything" (209). As a gentleman addressing another man's woman, he stops. The next chapter, written from her point of view, opens with "Alec was in love with her" (210). Later, she actually announces her love for him, "I love you" (357). The heroine's declaration is the strongest, but her doubt—her internal barrier—was the largest. In this novel the strength of the declaration balances the seriousness and height of the barrier.

In this instance, and in the case of many contemporary romances that have an internal barrier that hinges on the emotional lives of the characters, the declaration of a character to herself that she loves the hero (or to himself, that he loves the heroine) is as much a recognition as it is a declaration. It is part of the new information that will help fell the barrier, and in modern books, the key piece of information, the knowledge without which the book cannot go forward is "This is *love.*" Indeed, in *Again* the recognition is the psychological analysis that leads to these declarations of love. Both heroine and hero come to understand their pasts and how those pasts have made them behave. With this understanding they recognize their true selves just as if they had been disguised, which, of course, was a common form of recognition in earlier comedies.

The betrothal takes place after the heroine seeks out the hero who has stopped coming to work at the studio. Recall that by this action he reverses the classic ritual death in which it is the woman who disappears. Jenny explains to him why it is that he needs her (to keep him from ossifying into a man who is only and always the responsible one), and she tells him that she loves him. The role reversal—with the heroine seeking the hero who enacts ritual death—ends at this point. He proposes: "I don't want this to be a 'relationship,' Jenny. . . . I want us to be married" (363). She accepts, and the betrothal is complete.

Two of the three incidental but frequent elements of the romance novel are also present in *Again.* The wedding of Jenny and Alec is reported—it happens "off"—in a fond, funny memo by the soap opera's publicist to the editor of a soap fan magazine. The wedding, as a final action, defines how the old, corrupt society is reformed and made into a new society by the union of the heroine and hero. The old society had been corrupt, in part, because it was incomplete. It was a workplace, but Jenny had turned it into her entire society. By marrying Alec at his home in Canada, with her father in attendance, along with most of the cast and staff of *My Lady's Chamber,* Jenny and Alec subsume the old society into their newly formed one as Jenny's life becomes expanded to include a truly personal side, with a family other than the soap family. The change is not enormous; this reform impacts mostly Jenny and Alec (although when she stops treating the soap opera's employees as her family, they can, in turn, distance themselves from their workplace in a healthy way). The scapegoat, or, in this case, the scape-goats, are exiled from the celebration of the new society that this wedding represents. Brian, the false hero, and Rita, his new wife, are invited to the wedding but cannot afford the airfare to Prince Edward Island, where the ceremony takes place. This absence from the new society's celebration of unity and harmony does not commence their total exile from the new society because Brian and Rita keep their jobs as actors on the soap opera. The continued employment of the false hero and his wife by the heroine is one more signal that her society has been reformed—the soap opera is, after all, a workplace, not a family or a community.

The romance novel form is continuous from Jane Austen (and, as we shall see, from the birth of the novel in English) through Kathleen Gilles Seidel. Although writers will employ the form in different ways, Seidel in *Again* creates a complex, formally accomplished, vital romance novel. The form is neither moribund nor corrupt. Arguments about hack-work must confront *Again* and others like it being written and published today.

5

THE GENRE'S LIMITS

The eight essential elements of the romance novel represent the core of the genre. In addition to the three optional elements which appear in some, but not all, romance novels, other kinds of material, other sorts of scenes, are often incorporated. As long as the focus stays on the core, essential elements, the work is a romance novel.

When the writer focuses on other kinds of narrative elements, the novel is another kind of thing, a member of another genre. In all genres, however, love plots of various kinds are the norm rather than the exception. Considering only popular forms, there are love plots in science fiction, in which, traditionally, the hero gets the plucky girl as a sort of trophy after he completes the adventure plot. Their relationship is often not a courtship at all. It is represented by adventure scenes involving sexual tension and the couple's exit together at the narrative's end. In detective fiction a frequent pattern portrays a hero who is attracted to a woman who turns out to be a betrayer, or even the perpetrator of whatever crime is being solved. The detective-hero must expose her role in the crime so that knowledge of the crime (the goal of all detective fiction) and justice (the result in many instances) can triumph. There are love plots in the Western, in which the woman often represents the antithesis of the cowboy experience or an alternative to life on the range. The cowboy-hero sometimes marries this woman and sometimes leaves her. These love subplots usually lack one or more of the essential elements of the romance novel.

Chapter Five

A reader sometimes constructs a romance novel from the love plot in a given book whether or not the book contains all eight essential elements of the form. His or her knowledge of the genre—gathered from reading romance novels, or from situation comedies on television (most of which, in the course of their runs, contain all of the elements of the romance novel except the betrothal), or from film—guides such a reading. This reading is often inaccurate. It may include events that are not depicted or implied anywhere on the page. The reader, in other words, fills in missing romance novel elements. This reading is usually incomplete. The reader often discounts, skips, or otherwise disregards scenes that the writer did include but which contradict the romance novel paradigm that the reader is using to work through the novel she is reading.

Two popular love stories that are often misread as romance novels will illustrate the genre's limits: Daphne du Maurier's *Rebecca* (1938) and Margaret Mitchell's *Gone with the Wind* (1936). Both are "near misses." *Rebecca* contains fragments of a romance novel. *Gone with the Wind* has most of the elements, and, when misread in a very common way, seems to contain all of the elements of the genre.

Rebecca occupies fictional territory beyond the boundaries of the romance novel form. The barrier and point of ritual death reveal Rebecca's departure from the form and help define the limits of the romance novel. The work is certainly a love story between the heroine/narrator, who is never named, and Maxim de Winter, owner of an estate called Manderley. The barriers to the heroine's union with the hero are her youth (she is twenty-one, exactly half his age), station (she is a penniless orphan), and the impropriety of his courting her at Monte Carlo while she is employed as a paid companion to an older woman vacationing there. Maxim sweeps these impediments aside and marries her after a courtship that lasts less than a month and occupies about a quarter of the novel. The work of the romance novel is done at this point. The story of the courtship and marriage of a heroine has been told. There is a further barrier to the marriage—not to the courtship: Maxim's possible implication in the death of his first wife, Rebecca. The balance of the narrative splits its focus between solving the mystery of this woman's death and the heroine's efforts to fill Rebecca's place in the Manderley household. As the mystery is revealed the narrator becomes less dependent upon her husband; he, in turn, must depend upon her. The novel ends with the events surrounding Rebecca's death and Maxim's role in them known to the heroine but safely kept from the authorities. Maxim was in danger of being charged with murder; the heroine helps him save himself. The threat of a murder charge is his ritual death. He is saved by the heroine and is freed. But he is not freed to marry her—he has already done that. He is freed from the specter of his first wife.

Rebecca is a gothic tale. Like many such tales, it focuses on a house, Manderley, and the dark events that transpired there. The novel begins and ends with Manderley—in the heroine's dream at the outset and in ashes at the end. Romance novels can be gothic novels as well, but they must balance the focus on the house typical of gothic novels with a correspondingly strong focus on the courtship and betrothal. *Rebecca* depicts the courtship and betrothal, but does not focus upon them. They are preconditions for the story that follows rather than being, themselves, the story.

Gone with the Wind is a nearer miss than *Rebecca*, but still fails to be a romance novel. It is, as everyone knows, a gripping love story. Mussell sees this very popular work as an "antiromance" because the heroine, Scarlett O'Hara Hamilton Kennedy Butler, loses Rhett, the man she loves (*Women's Gothic* 13). All eight essential features of the romance novel are present in the work, but the barrier never completely falls. In addition, *Gone with the Wind* focuses on the effect of the Civil War on the way of life in Georgia, which further removes it from the territory of the romance novel.

Although the love plot does interest her, Mitchell devotes far more space to showing us Scarlett's career as a widow whose land, family, fortune, and society have been ravaged by the war. She shows us Scarlett reconstructing herself from spoiled Southern belle to businesswoman. She shows us a heroine who keeps her family together, defends her land, and runs the businesses she buys. By the time she marries Rhett, she is twice widowed and the mother of two, which takes Scarlett some distance from the ingenue heroine frequent in romance novels.

The barrier between Scarlett and Rhett is chiefly Scarlett's love for Ashley Wilkes, but at other times it includes her marriage to Wade Hamilton, then to Frank Kennedy; the war itself, which carries Rhett into the Confederate army; and Belle, a prostitute whom Rhett takes up with. In the romance, when the wedding precedes the declaration, the marriage is one of convenience. *Gone with the Wind* employs this marriage-of-convenience sequence for ordering events. Heroine and hero are betrothed (page 827) without a declaration from the heroine. By the time Scarlett declares that she loves Rhett, (page 1015), he no longer loves her. At no point in the novel have the two lovers declared for each other at the same time. In other words, the barrier never completely falls.

The barrier created by Scarlett's desire for Ashley falls in Scarlett's recognition scene when she realizes she does not want him now that she can have him. Then Rhett offers her a divorce and announces that he does not love her anymore, speaking his most famous line: "My dear, I don't give a damn" (1023). In this antideclaration, Rhett erects a new barrier, and it does not fall before the end of the novel. Heroine and hero do not end up together, do not, together, remake society (Scarlett has done this single-handedly), and their child, that other promise of the society to come, is dead. We are left with an image of Scarlett standing alone. *Gone with the Wind* is not a romance novel.

Why, then, do people think it is one? It is a love story, and love is the emotion on which the romance novel is predicated. But not every love story is a romance novel. Many readers, I think, read for the scenes between Rhett and Scarlett, even though in the novel there are far fewer of them than the film would imply. They see in those scenes many of the elements of the romance novel. They ignore Rhett's request for a divorce, overlook his having assumed Ashley's old values, overlook Bonnie's death, and credit instead Scarlett's statement that she will get him back. This selective reading results from the genre expectations that readers assume once they have become familiar with a given genre such as the romance novel. These expectations permit a reader to weigh some events in the narrative more heavily than others. The screenwriters did the same when they eliminated one of Scarlett's marriages and both of the children she had before marrying Rhett. In making her the childless widow of only one man killed in the war they restore some of Scarlett's ingenue status. The screenwriters make her into a romance novel heroine.

In both *Rebecca* and *Gone with the Wind* the marriage of heroine and hero in the middle of the book arouses our suspicions that the works are not romance novels. *Rebecca* fails to include several other essential elements. Maxim, for example, never actually undergoes a recognition of his love for the heroine. *Gone with the Wind,* despite its inclusion of the eight essential elements, never manages to deliver a barrierless relationship between hero-ine and hero, and that unconquered barrier, along with the novel's extensive depiction of Scarlett's life as a twice-widowed businesswoman, prevents *Gone with the Wind* from being a romance novel.

Love plots abound. Sometimes they can drive the reading of a book. Nonetheless, only some of these love-driven books are romance novels.

PART III

THE ROMANCE NOVEL, 1740–1908

6

WRITING THE ROMANCE NOVEL'S HISTORY

In Part III I trace the history of the romance novel in English from the beginning of its modern ascendancy in the mid-eighteenth century to the twentieth century when the form becomes a wholly popular one. Most critics writing about "the romance" pay, at most, lip service to the forebears of contemporary works. This practice robs the genre of its most distinguished representatives, marooning it in the present, and reducing it to the few works that a given critic has chosen to analyze. As we have seen, the typically narrow selection of texts has not stopped critics from making sweeping statements about the genre as a whole. This history, then, serves as a corrective to the blinkered vision of the romance novel.

It serves, too, as a map of territory in the eighteenth- and nineteenth-century novel that traditional histories of the novel have discovered but not explored. It thus serves as an addition to the usual history of the novel, which, as originally written, was a history of male forms (with Jane Austen made an honorary male by virtue of her irony). The romance novel, the most female of forms, was dismissed as an accidental choice. Overlooked with the genre itself was its power to convey ideas and issues essential to the heroines who were put at its center.

Standard histories of the novel marginalize the romance novel. We can find the beginnings of this treatment in Ian Watt's influential *Rise of the Novel*. Speaking of Samuel Richardson's invention of the romance novel in its modern form, Watt finds it "odd that so fateful a literary revolution should have been brought about with so ancient a literary weapon" (135). That this oddity would persist to become the most popular form of the novel has not garnered it any more respect from contemporary critics. Writing in 1994, Toni O'Shaughnessy Bowers identifies Augustan amatory fiction ("sensational tales of sexual intrigue published by and for English women in the late seventeenth and early eighteenth centuries") as the direct predecessors of today's romance novel which she typifies as "modern supermarket romances with their . . . sexually demanding men and innocent, desirable, passive women, and their insistence on sexual violence" (50, 59). This characterization of the modern romance novel is predictably hasty in its generalizations—not all, or even most romance novels have sexually demanding men, or innocent, passive women, nor do they all insist on sexual violence (in fact, this is rare in the 1990s). This characterization also condemns early amatory fiction for leading to its mischaracterized successors—romance novels. The grounds of marginalization have shifted: the romance novel is no longer simply an oddly chosen ancient literary weapon; its modern exemplars cast aspersions back through the centuries poisoning the literary history of their unsuspecting predecessors. The romance novel has never been considered in its own light.

When Cawelti began the study of popular fiction in his *Adventure, Mystery and Romance,* he devoted only two pages to the romance. David Perkins, writing on the practice of literary history, notes that literary historians of neglected groups, such as the romance novel, "confer cultural importance" on the group (181). However suspect the result of literary history—the canon—might be, however incomplete, it serves as a map of literature. Students of literature refer to that map, albeit with less than the absolute trust once attributed to it. Yet the romance novel, despite its long history and immense popularity, is on the map only through distorted, incomplete, and hostile representations. Where a clear outline of the romance novel should appear, we find instead the legend: "Here there be dragons."

The definition of the romance novel established in Part II—a work of prose fiction that tells the story of the courtship and betrothal of one or more heroines—provides a litmus test to determine if a novel is a romance novel. The narrative elements of barrier and point of ritual death—which are, as we have seen, two of the elements at the core of the romance novel— together suggest an analytic tool for the discussion of the early romance novel. Focus a romance novel through the lens of barrier and point of ritual death, and the result is a snapshot of what is at stake in that novel. Focus a chronological series of romance novels through this lens and it yields a moving picture of the concerns of the genre itself as it develops and changes through time. This method avoids the two primary pitfalls of earlier attempts to characterize the genre—it evaluates essential elements rather than accidental ones such as sex scenes (for most of its history, the romance novel did not *have* sex scenes), and it addresses texts across the whole span of the romance novel's history. No literary history of the genre can pretend to comprehend it entirely, and I do not make that claim here. Even a partial history, however, is useful, as long as readers understand that it is incomplete.

I have chosen for analysis Richardson's *Pamela*, Jane Austen's *Pride and Prejudice*, Charlotte Brontë's *Jane Eyre*, Anthony Trollope's *Framley Parsonage*, and E. M. Forster's *Room with a View*, first with an eye to their chronological distribution. This selection of texts provides a reasonable chronological distribution from the English novel's ascendancy in the eighteenth century to the early twentieth century: representatives from the Augustan (Richardson and Austen), romantic (Brontë), Victorian (Trollope), and Edwardian (Forster) eras. Second, I have considered the quality of the writing. For example, I passed by the good novels of Fanny Burney in favor of a truly great one of Austen. A third consideration has been the heroines. Pamela Andrews, Elizabeth Bennet, Jane Eyre, Lucy Robarts, and Lucy Honeychurch are vivid, assertive characters. They stand out as heroines in romance novels. In a genre whose focus is the heroine, novels portraying intense, vigorous women provide the purest account of the genre. Finally, I have chosen novels that sold well and were popular in their own day and yet hold places in today's canon; when they were first published, these six books were indistinguishable from other best sellers. The survey of the twentieth-century romance novel in Part IV includes few, if any, canonical works. The popularity of these older works assures continuity with the newer books in Part I, and is proof against the accusation that the virtues that I find in these older representatives of the genre are those of high art and not those of popular culture. *Pamela, Pride and Prejudice,* and the rest were part of popular culture in their day.

The romance novel steps forward as a dominant genre in English letters at a time of changing values and practices concerning courtship and marriage. This change brought about conflict, which is reflected in the pages of the romance novels in Part III. As a result of this change in values, three broad social trends meet and clash on the pages of the romance novel: the rise of affective individualism, the importance of companionate marriage, and English law as it applied to married women. Authors of the romance novel confronted all of these issues as they told the story of the courtship and betrothal of their heroines.

Marriage has, for centuries, been simultaneously the lot and the goal of most women. Historian Olwen Hufton states, flatly, "Most women in fact married." Speaking of the period during which the romance novel emerged, she notes "between 1550 and 1800 the proportion of women who died above the age of 50 in the celibate state varied from 5 to 25 percent" (26). Between 75 and 95 percent of all women married. This proportion has not decreased despite revolutions in sexual conduct and increased tolerance of couples living together unmarried. The proportion of women between the ages of forty-five and fifty-four in the United States who had never married was just 5 percent in 1990 (Wright 303). Ninety-five percent had married. In the twentieth century as in the sixteenth, most women married. The romance novel operates within this fact of female life.

"Affective individualism," a term coined by Lawrence Stone to name the shift in social relationships that he perceives in the late seventeenth and early eighteenth centuries, denotes the increase in feeling or emotion (that is, in affect) in family relationships and the advent of the idea that the individual's fulfillment is the end of life itself (221–69). This new set of values "placed the individual above the kin, the family, the society and even, in some eighteenth-century judicial pronouncements, the state" (224). Called "freedom" or "liberty" by contemporaries, these values "modified and mitigated the rigidities of a society whose fundamental cohesion was preserved by habits of obedience to legitimate authority, two of the most important aspects of which were the subordination of children to parents, and of women to men" (223).

We have seen that the form of the romance novel always involves freedom. The release from the barrier and the escape from ritual death provide, in the workings of the plot, this fundamental release from inhibition to action, from constraint to choice, from bondage to freedom. This formal feature was a part of the courtship plot long before the romance novel gained prominence. It was there in early forms—in Shakespeare's comedies, most notably—ready to be transformed when social forces in the late seventeenth and early eighteenth centuries promoted a new idea of individualism, which expressed itself as a demand for freedom and liberty, as well as a new, greater emphasis on the importance of feeling in family life, including the relationship between spouses. A genre which included freedom as a consequence of its formal features was the perfect vehicle for the expression of these new social forces. It is not a coincidence that a new genre—the romance novel—distinguished itself from other comedies in order to express these new social values.

At the same time that a belief in individualism was changing the expectations of the individual, a related belief in companionate marriage was changing individual ideas of courtship. A companionate marriage is one in which the chief end of a union is mutual comfort and support, including love, between spouses. Stone tells us that such a reason for union was preached from the pulpit in England as early as 1549, and the idea gained force during the latter part of the sixteenth century (136). Traditional reasons for marriage, such as procreation and the avoidance of fornication, became subordinate to the all-important love between spouses. Other social historians find that love itself was an old idea in English life. Alan Macfarlane reviews the expression of love in English literature to demonstrate the age and ubiquity of the importance of love in this culture, noting that "by the eighteenth century [moralists and philosophers] took it for granted that marriage was based on love" (175).

However old the idea is, by the time the romance novel assumes prominence in English literature, love is the primary reason that people marry. The traditional comedic courtship plot often depicts a hero who falls in love with the heroine at first sight. The romance novel emerges from, but shifts the focus of, this tradition. It often depicts a heroine who falls in love with the hero gradually. Telling the story of this slowly developing love and the courtship that structures this love becomes the major focus of the narrative.

The final social trend, if trends can be static, concerns the status of wives under English law, which is best reflected in their property rights, or lack thereof. Legal historian Lee Holcombe summarizes the situation: "Unlike single women or widows, who had the same property rights as men, except the right to vote, married women had legally no rights over property. . . . wives were reduced to a special status, subordinate to and dependent upon their husbands" (25). Sir William Blackstone, an eighteenth-century English jurist, wrote, "By marriage the very being or legal existence of a woman is suspended, or at least it is incorporated or consolidated into that of the husband, under whose wing, protection and cover she performs everything, and she is therefore called in our law a *feme covert*" (Holcombe 25). These laws pertained to all of the woman's property—real estate, rents from land, interest in a business, gifts, wages, inheritance, and dowry. All of it became the property of her husband when she married him. This legal eclipse of a woman's property rights upon her marriage was in place well before the emergence of the romance novel in the eighteenth century, and persisted until 1870 when the Married Women's Property Act assigned "the wages and earning of any married woman . . . to her separate use, independent of any husband to whom she may be married"(Holcombe 243). Of the heroines in the books analyzed below, only one, Forster's Lucy Honeychurch, courts and marries after the passage of this act.

There were ways around this law for women who had access to lawyers. Susan Staves notes that such categories of payment as jointure, pin money, and other forms of financial settlement could be made through a wife's trustees (27–161). In the novels of the eighteenth and nineteenth centuries, these trustees are referred to as the "friends" of the woman, and any marriage settlement made on a woman about to become a *feme covert*, a woman about to marry and lose her legal status altogether, would be made through these friends. Of course, the "friends" were actually legal trustees who owned and controlled the assets, but the married woman would at least derive income from these assets, independent of her husband's control. Husbands could, and did, beat their wives. Husbands could, and did, forcibly limit their wives' travel and associations. Husbands could, and did, so limit their wives' access to household money that their own children did not have enough to eat. In the face of an authority that could be so arbitrary, independent money for the wife (then as now) was a protection against some of the husband's potential abuses of power as well as a means of providing the couple with a higher standard of living.

The almost absolute dependence of the wife on the husband for the roof over her head, food to eat, clothes to wear, medical attention, and support for their children made courtship a momentous time in a woman's life. For centuries, choosing a husband was *the* crucial decision for most women. The romance novel emerges as a dominant form of the English novel just as the expectations surrounding the choice of a husband shifted. Affective individualism added to the choice a desire for liberty, and the shift from older forms of union to companionate marriage added a requirement that the wife- and husband-to-be love each other. The woman's search for liberty and love in marriage, a lifelong commitment that resulted in her loss of property rights, made courtship a time of conflicting goals. Of course, older assumptions about marriage had not died, and the goal of individual self-fulfillment had to be measured against the need for financial support and the desire for love. With one chance to make the right choice (divorce was rare and difficult, particularly for a woman), courtship became a battleground for the working out of these sometimes conflicting values. The literary form that took courtship as its subject—the romance novel—provided an obvious vehicle for the depiction of the clash of these values.

For centuries courtship as depicted in comedy focused on one or more heroes; with the advent of the romance novel, authors regularly began to place the focus on the heroine. One such hero-centered courtship narrative is *Incognita: Or, Love and Duty Reconcil'd* (1692), which was published in the early days of the English novel, just as the social changes outlined above were taking hold in English society. William Congreve (1670–1729), best known as a dramatist, as author of the comedy of manners *The Way of the World*, wrote this comedy of errors set in Shakespearean time and space. It is a confection: its tone is light; the action improbably telescoped; its purpose, delight. Examining this tale of heroes' courtship and betrothal from the early days of the English novel permits us to see the conventions that the authors of the romance novel—with its focus on the heroine—rejected, manipulated, and transformed.

Incognita's two heroes, Aurelian and Hippolito, journey to Florence, where the novel is set, where they learn that a public celebration of a noble marriage is about to begin. They disguise themselves by exchanging names and contriving costumes so that they may share in "the publick Merriment" without Aurelian's father, a Florentine nobleman, realizing that his son has returned. Aurelian, in physical disguise and calling himself "Hippolito," meets a masked woman calling herself "Incognita" (the unknown lady) and immediately falls in love with her. The real Hippolito meets Leonora and immediately falls in love with her. In both cases this is love at first sight, despite the disguises that both men and both women wear. Aurelian's father has betrothed him to one Juliana. In the confusing atmosphere of "Balls and Masques, and other Divertisements" where disguise, near abductions, partially destroyed letters, and sword fights in the dark are commonplace, the woman calling herself "Incognita" turns out to have been Juliana all along, and Aurelian, throwing off his disguise and disclosing his real name, the man who has been courting her (11). The fathers' wishes (both Aurelian's and Juliana's) are answered. Both pairs of lovers marry. Duty—following one's parent's orders—and love—marrying a person with whom one is in love—are thus reconciled.

Congreve's focus in *Incognita* is on the heroes. Their arrival in Florence sets the slight plot in motion, and their confused identities, near deaths, and determined searches for the disguised heroines constitute the greater

part of the narrative. Yet, in his treatment of Juliana/Incognita as she contemplates her father's decree that she marry someone not of her choosing,
Congreve anticipates the romance novel's focus on the heroine's delibera-
tion and choice of the hero. She represents her choices as running away to
a monastery where she has an aunt who opposes the arranged match (thus
saving herself for the man she has chosen), or remaining in Florence and,
in her words, "being taken by some of my Relations, and forced to a thing
so quite contrary to my Inclinations"—that is—being forced to marry the
man to whom her father has betrothed her (57). Congreve faces his heroine with the burden of assuming her liberty. In placing her own happiness
over the demands of filial duty, Juliana/Incognita acts from the values of
affective individualism.

In its treatment of love, Congreve's *Incognita* adheres to older conventions. In it, love is a largely male affair. Aurelian is smitten with Juliana the
first time he sees her. Love at first sight, although not unknown among
heroines in the literature of love, is largely a male phenomenon. In fact,
Juliana, wearing a mask and calling herself Incognita at a masquerade, gives
Aurelian a choice "whether he would know whom she was, or see her Face"
(28). He chooses sight over knowledge. In the romance novel, with its
focus on the heroine, love will rarely be at first sight, and knowledge will be
an important part of the courtship that is the very reason for the book's
being. In *Incognita*, disguises physically block sight; these disguises are the
reason that Congreve even has a story to tell. The romance novel will turn
the physical disguise so prevalent in older comedy into a lack of knowledge
about the hero's or heroine's inner self. Aurelian has obscured his name and
his appearance, and so has Juliana. In the romance novel, knowledge of the
beloved's personality, values, beliefs—identity in the psychological sense of
the word—replaces knowledge of their physical identity obscured by disguise and assumed names. The importance of sight becomes the importance of insight.

In the romance novel the kind of barrier that we typically see differs
from that in a traditional comedy such as *Incognita*. Aurelian and Juliana are
prevented from betrothing themselves to each other not only by issues of
physical identity—neither knows who the other actually is until the final
scene—but also by their fathers' having already betrothed them, so they
believe, to another. Parents are traditional blocking characters, and these
parents provide a barrier to the lovers' betrothal in the most fundamental
way. In promising their children in marriage, they enact a kinship exchange,
a union of their offspring to cement the two families' ties. The prospective

marriage partners' preferences in the matter are secondary—if they are even consulted. *Incognita* is forward looking in the insistence (on the part of the eligible men and women) on a love match, even if, as we have seen, this match is viewed primarily from the hero's perspective. The romance novel will augment this external barrier with internal ones which focus the novel on issues of a love achieved after careful reflection.

In his treatment of property in *Incognita*, Congreve adheres to the earlier form of comedy. He sets his novel in Shakespearean time and space: the time period is unspecified, some indeterminate "present" in which romantic heroes and heroines enact a timeless drama. Florence is exotic, simultaneously nowhere and everywhere. The characters are nobles; perhaps we are to assume that property will not be a problem for these young people. In the end, too, they do their parents' bidding with, one assumes, the marital settlements of property that reward obedient children who fulfill a marriage contract between wealthy, powerful families.

The romance novel will focus on the vulnerability that all women in English society had imposed upon them by the legal doctrine of the *feme covert*. If the romance novel form reflects social changes in its treatment of affective individualism and love, it also highlights problems with the long-established practice that eliminates, in law, the very distinctions that affective individualism and love between spouses implied. Individualism and love focus on each partner in the union—her feelings, his feelings; her preferences, his preferences. Feelings and preferences extend to property as well, and property is often the medium through which individuals express their feelings and act to secure their preferences. For centuries, English law simply erased one partner when the betrothal became a marriage. The woman became a wife based on her individual choice and her feelings towards her new spouse, but at the same time, she lost her ownership—and control—over all that she once had owned. Personal property is an important vehicle for individual choice. Paradoxically, in exercising her individual choice of a spouse, a woman was forced to surrender that range of individual choice provided by ownership of property. Society granted her autonomy as long as she was an unmarried woman, then removed it the minute she married. No wonder a woman's choice of a spouse was so fraught with drama.

The six novels chosen to represent the history of the romance novel in English from its inception to the beginnings of the twentieth century evince a form that was particularly suited to depicting the social changes, especially as they affected women, who, in these books, would become heroines.

7

THE FIRST
BEST SELLER

Pamela, 1740

My exploration of the history of the romance novel in English begins with *Pamela; or, Virtue Rewarded* (1740), the story of the courtship, betrothal, wedding, and triumph of lady's maid Pamela Andrews to Mr. B, the master for whom she works. Nominating a first novel in English is arbitrary, but *Pamela* is one of the works named to that honor. With it, Samuel Richardson (1689–1761), already a successful London printer and editor, advanced the quality of prose fiction, providing an early instance of the exploration of character that the novel would become known for. Ian Watt, an influential historian of the novel in English, notes that Richardson departed from earlier, episodic plots "by basing his novels on a single action, a courtship" (135). The courtship story would become a major force shaping the novel in English, and with *Pamela* Richardson brings the courtship plot, which is to say the romance novel, into more than prominence. He makes it famous.

If *Pamela* is not the first novel in English, nor yet the first romance novel, it is the first best seller. It was an immediate sensation. Richardson printed five editions in the eleven months following the novel's first appearance in November of 1740. Alan Dugald McKillop, one of the first modern critics to bring Richardson back into critical favor, typifies the novel's reception: "It is safe to say that almost everybody read it. It became the fashion, the best seller which it was compulsory to discuss" (*Samuel Richardson* 43). Its influence went beyond a mere novel—*Pamela* and Pamela became a phenomenon, what Eaves and Kimpel, Richardson's biographers, call a "vogue" (119–53). It was translated and adapted for the stage. Unauthorized sequels appeared. There was even *Pamela* merchandise—fans and teacups were painted with scenes from the book. And, of course, babies—and eventually their several times great-granddaughters—were named after the heroine.

Since its publication in 1740, *Pamela* has inspired fervent supporters, who came to be called Pamelists. A story, perhaps apocryphal, is told of the effect on some nineteenth-century English villagers who were hearing *Pamela* read aloud: "At length, when the happy turn of fortune arrived which brings the hero and heroine together . . . the congregation were so delighted as to raise a great shout, and procuring the church keys, actually set the church bells ringing" (McKillop, "Wedding" 323). This reaction is one we might expect to the happy ending of a romance novel in which a lady's maid (Pamela) marries her employer (Mr. B).

Anti-Pamelists have been present in force from the beginning as well. Henry Fielding immediately wrote *Shamela* (1741), a parody in which Richardson's sincere heroine is transformed into a scheming trollop who seduces and entraps B, now known as "Booby," by her sexual wiles. Fielding's skepticism about this Cinderella, rags-to-riches, servant-to-lady-of-the-manor story has been echoed by more recent critics of the novel. Watt discusses the economic and social background of the novel at length but gives scant attention to the text itself, dismissing it, finally, as a work "with the combined attractions of a sermon and a striptease" (173). McKillop responds to the theme of the work, and to its plot, as "the aftermath of ballad and romance. . . . The essential novelty of *Pamela* was in method rather than in theme" (34–5). Mark Kinkead-Weekes calls *Pamela* a "prentice-piece" (7). Eaves and Kimpel damn the plot with faint praise: "The plot has the advantage of unity and, at least for some readers, of suspense, but it is not calculated to appeal to readers of today" (103). Critics, on the whole, prefer Richardson's second novel, *Clarissa*, the story of the imprisonment, rape, and death of a pious young woman, a sort of *Pamela* with an unhappy ending. Pursuing *Clarissa*, Terry Eagleton takes a slap at *Pamela*, claiming that the heroine's absorption into marriage at the end of the novel changes her for the worse:

She is now the collusive victim of patriarchy, triumphantly elevated
into enemy territory. . . . it is difficult to imagine how Pamela could in
any sense be proclaimed as 'progressive.' The same question could be
asked of women's romances today: are they anything more than opiate
and offensive? In both cases, surely, the answer is guardedly positive.
Pamela tells the story of a woman snatched into the ruling class and
tamed to its sexist disciplines; yet it contains, grotesque though it may
sound, a utopian element. The novel is a kind of fairy-tale prerun of
Clarissa, a fantasy wish fulfillment in which abduction and imprisonment turn out miraculously well. . . . Like modern romantic fiction, its
main effect is thus anodyne and oppressive. (*Rape* 36–37)

What answer, beyond the ringing of church bells, can a contemporary
Pamelist make to anti-Pamelists such as Watt, McKillop, Kinkead-Weekes,
and Eagleton? Is Richardson merely riding on the coattails of earlier forms,
unaware of the sort of novel he is writing, in which Pamela is merely a Cinderella figure, untouched by more serious issues? Richardson mastered the
form of the romance novel and fully understood Pamela's financial vulnerability, both before and after her marriage to B. When Richardson chose to
focus upon a courtship, he accomplished more than simply avoiding the
fragmented episodic plot at work in the fiction of his contemporaries (for
example, Defoe). In choosing to write a romance novel—the story of the
courtship and betrothal of one or more heroines—he had at his disposal
the elements of the form defined and analyzed in Part II, and he exploited
them to full advantage. Far from stumbling upon a convenient form,
Richardson knows from the beginning its possibilities. A look at the barrier as well as the point of ritual death in Richardson's purest romance
novel, *Pamela*, will demonstrate the perfect fit that Richardson has crafted
between the form and its ideas.

The barrier, as we have seen, always involves freeing the heroine (and
hero) from restraint; in *Pamela* the heroine is *literally* restrained—that is, she
is physically imprisoned by the hero. Her liberty is literally at stake in this
most important barrier element. The ideas put into play by the barrier as
well as its literal content are Pamela's liberty and property, including
Pamela's ownership of herself. The point of ritual death, as we have seen,
always marks the seeming impossibility of the union between heroine and
hero, often with a death or a deathlike image; in *Pamela* the threatened death
is Pamela's own, as well as the hero's. At issue on the realistic level of inci-

dent and plot in this first best-selling romance novel are life, liberty, and property. In *Pamela*, Richardson devises a plot that not only embodies the formal features of the romance novel, it reflects the central meanings of those features in a starkly unmetaphorical way. He understands the new form from the beginning and simultaneously perfects it and inaugurates it as one of the main paths that the novel would follow.

In this, Richardson shows himself the product of the age that was embracing affective individualism with its emphasis on personal fulfillment. He is also the product of one of the intellectual workings-out of this notion, a product, in fact, of the Glorious Revolution and its best-known theorist, John Locke, whose triad of "life, liberty, and property" became the basis for revolutions and governments in the century that followed and beyond. Jocelyn Harris notes the importance of Locke to Richardson's thought, specifically his stated preference for "the Principles of LIBERTY" (*Samuel Richardson* 1–3). Pamela spouts the virtues of Locke's *Thoughts on Education* in *Pamela II*, the continuation that Richardson wrote to compete with the sequels that others were writing to his novel. The insistence in *Pamela* on his heroine's rights to her life, to her liberty, and to her property might also have come from the imaginative effort that it took for a fifty-year-old businessman to write and speak for a girl of fifteen. As a financially independent adult male, Richardson would naturally think himself entitled to life, certainly, but also to liberty, and most especially to his property, the fruits of his labor. It is not hard to imagine him transferring that kind of self-regard to the young heroine he placed at the center of his first novel. As a successful printer who had begun as an apprentice then accumulated a stake so he could set up his own shop and marry, Richardson was naturally sensitive to issues of property. His understanding of the romance novel's barrier, whose essence is a lack of freedom, and of the point of ritual death, whose essence is life itself, implies an artistic insight, a degree of self-consciousness as an artist often missed in critical portraits of the earnest printer (Harris 11). In his insight into the formal possibilities of the romance novel, Richardson gives us the means to decide between Eagleton's reaction—damning the novel with praise so faint that it can hardly be heard—and the villagers' response—the din of church bells ringing to celebrate the marriage of a character in a novel.

In *Pamela* every apparently exterior barrier has an interior component. Indeed, the novel is one of the first to probe psychological states, a consequence of its epistolary form. Still the barrier elements can be arrayed from those that exist largely outside the heroine and hero, to those that exist almost wholly within them, particularly within B. All of the barrier elements put into play issues of liberty and property.

The barrier with the largest exterior component is the heroine and hero's unequal wealth and status. Pamela measures her poverty against B's fortune and calls herself "a creature of unequal condition" (278). A constant reminder of this inequality is her relationship to B for fully half of the novel—she is his employee. Pamela, fifteen at the novel's beginning, is a lady's maid, a servant, and has been one since she was eleven. Olwen Hufton has found that 80 percent of eighteenth-century country girls like Pamela left home at around age twelve to go into service. Pamela's age and status are thus unremarkable for a girl who could not look to her family for financial support: "While sparing her family the cost of feeding her, she was in the business of accumulating a dowry and work skills to attract a husband" (Hufton 17). B, with his fortune, would expect to marry someone from his own class—the landed gentry—and would expect his future wife to bring to the marriage a handsome sum, one many times larger than any that Pamela could accumulate in her working life. Eaves and Kimpel note how "distasteful" a match between a servant and her master was to many of Richardson's contemporaries (151). This inequality forms an important part of the barrier to this union, both in the eyes of the society in which the novel is set and in the mind of B.

False suitors, when they appear in romance novels, always contribute to the exterior barrier. Marrying someone other than the hero is, after all, a rather large impediment to marriage to the hero. If the heroine is in love with the false suitor, the barrier has an internal component as well. In Pamela's case, however, the false suitors form part of the exterior barrier. Imprisoned by B in his Lincolnshire estate, Pamela reluctantly agrees to marry Parson Williams because the ruin that B threatens—her rape—is far more dire than marriage to a man she does not love. B, learning of the plan, exercises his power as a justice of the peace and has Williams imprisoned for debt, thus removing a potential protector for Pamela. Williams, then, represents the wrong man to B, and, for different reasons, to Pamela as well. A second "wrong man," a mirror image to Williams, is B's retainer Colbrand, whom B proposes as a husband for Pamela. As B's paid conspirator, Colbrand would then serve as a procurer for B, enabling the would-be rake to have what he claims to want through fully half of the novel—Pamela's sexual favors. Both the rescuing parson and the pandering toady serve as part of the impediment to the marriage between heroine and hero.

Geography, that most traditional of barrier elements that keeps heroine and hero from marrying simply by keeping them apart, has a complex role in this novel. Under the guise of returning her to her parents, B has Pamela kidnapped and taken from one of his estates to another—from Bedfordshire to Lincolnshire—where his servants imprison her. In imprisoning her, B has obviously removed her liberty. In response to her attempts to escape, B has Pamela confined more and more closely in Brandon Hall. First he forbids her to attend church. Then he confines her—contracts her world—to a bedchamber which becomes the setting for B's attempts to rape her. Thus confined, Pamela is, of course, also prevented from earning anything—she cannot work. No longer an employee, she is now a prisoner, her livelihood and her well-being in the hands of someone else.

Property is at stake here as well. Jocelyn Harris notes that in imprisoning Pamela, B has violated her property rights in herself (*Samuel Richardson* 20). John Locke says, "every Man has a Property in his own Person" (2:27, 305). Pamela asks Mrs. Jewkes, B's housekeeper and Pamela's jailer, "How came I to be his property? What right has he in me, but such as a thief may plead to stolen goods?" (163). He also has her shoes taken to impede her escape on foot. In addition to her shoes, he orders Mrs. Jewkes to take Pamela's money, which she would need to make good any possible escape from the house itself.

Money is also the means to Pamela's future. Hufton notes that "in her mid-twenties a maidservant who had managed to become a . . . lady's maid would have a respectable capital sum, the amount depending upon her ability to accumulate without cutting into her wages to help her family or to cope with periods of illness or unemployment" (22). Pamela's escape to her parents to preserve her virtue is a sacrifice of the chance to accumulate that sum. Pamela's parents are in debt; indeed, *she* sends *them* money (44). Her father is a failed schoolmaster forced into "hard labour" (48). In urging her to come home, Pamela's father tries to be optimistic: "you are the staff of our old age, and our comfort. . . . we cannot do for you as we would . . . what with my diligent labour, and your poor mother's spinning, and your needle-work, I make no doubt we shall do better and better" (69). As Hufton tells us, what Pamela (like all young women) needs, is a dowry, but her parents cannot "do for her"—cannot supply it. She left home to ease their burden. Returning is a step backward. Imprisonment denies her the chance to earn money, to earn her stake in her own future.

B's purpose for imprisoning her—to rape her—also jeopardizes her future. Pamela refers to this usage as B's attempt to "ruin" her, and such ruin is more than simply a deflowering (252). Hufton notes, "A maidservant who became pregnant was simply dismissed" (22). Pamela's virtue was essential to her future.

All of these actions to deny Pamela her liberty and property are proof of B's inability or unwillingness to recognize Pamela as a person with rights. This is, at bottom, the real barrier to this marriage. Pamela refuses all entreaties to surrender to B outside of marriage. In doing so she seeks to preserve her virtue, her self-ownership (i.e., her property in herself) and her self-determination. It is more than mere piety, although she is certain that this is God's will. It is also more than obedience to her parents, although she knows that they wish her to remain virtuous. It is a preservation of her inner self, of her freedom. Frye says, "Virginity is to a woman what honor is to a man, the symbol of the fact that she is not a slave. . . . Deep within the . . . convention of virgin-baiting is a vision of human integrity . . . always managing to avoid the one fate which is really worse than death, the annihilation of one's identity" (*Secular Scripture* 73, 86). Liberty and property, including self-ownership, are the terms in which Richardson casts this identity.

The constraining nature of all barriers becomes, in Richardson's hands, actual, physical constraint. For Pamela, release from this barrier is actual, physical release. Indeed, the moment that Pamela is free the declaration scene occurs, and B proposes marriage, putting the betrothal in motion. In this part of the novel, the events of the courtship are driven by the mechanism of the romance novel's formal elements. When the barrier is removed, the next steps occur automatically, as if a dam has broken. Explanation of the psychological insight into the characters' motives for this change comes after, constituting a mopping up operation. The romance novel typically insists on this explanation. When declaration and betrothal follow mechanically upon the removal of the barrier, the romance novel's debt to comedy is evident. When it probes the motivation for declaration and betrothal, it concerns itself with matters typical of the newer form.

If the barrier that B has constructed consists of assaults on Pamela's property and liberty, the point of ritual death puts life at risk—both Pamela's and B's. Heroine and hero both undergo ritual death, with Pamela actually contemplating suicide as a way to escape imprisonment in B's household and defilement at his hands. The action is complex. In an escape attempt Pamela climbs out a window in her locked room, fakes her drowning by throwing clothes in the pond behind the house, and tries unsuccessfully to unlock the garden gate. She knocks herself unconscious when her attempt to climb the garden wall brings a loose brick down upon her head. Unable to escape, she considers actual suicide: "What to do, but to throw myself into the pond, and so put a period to all my terrors in this world!" (211). The faked suicide, being knocked out, or the contemplated suicide—any one would serve as a ritual death. Richardson gives us all three. Like all ritual death, it marks the nadir of hope for the potential union between heroine and hero. However, this death is more than mere ritual because Pamela actually contemplates suicide. Continuation, procreation, society renewed—all of the things that the romance novel promises—are impossible in the face of the heroine's suicide. Later Pamela loses consciousness again in the final rape attempt as B, who disguises himself as a maid, has Mrs. Jewkes restrain Pamela and begins to rape her. She faints twice, mimicking in her unconscious state the deaths that the narrative had just projected. B and Jewkes think the worst: "They both, from the cold sweats I was in, thought me dying" (242). Fainting is Pamela's last resort. She cannot run or struggle, but she can absent herself. Throughout the book, when Pamela faints, B stops assaulting her; sex with an unconscious, bound partner apparently is not what he had in mind. (Sex with a conscious, bound partner seems to be another matter.) Fainting is a simulacrum of death, common at points of ritual death.

B suffers a ritual death as well. Soon after he relents in his attempts to rape her and arranges for Pamela to return to her parents, he falls ill (286, 290). This series of suicides faked and contemplated, of consciousness lost in the garden and in bed, and of illness upon separation marks the impossibility of the union. In this novel, ritual death is almost made actual—the heroine not only mimics death, she contemplates its reality.

Pamela's ritual death reflects on the barrier as well. Constrain liberty closely enough, and life itself is jeopardized. And Pamela is held ever more closely as a prisoner until physical resistance is denied her and rape is imminent. Rape itself is a fundamental denial of liberty, a violation of Pamela's self-ownership, and a serious threat to her career as a servant. Pamela (and B) are not only freed from the barrier, the barrier is about not being free. Pamela is not only delivered from mythic or symbolic death, she is delivered from suicide. The meaning of these formal features and the plot itself coincide, as Richardson creates the closest possible correspondence between form and event, between genre and plot. Richardson well understood the form he chose for Pamela, the "ancient literary weapon" called the romance novel.

When B and Pamela marry the novel is only three-quarters complete.

This extension of the action beyond the marriage, which John Allen Stevenson reads as an "anticourtship narrative," is actually a working out of the consequences of Pamela's choice to marry B and an attempt to mitigate the more serious implications of Pamela's new legal status as a married woman (474). This quarter of the work that extends beyond the traditional ending of the romance novel testifies to the difficulty of settling this particular heroine into her new-found state of pragmatic freedom.

With the demise of the barrier and the release from ritual death, B is freed of the view he has held of Pamela as something less than fully human. Pamela is delivered from death and freed of the barrier's threats to her liberty and property. At this moment, she has the liberty to make an uncoerced choice. Given Pamela's case, what does an assumption of pragmatic freedom mean for a heroine? Comedy assumes that men inhabit—or should inhabit—a state of nature; the artificial (Frye would say absurd) claims of the barrier interfere with this state. Indeed, this is true of B. Lady Davers, his sister, is depicted as a creature of extreme temper and will to illustrate the absurdity of society's objections to B's marriage. As these artificial, absurd constraints are removed, the hero inhabits that state of nature, and society adjusts itself to the newly freed man in its midst. We see B dealing imperiously with Lady Davers. She must accommodate him.

Women, however, when freed from the constraints of the barrier must confront the laws of men. Pamela's choice to return to B rather than home to her father must be seen in this light. As a heroine, she is denied the absolute freedom that men assume (and that B as lord of the manor and justice of the peace has). If she returns home, she becomes once again a burden on her parents. Her father is in debt. Her mother, who spins to contribute to the family income, has failing eyesight. Pamela is penniless, no closer to a dowry and independence from her parents than when she left home six years earlier. B, on the other hand, offers financial security, protection from some of the perils of pregnancy, legitimacy, and a large step up in status.

It is part of the work of the last quarter of the book to settle Pamela financially. To accomplish this, Richardson supplies all of the details of the usual marriage settlement. Susan Staves tells us that such marriage settlements were "common among substantial country freeholders"—B's status is higher than this—as well as among "city business . . . people," which describes Richardson's status (60). In 1752, while he would have been revising *Pamela,* Richardson negotiated the settlement for his eldest daughter Mary upon her marriage to a Bath surgeon. Recall that when a woman married, when she became a *feme covert,* she "in effect made a gift of her property to her husband" (Holcombe 18). Richardson, a prosperous city businessman, was displeased with the provisions made for his daughter, noting that his "reasonings were not attended to" and further that the bridegroom had been left with too much discretion by the final settlement. He writes in his diary, "Mr. D. [the groom] whatever kind things he may do by his Wife [Richardson's daughter Mary], has it now in his Power to do them or not" (Reed 231).

Pamela in her settlements fares better than Mary Richardson Ditcher. B settles on Pamela both forms of married women's property that circumvented the usual denial of women's property rights: pin money and jointure. Pamela entered her marriage with nothing, but B manages to provide for her in settlements that would ordinarily have been made before marriage. B moves Pamela's parents to property he owns in Kent, where they can live and farm for the rest of their lives, with an income over and above that of the farm (390). B allows Pamela "two hundred guineas a year, which Longman [the steward] shall constantly pay you, at fifty guineas a quarter, for your own use, and of which I expect no account" (391). This is "pin money," defined by Staves as "payments under a contract by a husband to a wife during coverture [marriage] of a set annual sum." Often the contract was the marriage settlement, but sometimes husbands entered into other pre- and postnuptial agreements to pay pin money (132–33). This postnuptial settlement is quite handsome—some ten times the annual wages of the average working man—and the sort of generous dealing that B never displayed during the courtship. In fact, he had offered Pamela a contract to become not his wife, but his mistress.

In addition, he provides a jointure, first explaining that he does not determine the disposition of property that came to him through his mother and refusing "to leave my Pamela at the mercy of those to whom my *paternal* estate . . . will devolve" (510). B refers here to Pamela's dower rights. Dower, Staves tells us, is "the legal right or interest which the wife acquired by marriage in the real estate of her husband." Usually this amounted to one third of all the real property of which her husband had been the legal owner at any time during the marriage (235, 27). If the widow Pamela B were to claim her dower rights, she would receive the income from one third of B's land. But the land itself would be owned by, and under the direction of, his heirs, probably his nearest male relatives. Pamela's income would depend on their honoring her dower rights, a reliance that B seems unwilling to make. He substitutes a jointure, "a provision of land or income made in the marriage settlement for the wife should she survive her husband" (Staves 238). This makes Pamela "absolutely independent" and "put[s] it out of anybody's power to molest [her] father and mother" (510).

In the carriage on the way home to her parents, Pamela was free but not secure. Her future was grim. Overcoming her family's poverty would have required health, intelligence, and luck. In love with B, she chose to return, and within the oppression of English property laws as they applied to women, he secured both her and her parents' future. The novel frees her to choose—but only within the constraints of the law and of the society of the day. As Samuel Richardson understood, the institution of marriage itself is part of that society and the determining factor in an English-woman's relationship to private property, .

Are the bell-ringing villagers simply stoned on an "opiate"—that is, on the novel they have been listening to? Is Pamela's triumph merely "conso-latory myth" as Eagleton claims? In *Clarissa* Richardson certainly rejects the marriage that he embraced in *Pamela*, despite the supplications of his read-ers that he write a happy ending for the heroine they had come to love. In Eagleton's critique of the romance novel, the consolation, the anodyne, *is* the marriage. There is, finally, no room for marriage at all in the literary views of critics like Eagleton. Yet throughout the period studied in this book, the middle of the eighteenth century through the twentieth, most women married. A literary form that depicts that decision as fraught with difficulties in the making but ultimately happy, in other words, a romance novel, offers insight into the state itself, and, as Eagleton grudgingly admits, critique. This story can be called oppressive, I think, only if one believes that marriage itself is an institution so flawed that it cannot be good for a woman. There would be no romance novels if everyone agreed that marriage was invariably good and that the decision to marry was not difficult or fraught with peril. But to conclude that every fictional depic-tion of the decision to marry is "oppressive" is to ask one genre to become another—to ask a romance novel like *Pamela* to become a prose tragedy like *Clarissa*. This is unreasonable. The villagers would say it is undesirable as well.

Richardson's journey to the essence of the romance novel form—recorded in *Pamela*—reveals not only the depth of his self-consciousness as an artist, but also the capacity of the form to explore the most fundamen-tal issues surrounding a woman's decision to marry. As we progress through other decisions to marry depicted in the romance novels examined here, we will see the institution of marriage interrogated as the role of women in society comes under sharp, skeptical scrutiny. The freedom that the removal of the barrier and ritual death provides for a heroine is partial, pragmatic. Exploration and expansion of the sphere of this pragmatic freedom—the expansion of the sphere that society will permit women—is the work of the romance.

8

THE BEST
ROMANCE NOVEL
EVER WRITTEN

Pride and Prejudice, 1813

Jane Austen is the master of the romance novel. She published six but had she written only *Pride and Prejudice* (1813), her command of the form would be indisputable. For this reason *Pride and Prejudice* served as the case study in Part II to illustrate the elements of the romance novel. I return to her here in part because the brief discussion in Part II of barrier and point of ritual death, the lenses through which I focus my analysis of the romance, deliberately ignored a large segment of the barrier and did not deeply explore the significance of the point of ritual death. I also return to this work because the form of Austen's novels has attracted critical attention. Here I place the analysis of her achievement in the romance novel form in the context of the critical debate on Austen's works.

Austen accurately described this particular novel as "light and bright and sparkling," worrying, needlessly, that it was too much so. Austen's familiarity with the romance novel was the result of her voracious reading, a family trait. Her reading would have included various lesser novelists (whom she parodied in *Love and Freindship* [*sic*] and other burlesques written as a teenager), as well as, importantly, Richardson. She set his *Sir Charles Grandison* for the stage (amateur theatricals were a part of the Austen household). The characters of this, his last novel were her "living friends" and provided inspiration for *Pride and Prejudice*; her own genius made Austen's the better book (Harris, "Influence" 94).

Pride and Prejudice was well reviewed and much talked about. It sold out its modest first printing and its influence extended as far as the Prince Regent, who asked that Austen's next work be dedicated to him. *Emma* indeed is so dedicated by "His Royal Highness's Dutiful and Obedient Humble Servant," but Austen made the dedication reluctantly—the Prince was a rake and she sided with his wronged wife (Halperin 210, 282).

Unlike *Sir Charles Grandison*, *Pride and Prejudice* focuses on the heroine. It contains the most complete exploration of marriage in all of Austen's works. Indeed, Julie Shaffer notes that the novel "revolves almost obsessively around marriage" and finds that it demonstrates the proposition that "some views of marriage are less adequate than others, but also that no view of marriage should be embraced without question" (*Confronting* 139–40). All of Austen's novels end in one or more marriages, and all depict the path to those marriages. *Pride and Prejudice,* more than any of the other five, explores marriage itself as the primary theme of the work.

Austen was a genius. Her chosen form was the romance novel, and she never deviated from it. As a result she has, of course, attracted the same sort of criticism that we have seen directed toward twentieth-century popular romance novels and Richardson's *Pamela*.

Wayne Booth reconsidered his earlier approbation of Austen in *The Rhetoric of Fiction* (243–66) to examine, in *The Company We Keep*, "the indictment" of Austen by feminist critics (423–35). Booth's discussion concerns *Emma*, but his case against that book can be generalized to the other Austen novels because it is, finally, an argument about the form of the works. Booth asserts the now-familiar argument that *Emma* perpetrates a "reinforcement of . . . deep-seated sexist beliefs . . . that women are indeed the weaker sex, that unlike men they cannot be whole, cannot find maturity, without the protective instruction and care from the right kind of man" (429). Booth also addresses the portion of this argument that condemns the form, the fear that "many readers will succumb morally to what was simply required formally" (431). In this view the form's requirement for a "resounding ending"—the marriage—demanded of Austen a lamentable sacrifice of morality to formal conventionality (430). He rehearses the claim that the ending requires a moral compromise that harms readers. Unlike other critics we have seen, he then answers his own indictment. He invokes Austen's celebrated irony: "unless we can somehow incorporate something like an ironic vision of the ending—even while pretending not to, even while enjoying the fairy tale to the full—we are indeed confirming its capacity to implant a harmful vision of the sexes" (435). For Booth, Austen's vigorous ironic questioning of women's roles, of status, of virtually every situation that contributes to the marriage, puts the marriage itself in a critical light. Although this may be an answer for Austen, for whom irony was a usual practice, the same condemnation of the form will stand unchallenged in another, unironic author (Richardson, for example).

Pointing to the characters of heroine and hero, Julie Shaffer finds that their construction as fallible beings who learn and grow modifies the meaning of the marriage ending. In *Pride and Prejudice* she describes the convention of the "perfect heroine" as in conflict with that of the male lover-mentor: Elizabeth is not quite the perfect heroine that, say, Pamela was, and Darcy is not the infallible lover-mentor that some romance novels present. Despite Elizabeth's fallibility, and because of Darcy's, in *Pride and Prejudice* Austen eschews a work that presents women as "subordinate and inferior creatures" writing instead a work "that granted women greater autonomy and respectability" than was usual in society or in the novels of the time ("Not Subordinate" 52). When the equally fallible heroine and hero marry, that marriage is "precisely that which is the most central to the preservation of the world as it ought to be, when the institution involves a husband and wife who are willing to improve each other, be improved by one another, and to extend that mutual improvement to a larger community" (66). It is not only Austen who thus challenges the stock characterization of heroines as merely subordinate and of heroes as invariably superior. If Richardson draws Pamela as a "perfect heroine" (and he does, much to the amused ridicule of Fielding in *Shamela* and generations of critics who followed him), he certainly draws B as the very opposite of the lover-mentor, at least for three-quarters of the novel.

The improvement that heroine and hero offer and receive is a primary vehicle for the remaking of society that marriages in the romance novel (as a legacy from comedy) bring about. Laura Mooneyham White reads the ending of the romance novel as "psychic integration through the power of wedding bells at a narrative's close" (77). In this she echoes romance writer Laura Kinsale who calls the "oft-derided happy ending" an "integration of the inner self" (39). White calls for a rethinking of the marriage plot's meaning in the face of its tenacity: "We must . . . acknowledge the persistence of a plot that currently offends and offer room for explanations of that plot's persistence that go beyond the most-traveled ground of critique, that of dissatisfaction with particular historical and social practice, toward some elementals of human experience" (83). The elementals of human experience are, for Austen and Richardson, genuine growth.

In addition to Austen's irony, in addition to the fallibility she invests in the heroine and hero she draws, in addition to the psychic integration at the close of a romance, there are the other elements of the form itself that contribute to the meaning of the ending. As in Richardson, in Austen we will again see that the barrier and ritual death provide formal features other than the marriage whose meanings can be read, whose meanings, moreover, are the opposite of the closing down of possibility that a myopic view of the marriage ending often yields. As in *Pamela*, freedom and life will be their message. In *Pride and Prejudice*, marriage itself may not be renovated, but it is rethought from within. The law and society's institutions cannot be changed by one heroine, but she can obtain maximum freedom within them.

The barrier in this novel preoccupied with marriage is neither single nor constant. Austen writes a different barrier for the marriages whose courtships the book records, embodying these barriers in various characters who actually impede or suggest impediments to the unions of Charlotte and Mr. Collins, Lydia and Wickham, Jane and Bingley, as well as Elizabeth and Darcy. Characters make claims or embody an attitude or attribute which seem to impede a given marriage. In placing such objections in the mouths or actions of her characters, Austen refrains from objective authorial comment, leaving readers, as well as the heroines and heroes, to evaluate the force and relevance of each barrier. At stake in the barriers is the nature of marriage itself. *Pride and Prejudice* poses the question, "On what basis should marriage go forward?"

The simplest courtship in the novel is between Charlotte and Mr. Collins, who agree to marry almost as soon as it is clear that Elizabeth, to whom Mr. Collins first proposes, will not accept him. Elizabeth represents in this instance the claims of landed interests. A match between Elizabeth and Collins would cushion the force of the entail on the Bennet family. The entail required that the land and house that Mr. Bennet owned be inherited by a male. Elizabeth has only sisters; Mr. Collins is Mr. Bennet's nearest living male relative, and hence his heir. If anything were to happen to Mr. Bennet, Mrs. Bennet and the sisters would be summarily turned out of what had always been their home. They would lose the income from the land as well. Mrs. Bennet champions Mr. Collins's proposal out of a legitimate fear of poverty. If Elizabeth, in her potential marriage to Collins, represents the ancient values of the land, she speaks a more forward-looking doctrine when she pronounces as "not sound" Charlotte's pragmatic view of marriage, that "it is better to know as little as possible of the defects of the person with whom you are to pass your life" (19). When Charlotte acts on her philosophy of marriage and weds on short acquaintance the pompous sycophant Collins, Elizabeth is appalled but must admit that the marriage is far more successful than she would have thought, given Collins's qualities. This courtship is undramatized and brief. There is no declaration between the heroine and hero, and no recognition. Charlotte never pretends to love Collins, and, in wishing to know "as little as possible" of him, she rejects the action essential to a recognition. The barrier of Elizabeth as the "other woman" is surmounted almost immediately. The reader might feel relieved at Charlotte's prospects for prosperity—Collins, as heir to the Bennet lands and as a favored clergyman of a powerful patron, is a good catch from an economic point of view. The reader might also feel appalled at her willingness to overlook so obviously flawed a personality in her husband—Collins, after all, is a pompous ass. Each reader must decide if the marriage is a success.

The next marriage contracted is between Lydia Bennet, Elizabeth's youngest and least disciplined sister, and Wickham, son of Darcy's father's steward. This courtship is also not dramatized, but the barrier is quite fully elaborated. It is represented by Elizabeth, a Miss King, and by Wickham himself. Elizabeth represents the claims of the older sister, who would naturally take precedence over a much younger sister like Lydia. Wickham had first been attracted to Elizabeth, and she to him. When Elizabeth learns that he is a gambler, rake, and seducer, her regard for him vanishes. He pursues Miss King, an heiress, but is unsuccessful in that quest. She represents money, which Lydia, like all of her sisters, does not have. Wickham himself is the final barrier. Having eloped with Lydia, he does not marry her, representing in this action the hope of the rake to stay in play, as it were, and wait for the next chance. Darcy offers Wickham enough money to secure his agreement to marry Lydia. The nature of this barrier characterizes Lydia's union: first an older sister warned off by the evil reputation of the suitor, then an heiress hunted for her money, and finally the rake himself, willing to seduce and abandon young women. The reader must decide if Lydia's being made an honest woman outweighs her choice of a husband.

Between Jane and Bingley there is only Darcy. Their courtship, mostly dramatized, advances quickly when they are together. When they are separated, it languishes, and Darcy is the mechanism of that separation. He thinks Jane an imprudent choice for his friend Bingley, so he engineers Bingley's removal from Jane's Hertfordshire neighborhood and later, in London, conceals from Bingley Jane's presence in town. In thus keeping them apart he creates the most primitive barrier, geography. The moment Darcy confesses his manipulations to Bingley and brings him back into Jane's society, which is to say, the moment this wholly external barrier is removed, the courtship advances apace. Neither lover endorses Darcy's reason for separating them; their match seems suitable to them, and they conclude it with dispatch. Again, the nature of the barrier characterizes Jane's union: a spurious argument about imprudence and a stage-managed separation. Neither lover had any part in the barrier. It was completely external to both. The reader must decide if the ease with which Darcy prevented—then later precipitated—this union reflects badly on the union itself: is Bingley too easily influenced, Jane too easily rendered passive?

Between Elizabeth Bennet and Fitzwilliam Darcy stands a long list of characters. In approximate order, they are Caroline Bingley, Mrs. Bennet, Wickham, Lady Catherine de Bourgh, Mr. Bennet, Darcy himself, and Elizabeth herself. Through this elaborate barrier Elizabeth's marriage receives the closest scrutiny. In the end, only the interior barriers require overcoming.

Caroline, who has her eye on Darcy, represents familiarity, fortune, and the shared values of his social set. By contrast Elizabeth is a strange, poor, rustic outsider. Caroline also sounds the note that will echo throughout the elaboration of the barrier. In regaling Darcy about his supposed marriage to Elizabeth, she cites Mrs. Bennet's bad behavior—"give your mother-in-law a few hints," she advises Darcy (45). Mrs. Bennet's crassness is indeed a barrier issue, and it becomes a moral issue when the behavior of the younger daughters goes unchecked. Her bad judgment contributes to Lydia's elopement and to the near ruin of the other sisters' futures. Caroline associates Mrs. Bennet's crassness with the lowness of her connections: her money is from (and her relatives in) trade.

Wickham's brief attentions to Elizabeth represent the threat of seduction based on lies. As a rake he endangers every woman he comes into contact with. He embodies the risk of sex appeal without morals, of attractiveness paired with shark-like acquisitiveness and ready claims of victimhood. He is, for a time, the other man. Darcy disarms his ploy through the simple act of telling Elizabeth the truth about Wickham.

Lady Catherine, Darcy's aunt, advances the claims of Darcy's prior engagement to Anne de Bourgh, Lady Catherine's own daughter. This marriage, talked of by Lady Catherine and Darcy's late mother, was designed to unite Lady Catherine's status with Darcy's land and wealth. It represents the claim of kinship bonds as a basis for marriage. Neither the heroine nor the hero admits its importance. This older form of marital union is advanced and rejected in a single scene, but it is nonetheless put into play in the novel, albeit in the mouth of a fairly weak spokeswoman.

Mr. Bennet's financial improvidence and moral ineffectiveness also form a barrier to the marriage. Darcy cites him, as well as Mrs. Bennet, when he complains in his first proposal to Elizabeth of her embarrassing family. In not preventing Lydia's trip to Brighton, Mr. Bennet enables her elopement with Wickham. He is a weak parent, and Elizabeth's union is threatened as a result. The *senex* common in hero-centered comedy has been transformed into a moral threat in this heroine-centered work—equally menacing, if from a different motive.

The internal barriers, Elizabeth's prejudice and Darcy's pride, are the last to fall. Heroine and hero both surmount their own distorted view of each other and of the world through a process of mutual correction. Darcy teaches Elizabeth. This we would expect. But Elizabeth teaches Darcy as well, and that instruction is indicated as continuing after their marriage. There is a way in which all of the other barriers, the external ones, are interior as well. Darcy must overcome some of them—the sense of financial inequality between Bingley and Jane, for example, or the behavior of the elder Bennets. The barriers in this book hold sway only if the heroine and hero wish to credit them, or only if they cannot grow and change enough to overcome them. Darcy is Austen's wealthiest hero—he would have been one of the two or three richest men in England at the time. What she buys with this wealth, so to speak, is the power on the part of her heroine and hero to choose each other without any collateral worries.

The reader may also stand between Elizabeth and Darcy, given the shifting nature of the barrier, its embodiment in characters of varying credibility and beliefs (contrast Charlotte's view of marriage with Elizabeth's, and both of theirs with Lady Catherine's). The task of the reader is to remove him- or herself from between the lovers. Imagine a reader sympathetic to Charlotte's hard-headed view of marriage. This reader must amend this view, or risk being left behind at Elizabeth's refusal of Mr. Collins. Such an amendment is helped along by Mr. Collins's hilarious sycophancy, but it is still an amendment. As character after character presents or represents a case for one view of marriage or another, the reader must engage in a process of self-renovation or risk being part of the barrier. Like Darcy and Elizabeth, readers must free themselves from impediments to the marriage.

Elizabeth reforms and is freed of self-delusion. Darcy reforms and is freed from his pride, which is to say, his allegiance to many of these other considerations. The ending isolates them in their mutual choice, while it inserts the new union based on that choice back into society which includes the characters who embodied the barrier. The power of choice to create this freedom has attracted the notice of critics. Marvin Mudrick considers choice the most important element of Elizabeth's makeup: "the central fact for Elizabeth remains the power of choice" (95). Joseph Wiesenfarth places freedom at the heart of this novel: "Jane Austen dramatizes the growth of individuals to a freedom of action based on intelligence and affection in Pride Prejudice" (270). So does Susan Morgan: "Pride and Prejudice explores the special question of the meaning of freedom . . . Elizabeth's freedom is basically the freedom to think for herself" (85). Julia Prewitt Brown ties the sort of freedom explored in Pride and Prejudice to political and social movements: "The increased freedom of choice in marriage led to an emotional force behind the feminist movement of the early nineteenth century and is perhaps the origin of what we understand to be modern womanhood" (20). This freedom, which results in a choice, is partly a consequence of the form itself, of the release of the heroine from the barrier. Like Pamela, Elizabeth's liberation from the barrier frees her to choose.

Elizabeth defies the older order of obedience to authority and marriage for kinship exchange. She personifies the assumptions of affective individualism throughout the novel, holding out for her happiness against her mother's insistence that she marry her distant cousin Collins to secure their home against the entail. She holds out as well against Lady Catherine's insistence that she not marry Darcy so that he might marry his cousin to unite the lands, wealth, and status of the two families. She chooses individual happiness. Of course, Elizabeth's choice is also based on the ideals of companionate marriage. She refuses to marry without love.

As the brief discussion in Part II indicated, the point of ritual death is partly the social exile that Lydia brings upon herself when she elopes with Wickham. The point of ritual death also dramatizes the daringness of Elizabeth's choice. Cynthia L. Caywood reminds us just how remarkable this choice is: "When looked at realistically, Elizabeth's belief in choice is astonishing. . . . [She] never worries overtly about the entailment or about marrying" (35).

Karen Newman, claiming that Austen's heroines "live powerfully within the limits imposed by ideology," observes that "[i]n Pride and Prejudice, everything about Elizabeth—her poverty, her inferior social position, the behavior of her family, her initial preference for Wickham, and her refusal of Darcy's first offer of marriage—all these things ideologically should lead if not to death, at best to genteel poverty and spinsterhood" (705). At the point of ritual death, Lydia is not only the agent of the family's disgrace, she is also Elizabeth's stand-in. She is the younger, less wise, less well-informed Bennet who elopes with the man who had tried to seduce Miss Darcy and who had enchanted—and lied to—Elizabeth. Despite Elizabeth's rejection of him he almost ruins her anyway. Her financial vulnerability is extreme—exactly the same as Lydia's. Lydia's disgrace threatens social death for the entire family, including Elizabeth.

Mr. Bennet, who should have prevented Lydia's elopement in the first place by better governing her behavior, is utterly ineffectual at finding the runaways. Had he found the couple, he would have had difficulty meeting Wickham's financial terms, thus failing to salvage Lydia's reputation and permanently harming the good name of his family. This, in turn, would have directly affected the remaining sisters' marriage choices. Or perhaps he would have impoverished himself, and his children, in the process of buying a bridegroom for Lydia. Or perhaps Mrs. Bennet's worst fears for her husband would have been realized. She whines, "I know he [Mr. Bennet] will fight Wickham, wherever he meets him, and then he will be killed, and what is to become of us all? The Collinses will turn us out, before he is cold in his grave" (253). This version of a future placed in the mouth of one of the least credible characters in the novel is nonetheless one possible outcome.

The ritual death in *Pamela* placed at stake life itself. In *Pride and Prejudice* ritual death places at stake the social life of one family, which must rely upon society to bring husbands for daughters who, as spinsters, would be scantily provided for. Freed from social death and from the barrier, Elizabeth gets to choose, against stiff odds, to marry one of the richest men in England, a man whom, not incidentally, she loves.

Elizabeth's marriage at the end of this novel results from the removal of the barrier, the most serious portions of which were internal. Freed not from impediments that the world presents, but from those in her own mind, she exercises her freedom by choosing Darcy. Her marriage also results from her survival of ritual death. Her (social) life preserved and her freedom secured, she becomes Mrs. Fitzwilliam Darcy. Booth, as we have seen, reads this marriage as ironic, lest it "implant a harmful vision of the sexes" in the reader. But how could marriage invalidate the choice that Elizabeth was freed to make? Given the possibilities open to women, marriage is her best choice. In the first decades of the nineteenth century, it was still women's lot, still a fact of female life. We can regret this fact, but expecting Austen to do so as well is both unreasonable and anachronistic. The romance novel will question marriage itself, but not yet.

9

FREEDOM AND ROCHESTER

Jane Eyre, 1847

Charlotte Brontë's *Jane Eyre* (1847) received the same sort of popular acclaim as *Pamela* and *Pride and Prejudice* (Allott 20). The critic writing for the *North American Review* described the book's popularity in New England as "Jane Eyre fever" (Allott 97). Thackeray, who was issuing *Vanity Fair* in monthly install-ments at the time, called Brontë a "genius" and explained in a letter to the person who sent him *Jane Eyre* that he could not put it down: "I lost a whole day in reading it. . . . Some of the love passages made me cry" (Allott 198, 70). Brontë's biogra-pher, Winifred Gérin, summarizes the critical pronouncements on this novel as "near unanimity of praise" (344). From the beginning, *Jane Eyre* received acclaim from novelists, profes-sional reviewers, and the reading public. It is one of those rare canonical novels that is read outside of the literature classroom. Jane's story compels.

But what kind of story does Jane tell? *Jane Eyre* is a romance novel, but, as critcs have noted, one which demonstrates the flexibility of the form. Helene Moglen notes that "the form and structure of *Jane Eyre* approximate the form and structure of romance which Northrop Frye describes" (108). Recall that the romance novel exists in the overlap between comedy and romance in this larger sense. Sandra Gilbert finds that Brontë has "[b]orrow[ed] the mythic quest-plot . . . of Bunyan's *Pil-*

grim's Progress" (254). Harold Bloom claims that the genre that *Jane Eyre* belongs to is new: "Between them, the Brontës can be said to have invented a relatively new genre, a kind of northern romance, deeply influenced both by Byron's poetry and by his myth and personality, but going back also, more remotely yet as definitely, to the Gothic novel and to the Elizabethan drama" (1). Bloom doesn't see that romance in this larger sense, as well as Byronic influence, are compatible with the romance novel. Cynthia Carlton-Ford also finds in *Jane Eyre* a new genre: "Brontë fuses two separate stories, the love story and a feminist statement, but the two are so tightly interwoven that the reader may read the whole novel seeking only one of them. . . . The emergent genre is an original one—the feminist fairytale" (342). The term "fairytale" is a backhanded naming of the romance novel, which can (and in the case of *Jane Eyre,* does) include a "feminist statement." Gill Frith finds a familiar genre in *Jane Eyre:* "Brontë's novel is also a romance, the 'mother-text' of all those novels—written, and read, primarily by women—in which innocent heroine meets brooding hero and lives happily ever after"(172). "Romance" in Frith's sense is the "romance novel" as defined in Part II. This particular romance novel incorporates the quest-plot, the northern (England) gothic, and overt feminist statements.

The novel also incorporates elements of *Bildungsroman,* the novel of education. If the action ends with Jane's marriage, it begins with her exile from her home to school at Lowood. The heroine's education is often at issue in romance novels. (Elizabeth Bennet, it could be argued, must learn to judge others less quickly and to be more skeptical of the information that she hears.) We follow Jane's education from the age of ten until she is grown and has a profession that will sustain her. The account of this formal training lasts for about one quarter of the novel. The great theme of independence introduced in this section governs the entire novel, and its attainment guides Jane through the courtships that she must navigate to reach Ferndean and Rochester. Indeed, the remaining three quarters of the work are devoted to courtship.

The structure as well as the genre of Brontë's novel has attracted critical attention. R. E. Hughes, seeking a pattern in a novel that had once been thought "chaotic" discovers a "five-part action" which he identifies as "the Reed action," "Lowood," "Rochester (A)," "St. John Rivers," and "Rochester (B)" (116). For him the courtships form the last three "acts" of *Jane Eyre.* Eagleton notes that "[t]he fundamental structure of Charlotte's novel is a triadic one" (*Myths* 74). Characters, especially, are tripled up, as are the courtships. Whereas Hughes sees the final "act" as

"Rochester (B)," I believe a better name for this final section would be "Jane." The first two courtships are indeed Rochester's and St. John's. They both court Jane. In the final courtship, however, when Jane leaves Marsh End to travel first to Thornfield and then to Ferndean to find Rochester, it is *she* who courts Rochester. This final courtship cements Jane's freedom. As an examination of the barriers and points of ritual death in the novel will show, freedom, for Jane, is independence—emotional, financial, and physical. In the course of the novel, she becomes self-possessed. She controls her emotions. She gains and then acts from a base of financial independence. She governs her movements—where she will live and how. She is, in short, free, and Brontë finds the romance novel form a natural medium for this theme of freedom.

Barriers to Rochester's courtship of Jane when she is governess at Thornfield are at first manufactured and stage managed by Rochester. Blanche Ingram, noble and rich, is beautiful and accomplished: "Blanche was moulded like a Diana. . . . She played . . . she sang . . . she talked French" (151). Jane assumes what everyone else does—that Blanche and Rochester will marry. Yet she has admitted to herself that she loves Rochester: "I have something in my brain and heart, in my blood and nerves, that assimilates me mentally to him" (154). The beauty and wealth of Blanche contrasted with her own plainness and poverty define for Jane the height and breadth of this particular barrier. She plans to leave Thornfield, and tells Rochester, "[I]f God had gifted me with some beauty and much wealth, I should have made it as hard for you to leave me, as it is now for me to leave you" (222). But this barrier has been erected by Rochester himself, who feints behind it waiting to hear Jane commit herself to him.

After the first proposal scene, in which Rochester asks—"My bride is here . . . because my equal is here. . . . Jane, will you marry me?"—and Jane, after cross-examining him, accepts him, the courtship enters a new phase. The barrier shifts to Jane's lack of freedom, expressed in images of oriental slavery. Rochester has tried to buy her extravagant dresses and jewels. Jane feels "annoyance and degradation" and thinks, "It would, indeed, be a relief . . . if I had ever so small a [financial] independency" (236). She regards him as a "sultan" and threatens to "preach liberty to them that are enslaved—[his] harem inmates amongst the rest" (236, 237). He sings a love song to her: "My love has sworn, with sealing kiss, / With me to live— to die," and Jane insists that "I had as good a right to die when my time came as he did; but I should bide that time, and not be hurried away in a suttee" (240). Rochester is sultan-like; Jane refuses to immolate herself on his funeral pyre. The East is associated with slavery—and with bigamy in the reference to Rochester's harem. The lovers' "Eastern" banter equates money with an overheated, purchased sexuality.

Rochester's stage-management of the courtship comes to a halt as Jane reasserts her independence by imposing a professional distance between her and her employer. He protests, "You will give up your governessing slavery at once." She replies, "Indeed! begging your pardon sir, I shall not" (238). He precisely mistakes the nature of Jane's enslavement. He thinks her a slave to her job. She is, in fact, a slave to his money, unless she can assert some independence. She does this by insisting on her role as employee—as governess. Her profession provides the known territory from which to be courted by Rochester. It stands in for the family she does not have, for the home she cannot return to, for the financial independence she longs for but has not yet achieved. Jane masters the last apparent barrier element as she asserts herself and places her relationship with Rochester on a more rational footing.

For Pauline Nestor, "the novel is a triumph of achieved balance for the heroine." Her survival "depends on her ability to mediate between the potentially destructive extremes of her own character:—between the poles of Reason and Feeling, absolute submission and determined revolt" (74–75). The submission, the slavery that Jane felt in Rochester's treatment of her, has been replaced not by revolt, but by the control that a professional relationship affords her. At this point in the courtship, Jane controls it, and she does this from the platform of her profession. She limits her time with Rochester, asserts the importance of activities other than those he dictates, and even controls his love-making (in the nineteenth-century meaning of the term) by insisting on her status as governess in his household. She is thus free from Rochester's control of the courtship—one element of the barrier—but not yet free from the whole of the barrier. Rochester's wife, Bertha Mason Rochester, stands between Jane and Rochester.

The point of ritual death comes on the steps of the cottage at Marsh End, where Jane has wandered in her flight from Rochester. She is at first turned away, and thinks, "I can but die" (295). She has inserted the barrier of distance between herself and the married Rochester, and this self-exile from the object of her love is punctuated by her wish for death. Jane's own life is put at stake: she is in danger of dying from exposure. This effort to free herself, however, ends not in death, but in life; Jane finds family and wealth. Unbeknownst to her, her own cousins live within. They rescue her and through them she claims an inheritance that establishes her financial independence. It does not restore her to Rochester however; rather, it delivers her to a second courtship.

The barriers to the St. John–Jane courtship are another woman, the lack of love between the would-be hero and the heroine, and, as in the Rochester courtship, Jane's suitor's attempts to dominate her. St. John tries to rule Jane's will much as Rochester did. More than money and beauty (although she has both) the other woman, Rosamond Oliver, is a barrier because she represents the real object of St. John's love. St. John offers Jane useful work as a missionary to India, a powerful draw for the serious-minded young woman who no longer needs to work for her living. He couches Jane's domination in terms of an Eastern-style slavery reminiscent of Rochester's own overbearing assumptions about Jane. She is studying languages; he tells her, "I want you to give up German, and learn Hindostanee" (349). St. John conducts a long siege of Jane's resistance to marriage without love, invoking God and abandoning cordiality. She replies with her own condition: "I'll agree to go to India, if I may go free" (356). She will go as his adopted sister, but not as his wife: "[Y]ou and I had better not marry" (357). Jane has delivered an antiproposal. This courtship is incomplete. The barrier remains.

Rochester, too, undergoes ritual death. The hero calls to Jane, hoping that he "might soon be taken from this life, and admitted to that world to come, where there was still hope of rejoining Jane" (393). He does not know where she is, or even if she is alive.

It is Jane who conducts the final courtship of the novel. First, she closes the geographical distance between them, abruptly abandoning her newfound family and rushing first to Thornfield, only to find it destroyed, and then to Ferndean. All remaining barriers are in Rochester's mind and are utterly within Jane's power to sweep away. Rochester believes that there is another man, St. John Rivers; he believes that the injuries that he suffered in trying unsuccessfully to save Bertha will keep Jane from wanting him; and he believes that he is too old for her. The heroine frees the hero from these barriers to their marriage. She then stage-manages the proposal. He explains:

> "Ah, Jane. But I want a wife. . . . I will abide by your decision.
> "Choose then, sir—*her who loves you best.*"
> "I will at least choose—*her I love best.* Jane, will you marry me?"
> "Yes, sir." (391–92)

In freeing Rochester from the barrier, Jane frees herself from it as well. We celebrate this release, and the escape from death that both heroine and hero enjoy. In the case of *Jane Eyre*, however, the freedom motif is doubled. John Hagan observes that *"Jane Eyre* is a novel of liberation. A series of quests by Jane for 'freedom' and her final attainment of that goal constitute its principal action" (187). The freedom that Jane has achieved in the novel results in her ability to overcome the final barriers to her marriage to Rochester. In traveling to him, in sweeping aside the barrier in his mind, in stage-managing the proposal and, one might add, his life after their union, Jane comes into the full possession of the freedom that she has sought throughout the novel. The heroine's own agency provides the final freedom for both her and the hero. "Reader, I married him" (not "Reader, he married me") thus rings as a double assertion of freedom: a free woman securing an additional freedom—from the barrier to the marriage she has proposed. The form reinforces the theme.

Both Terry Eagleton (ubiquitous in his antibourgeois crusade) and Shirley Foster find the novel's ending contrived. Eagleton sounds his familiar theme of the unreality of the resolution in marriage: "By the device of an ending, bourgeois initiative and genteel settlement, sober rationality and romantic passion, spiritual equality and social distinction, the actively affirmative and the patiently deferential self, can be merged into mythical unity" (*Myths* 32). Foster notes that *Jane Eyre,* like other Victorian women's novels, remains ambivalent about the questions that Brontë raises in the novel: "[I]dealism about marriage as the supreme female fulfillment is often challenged; the heroines resist their socially-imposed roles and make valiant bids for freedom; the authors themselves frequently verbalize their anger and frustration at male-oriented definitions of womanhood. Yet sooner or later, romance triumphs" (217).

Other critics find that Jane's freedom—financial, emotional, and physical—enables her to live with Rochester on a footing of equality. Sandra Gilbert notes that "Charlotte Brontë appears . . . to have imagined a world in which the prince and Cinderella are democratically equal, Pamela is just as good as Mr. B., master and servant are profoundly alike" (266). This equality , and the freedom that gives rise to it, makes *Jane Eyre* a bit easier for critics to take, despite what Eagleton calls its "mythical" unity or what Foster ruefully claims is the "triumph" of romance. Jane's assumption of wealth and gentility is not "mythical" and not the result of her romance with Rochester (romance does not triumph in the sense of rewarding the heroine with things that she had not otherwise earned). She worked for her keep and achieved independence. Her inheritance makes this independence more carefree, but she had won it before she became an heiress. In returning to, courting, and marrying Rochester, she acts from the base of that independence, and extends it to her life with her new husband. In this she is profoundly bourgeois, but bourgeois values of independence, individualism, and freedom have been the goals of her quest; her marriage to Rochester is simply an extension of these, not a concession to literary form.

In *Jane Eyre* Brontë draws a character who pursues affective individualism in almost everything she does. She defies authority at every turn—her Aunt Reed, Rochester, and St. John. An orphan, she leaves her foster parents behind, returning only when her aunt is on her deathbed, and then, surprisingly, to forgive her. (Her aunt, to the end, finds Jane's refusal to recognize authority absolutely unnatural.) Jane refuses to marry St. John in the face of what he calls her Christian duty. She marries Rochester in the face of his own disapproval because she loves him. In this, of course, she pursues the goals of companionate marriage, the companionship in her case being particularly close: "to talk to each other is but a more animated and an audible thinking" (397). Brontë makes her heroine rich, and then implies that this independence will persist into her marriage with Rochester. Jane tells him, "I am an independent woman now. . . . My uncle in Madeira is dead, and he left me five thousand pounds" (382). We do not understand exactly how Jane's money is arranged to circumvent her position in marriage as *feme covert,* but we do understand that her independence, including her financial independence, is intact after the marriage.

Jane Eyre is the first orphaned heroine we have seen. They are common in romance novels. Who better to pursue the goals of affective individualism than someone who has no authority figures in the form of parents to defy? The orphan's lack of human attachment makes virtually every relationship a choice, thus increasing the scope of her freedom. Her marriage is absolutely her own choice because there are no parents to object or interfere. Orphanhood liberates a heroine to an interior struggle; it casts her upon her own resources, including her psychological resources. Jane Eyre is perhaps the most famous canonical orphaned heroine, but the romance novel chronicles many more.

10

The Romance Form in the Victorian Multiplot Novel

Framley Parsonage, 1861

In *Framley Parsonage* (1861) Anthony Trollope enjoyed his first popular success. It is the fourth of Trollope's Chronicles of Barsetshire—a set of six novels that share a fictional geography, interlaced characters, and a thematic preoccupation with the church in a Cathedral town. N. John Hall, notes: "From the first most people have over the years given pride of place to the six novels of the Barchester series. . . . Trollope's contemporaries set great store by *Framley Parsonage*" (505).

Framley Parsonage contains a first-rate courtship plot—a complete romance novel within the larger work—which has as its heroine the redoubtable Lucy Robarts, one of the most remarkable women ever drawn by Anthony Trollope, a novelist noted for his depiction of English women. In addition to the Lucy—Lord Ludovic romance novel plot (and no fewer than three other less detailed courtship plots) the work contains a "church" plot that focuses on the temptations and trials suffered by Mark Robarts, Lucy's clergyman brother, as he ventures into the morally fast society at Gatherum Castle. In its combination of a number of plot threads, *Framley Parsonage* is typical of the Victorian multiplot novel as well as of the Victorian romance novel. Examining the barrier and point of ritual death in this novel will illustrate not only what is at stake in the courtship plot, but how this plot complements the themes of the church plot.

Trollope himself was ambivalent about the Lucy-Ludovic courtship plot. At one point in his *Autobiography*, Trollope says, "The love of . . . [Lucy] for the young lord was . . . necessary, because there must be love in a novel" (142). Here Trollope's dismissal of the inevitable courtship or love plot sounds remarkably contemporary. Later in the same work Trollope admits that this plot is important: "The real plot consisted at last simply of a girl refusing to marry the man she loved till the man's friends agreed to accept her lovingly" (142). The other plot centers on Lucy's brother, Mark, a clergyman tempted by a style of living that he can ill afford, monetarily or morally. Trollope explains, "There was much Church, but more love-making. And it was downright honest love. . . . Each of them longed for the other, and they were not ashamed to say so"(*Autobiography* 142).

Critics have begun to reevaluate what some have called Trollope's "personal hostility to feminism" (Barickman et al., *Corrupt Relations* 199). They find that Trollope, for all his ridicule of "the debate about women in the nineteenth century: the problem of 'redundant' women, economic independence for women, reform of the married women's property laws, opening up the professions to women, education, and suffrage," did not write as a "bland apologist for orthodox sexual relations" (197, 199). His novels present, in their multiple plots, society's "fragmentation" in such a way that the various plots comment upon each other (200). Peter Garrett finds the multiple plots of Trollope and others to be in "dialogical opposition," in "tension" that goes unresolved (223). What some critics see as "fragmentation" is actually a whole, and what Garrett reads as "tension" is actually resolved. Trollope's claim that "there must be love in a novel" is like the magician's flourish that distracts the audience. The Lucy-Ludovic plot reproduces the thematic concerns of the church plot within the elements of the romance novel.

The heroine in this courtship plot, Trollope claimed, was "perhaps the most natural English girl that I ever drew" (*Autobiography* 143). Henry James notes Trollope's abilities in drawing a heroine: "He has presented the British maiden under innumerable names, in every station and in every emergency in life, and with every combination of moral and physical qualities. She is always definite and natural" (16). Robert Utter and Gwendolyn Needham, tracing the descendants of Pamela in fiction, find that "Lucy Robarts . . . is a favorite no less with Trollope himself than with his

readers" (375). This extraordinary heroine is one of the two foci of Trollope's book; Mark, her clergyman brother, is the other.

In *Framley Parsonage*, Lucy Robarts rightly refuses to join the society at
Framley Court—that is, she refuses to marry its lord—until it is clear that
she will incur no unpayable social debt in doing so. She fears that Ludovic's
mother, Lady Lufton, who lives at Framley Court and whose influence
extends beyond her household and her son's tenants to the wider community, will never accept her. She fears that if she marries Ludovic she will live
in a perpetual state of apology to her mother-in-law for what that lady sees
as her shortcomings. Mark Robarts errs in agreeing to join the society at
Gatherum Castle; in doing so, he incurs debts, both financial and moral,
that he cannot pay. Both plots hinge on the unpayable debt, the church plot
commenting upon and illuminating the courtship plot, and vice versa. The
barrier and point of ritual death in Lucy's plot illuminate what is at stake
for her and for society in her union with Ludovic; at the same time these
narrative elements provide ironic comment on Mark's difficulties in cor-
recting his behavior to accord with the morals and style of life appropriate
for a clergyman of his rank and station.

Barriers to the Lucy-Lufton marriage include another woman, Lucy's
pride, and Lady Lufton's disapproval. Each of these barrier elements is
reflected in the church plot.

The other woman is, for a short while, Griselda Grantly, daughter of an
archdeacon. Lady Lufton and Mrs. Grantly have decided, much in the manner of Lady Catherine de Bourgh and Mrs. Darcy in *Pride and Prejudice,* that
their children, Ludovic and Griselda, will marry. Their agreement, Trollope
tells us, was "[n]ot signed on parchment, and sealed with wax" but was,
nonetheless, "a treaty which between two such contracting parties would be
binding enough (132–33). Griselda, unlike Lucy, is beautiful and has connections.

Lucy's pride prevents her from accepting Ludovic when he asks her to
marry him. She fears "the sneers of the world, which would have declared
that she had set her trap, and caught the foolish young lord!" (198). She
brings no money or status to the match; Ludovic brings a title and a fortune.

Lucy, when she learns of Lady Lufton's opposition to her becoming the
"queen" of Framley Court, declares, "I will never marry him unless his
mother asks me" (380). Lady Lufton's objection as she explains it to her
son is that: "She is——insignificant. I believe her to be a very good girl,

but she is not qualified to fill the high position to which you would exalt her" (517). Lady Lufton herself sweeps this barrier element away when, in a remarkable doubling of the proposal scene in this novel, *she* repeats Ludovic's proposal. Only then does Lucy accept.

These barriers are paralleled in the Mark/church plot. Mark is a party to many "treaties" negotiated by Lady Lufton. He owes his job and his wife to this patroness. Mark is subject to the "sneers of the world" as he chases the fast life at Gatherum Castle. He engages in questionable behavior for a clergyman, he slights his duties in his own church, and he makes financial commitments—cosigning notes that ultimately fall to him for payment—that he cannot keep. He must overcome his own pride to accept the financial help that Ludovic offers. Although Lucy triumphs over her insignificance, Mark must confront his and submit to it. Climbing the social ladder at Gatherum Castle, filling a prebendal stall at Barchester Cathedral, these are above his station. He accepts help from his friend from school days—and he reforms his way of life.

The point of ritual death occurs when Lucy risks her life in caring for a typhus victim, Mrs. Crawley, wife of an impoverished clergyman. Typhus was "associated with filthy, crowded living conditions" and could have a mortality rate "as high as sixty percent among older . . . patients" (Biddle 154–55). In visiting the sick, Lucy thus assumes the position, and duties, that a woman of some standing (Mark's wife or even Lady Lufton) might assume. But Lucy does more than just visit. She returns to the sick woman's home, sends the Crawley children to Framley over the objections of their father, and nurses Mrs. Crawley back to health, sleeping on a pallet in the sickroom. Lady Lufton visits Lucy at the Crawley house to ask her to marry Ludovic.

The barrier places at stake Lucy's "significance." The old order, Lady Lufton, is pitted against the new, Lucy. The point of ritual death puts Lucy's life at stake, and proves her significance at the same time. Her freedom from death and from Lady Lufton's disapproval celebrates the ascent of an articulate, bright, feeling, funny, self-reflective woman to the "throne" of Framley.

James Kincaid notes that Trollope has used Lady Lufton as "both the pivot of the value system and the major blocking figure" in *Framley Parsonage* (122). She represents the values to which Mark must return after his experiment with the society at Gatherum. She also represents the values that she herself must repudiate in order that Lucy's courtship might end happily. Mark risked social ruin, and escaped—nine hundred pounds poorer, indeed, but an escape nonetheless. Lucy risked death and unhappiness and escaped to wealth, a title, and happiness. Lucy retreats, does good works, and is rewarded with advancement. Mark advances, acts rashly, and is punished with debt that will take him years to pay off; even his belongings are in the hands of the bailiffs. Lucy's ascent counters Mark's descent; her triumph over Lady Lufton's values counters his return to them. She achieves social advancement; he escapes social ruin.

Yet the commentary of the romance plot on the church plot runs deeper than this. When Lucy arrives at the Crawleys' to move in for a time, the dean of Barchester, who has arrived on horseback, is there as well. Lucy simply bustles into the Crawley household over the objections of Mr. Crawley, who does not wish his wife's illness to make the family into a charity case. The dean, meanwhile, cannot figure out how to dismount—what is he to do with his horse? And he knows that Crawley disapproves not only of the horse but of the dean's way of life as well. The church is ineffectual. Mark himself does no more than drop Lucy off and drive the children away after Lucy has spirited them out of the house and into the carriage. Lucy, by virtue of her status as a romance heroine, stands in ironic contrast to Mark, who nearly enacts a tragedy or at least a melodrama. On the level of myth and on the level of narrative event, she risks more and wins.

As Austen read and admired Richardson, Trollope read and admired Austen, claiming that *"Pride and Prejudice* was the best novel in the English language" (*Autobiography* 41). Barbara Horwitz has noted the extensive parallels between *Pride and Prejudice* and *Framley Parsonage*. Lucy and Elizabeth, she rightly notes, share many characteristics: Trollope parallels Lydia's disgrace with Mark's (33–34). This gives rise to the other plot in *Framley Parsonage*, which, unlike Lydia's fall in *Pride and Prejudice*, is completely dramatized and explored at great length. Trollope builds his novel on the scaffolding of Austen's, but in so doing, he opens his out, encompassing a world—the church—that Austen had little knowledge of even though she was a clergyman's daughter.

Trollope was the quintessential Victorian novelist—he was prolific (forty-six novels), and he wrote sprawling books with multiple plots. In his work the romance-novel plot often balanced a more worldly, usually male-centered plot, sometimes satirically (*The Way We Live Now*, 1875) and sometimes, as in *Framley Parsonage*, sympathetically. *Framley Parsonage* reflects the values of the romance novel. Lucy wins freedom as she is released from the barrier, which, finally, consisted of her future mother-in-law's condescending views of Lucy herself. She wins life as well, as she escapes from the threat of typhus. She chooses the hero, combining affective individualism and the value of companionate marriage: she consults her own happiness and she defies parental authority. Trollope understood full well how financial arrangements in marriage worked. (Marie Melmotte in *The Way We Live Now* claims not a husband, but a fortune, and keeps it, too, by moving to America before she marries). In *Framley Parsonage* fortune is not an issue. Lucy has none; Ludovic's is ample and beside the point. Lady Lufton's disapproval of Lucy has focused on her unsuitability to become the new Lady Lufton—her insignificance—which is more a matter of bearing and appearance than it is of wealth.

The two plots invite us to compare the sister and brother. Lucy holds fast to her values. Her "friends" caution her against marriage to Ludovic, and she frees him from the promise implicit in his proposal to her. (She accepts him after his *mother* repeats this proposal.) But she does not deny her love for him. All other forces in the book, especially Lady Lufton, the most powerful character in this novel, bend to Lucy's will. Mark surrenders his values. His friends caution him against his involvement with the fast crowd at Gatherum, but he ignores their advice and mixes with them anyway. In so doing he ignores his own duties, both to his parishioners and to his family: clerical and household disorder ensue. He must eventually bend to the moral forces in the novel, to the Luftons, who bail him out financially and return him to a sense of his proper duties. Lucy's romance plot delivers victory to her through an act of pure Christian charity—the point of ritual death is marked by Lucy deliberately risking her own death by caring for a woman with an often fatal, infectious illness. The church—in the guise of the woman's husband (also a clergyman), Mark, and the dean of Barchester—stands ineffectively by while Lucy nurses the woman back to health. The elements of the romance novel provide vivid moral counterpoints to the church plot. For all his denigration of love in the novel, the romance plot he inherited from Austen and others provided Trollope with the moral center of this novel.

11

THE IDEAL ROMANCE NOVEL

A Room with a View, 1908

Lucy Honeychurch marries George Emerson at the end of *A Room with a View* (1908). We see the heroine and hero for the last time in a pension in Florence, in an attitude of worship—on their knees, each whispering the other's name. E. M. Forster may have ended this novel happily, but he was by no means sanguine about happy endings in general. In his *Aspects of the Novel* he takes a pragmatic and skeptical stance with regard to love in the novel: "Love, like death, is congenial to a novelist because it ends a book conveniently. He can make it a permanency, and his readers easily acquiesce, because one of the illusions attached to love is that it will be permanent. . . . all our experience teaches us that no human relationship is constant. . . . Any strong emotion brings with it the illusion of permanence, and the novelists have seized upon this. They usually end their books with marriage, and we do not object because we lend them our dreams" (86). His biographer, P. N. Furbank, notes Forster's distrust of the institution of marriage: "He quite seriously, and on fully thought-out grounds, distrusted marriage as an institution and fretted at having to write 'marriage-fiction.' He suspected marriage might produce more harm than good; he was sure, at least, that there were finer possibilities outside it" (23). Forster had read the novels of Austen with great care, and admired her above all other novelists, moving him to exclaim, "How Jane Austen can write!" *(Aspects* 116). Yet her legacy of fiction about "love," that is, her legacy of romance novels, was one that he eventually felt compelled to move beyond. Indeed, *A Room with a View* is his only novel that ends happily. It is his only romance novel.

Perhaps because of his skepticism about marriage, or perhaps because literary fiction itself moves away from the romance novel form in the early twentieth century, critics are divided about the effectiveness of Forster's ending in *A Room with a View.* Bonnie Blumenthal Finkelstein calls it "an effective paean to heterosexual love and marriage" (87). Barbara Rosecrance links the homosexual Forster's hesitations to his sexual orientation, finding that "[t]he novel's conclusion represents Forster's only real victory for personal relations and marks his single harmonious association of personal fulfillment with heterosexual love" (83). Other critics are not convinced by the ending. John Colmer finds that "marriage as the happy climax . . .[a]ccounts for a certain falsity of tone that impairs its [the novel's] ending" (118). Judith Scherer Herz criticizes the "conventional happy ending," labeling it "mechanical and somewhat trivial." She believes that Forster, on the cusp of modernism at the beginning of his career, "take[s] a tradition two hundred years in the forming and simultaneously accept[s] and reject[s] it" (88). Rosecrance agrees, "[D]espite the happy ending, Forster implies a modern condition" (90).

The ending of *A Room with a View* is not ambivalent, but it is the result of a concentrated, almost extreme, manipulation of the romance novel's formal elements. Where Austen employed them quietly, submerging them in the narrative, Forster manipulates them brazenly. He doubles the point of ritual death, and shifts one such death about as far forward in the novel as possible. He not only alludes to the mythic basis of this element, he introduces a character named Persephone, and associates his heroine with this daughter of Demeter. The interior barrier is as elemental as possible—the denial of sexual attraction. Forster's characters actually speak the meanings that are ordinarily latent in the romance novel. Draped in layers of overtly evoked myth, peopled by characters whose dialogue forces the reader to confront the meanings generated by its formal elements, *A Room with a View* is a romance novel that guides its own reading and that provides the reader with an ideal instance of the form. Seen in this light, the ending is both a satisfying climax to Forster's novel and his valedictory to the form itself. Having written one such romance novel, he did not need to write another.

Two points of ritual death bookend the long middle barrier portion of the novel. The first is the chapter set in the Piazza Signoria, one of two chapters that Forster simply numbers, rather than naming. This "Fourth Chapter," like the "Twelfth Chapter," is about sex (Rosecrance 97). It contains the first of two points of ritual death in the novel. In this one, heroine Lucy Honeychurch undergoes ritual death and enters the dark middle of the novel. Recall the mythic underpinnings of ritual death in the romance novel: Persephone is carried off by Hades to the underworld to be his wife. Demeter, goddess of agricultural abundance, searches for her abducted daughter, leaving the earth barren. As Persephone is restored to her mother, returned from the kingdom of death, fruitfulness is restored to the earth.

The "Fourth Chapter" takes place in Florence, where the novel begins and ends. Lucy walks alone to the Piazza Signoria, where there was (and is), among other things, a three-arched loggia (a sort of porch on a grand scale) and a palace with a tall tower. The Uffizi, a large public building with its own porch or arcade, is nearby. "The Loggia," Forster tells us, "showed as the triple entrance of a cave, wherein dwelt many a deity, shadowy, but immortal, looking forth upon the arrivals and departures of mankind" (39–40). Lucy stands at the entrance to the underworld: "She fixed her eyes wistfully on the tower of the palace, which rose out of the lower darkness like a pillar of roughened gold. It seemed . . . some unattainable treasure throbbing in the tranquil sky" (40). This is a phallus, and Lucy is about to experience a symbolic initiation into sexual life at the same time that she undergoes ritual death. (Forster here, and throughout the book, stacks meaning upon meaning.)

There is a literal death. Near the Loggia one Italian stabs another. Before the dying man falls, he "bent towards Lucy with a look of interest, as if he had an important message for her. He opened his lips to deliver it, and a stream of red came out between them and trickled down his unshaven chin" (40). Lucy responds by fainting. This is a simulacrum of mortality that signals her own ritual death. She revives in the hero's arms; George Emerson, a few steps away in the piazza, had seen her fall and carried her to the arcade of the Uffizi. This is the first extended contact between heroine and hero; Forster has doubled this point of ritual death with the meeting element of the romance novel. Then he adds the awakening of sexual desire: Lucy felt that she "as well as the dying man, had crossed some spiritual boundary" (41). George is also aware of this. He tells Lucy, "[S]omething tremendous has happened" (42). Forster hints at what this something tremendous is: "[T]hey had come to a situation where character tells, and where Childhood enters upon the branching paths of Youth" (43). He exclaims, "I shall want to live, I say" (44). His resurrection from ritual death (for it has been his, too) is underway. Lucy, however, is concerned chiefly with how this unseemly episode will look to others

George has retrieved Lucy's parcel which she dropped when she fainted, but seeing it covered with blood, he throws it in the river Arno. It contained photographs of Botticelli's *Birth of Venus*, a nude painting which scandalizes Charlotte, her cousin and chaperone. Blood is a symbol of initiation into adult, female sexuality.

As Philip C. Wagner, Jr. has noted, Lucy "re-embodies Persephone" (276). Two chapters later, Forster explicitly identifies her with the daughter of Demeter. Wagner sees Lucy's subsequent journey to Rome as "Persephone's movement from the surface to Hades" (280). Jeffrey Heath also sees Lucy as Persephone, and identifies the "other man," Cecil Vyse, as King Hades (430 n. 10).

What, exactly, does this elaborate overlay of mythic suggestion mean in the story of Lucy and George? As Persephone, Lucy undergoes ritual death. The underworld that she enters is indicated by the cave-like Loggia, denizened by various gods (the statues within this structure). The Italian's murder and Lucy's subsequent fainting are death and her imitation of it. George's embrace is her initiation into physical attraction, marked by the blood on the photograph of Venus. The burden of the mythic is to make these larger meanings. In the story itself, Lucy does not recognize the moment for what it is—the beginning of her attraction to George which will culminate in their elopement and marriage. As Alan Warren Friedman notes, this marriage is "initiated by death" (105). But the impossibility of the immediate betrothal that would lead to this marriage is also initiated by the same death. Lucy rejects George, ignoring the meaning of this moment. She says, "How quickly these accidents do happen, then one returns to the old life" (43). She leaves Florence to get away from George. In Rome she meets and becomes betrothed to the other (wrong) man, Cecil Vyse. The entire rest of the book is an argument, conducted in symbols, for reuniting Lucy and the hero, George.

The barrier that keeps Lucy and George apart is internal, and it is Lucy's. She cannot admit her attraction to George—her response to him physically. Forster calls this "muddle," the "why" of depressive, inhibiting thought instead of the yes of direct action (25, 53, 77, 133, 191, 196, 198). Lucy expresses this disconnect between feeling and action in a song that Cecil gives her: "Vacant heart and hand and eye / Easy live and quiet die" (184). Her mother sees her becoming like her cousin Charlotte, a passive-aggressive spinster afraid of living (189). The outer manifestations of this interior barrier are engagement to the wrong man, Cecil Vyse (King Hades), and geographical removal from the hero. Eventually, Mrs. Honeychurch's disapproval is added to these very traditional barriers. Lucy, however, has it within her power at any time not to be "muddled." Forster has in an incidental way made Lucy financially independent (188); it is her spiritual independence that he is interested in, and the rejection of convention when it interferes with desire. At stake is Lucy's physical, sexual being.

Lucy's long sojourn in the underworld of engagement to Cecil is broken in the second point of ritual death. Mr. Emerson tells Lucy about the death of his own wife. In typical fashion, Forster stacks three elements of the romance novel form into this single scene: this point of ritual death is also the proposal scene (it is Mr. Emerson who proposes for his son) and Lucy's recognition scene.

All of these elements occur in the penultimate chapter, the most conventional place for a point of ritual death. Lucy has broken her engagement with Cecil and intends to run away to Greece. Ritual death this time is primarily George's. Mr. Emerson explains that his son is like his late wife, who became ill when George's typhoid fever was blamed on their failure to baptize him. George has sunk under the knowledge that Lucy will not have him. His father says, "He will live; but he will not think it worth while to live" (194–95). He provides Lucy's recognition: "You love George." He also proposes: "Marry my boy" (197). Having been shown "the holiness of direct desire," Lucy abandons her plans to go abroad and turns to George instead (199). The barrier, finally, was internal. Despite her family's opposition, she elopes with George, and the final chapter returns us to Florence and spring.

A Room with a View puts at stake the most basic requirement for a romance novel: the sexual attraction of heroine and hero. Cecil Vyse, having concocted the scheme to bring the Emersons into Lucy's neighborhood, thinks he is playing a grand joke and claims that "the cause of Comedy and the cause of Truth are really the same" (113). He speaks more truly than he knows, for the comedy being enacted casts him as the other man. This collapse of the geographical barrier between heroine and hero puts in motion the events that will free Lucy and George of self-denial and self-delusion. It will free Lucy of hypocrisy about sex and lead to her recognition that she had not yet understood the most basic reason to marry. Lucy and George are free to act on their love for each other, free to recognize it, free of the interior muddle that prevents that recognition. In this, Lucy is every heroine and George every hero. The work is universal and quintessential, an ideal romance novel.

Affective individualism in this novel is blocked from within. Lucy must understand that recognizing genuine sexual attraction when it occurs will make her happy. Its denial or falsification will consign her to years of misery in a "muddle." Companionate marriage is also blocked from within. The assumption of these two societal values has become, in this novel, solely a matter of getting out of one's own way to accomplish them.

Lucy courts and marries after the passage of the Married Women's Property Act in 1870. As she reminds her mother, once she reaches her majority, her money is her own (188). It enables her to elope with George, marrying him despite her family's objections to what they call her "hypocrisy." They are angry that she has changed her mind about whom she will marry, that she has rejected Cecil to marry George. Lucy's money simply permits the couple to carry out their threat of elopement if her family does not approve. They do not. The lovers elope. Forster endorses the marriage ending in *A Room with a View.* In fact, he makes Lucy and George the mythic stand-ins for every heroine and hero in every romance novel.

It would be his only romance novel. In a public address called "Pessimism in Literature," given in 1906, two years before the publication of *A Room with a View,* Forster explores the two endings possible to the novel: On the one hand, "let the lovers be united, to the sound of wedding bells" or, on the other, let the novel end with "some scene of separation" (135–36). Despite the marriage of Lucy and George, Forster finds that ending a book with a marriage is problematic: "A hundred years ago, or fifty years ago, this [the marriage ending] would have seemed a very good answer. But our social feelings are altering very rapidly. We of today know that whatever marriage is, it is not an end. We know that it is rather a beginning, and that the lovers enter upon life's real problems when those wedding bells are silent" (135).

The twentieth-century novel in English explores women's lives in at least two divergent forms. The novels that will come to be regarded as canonical explore the path of "separation" that Forster identifies at the start of the century. The romance novel survives and flourishes in its now familiar, popular form.

PART IV

❧

THE TWENTIETH-CENTURY ROMANCE NOVEL

12

THE POPULAR
ROMANCE NOVEL
IN THE TWENTIETH
CENTURY

In Part IV, I examine the courtship in a shelfful of the most popular romance novels of the past century. These twenty-five titles by five writers provide the beginnings of a canon for the twentieth-century popular romance. The five writers who belong in any list of canonical twentieth-century romance writers are Georgette Heyer, Mary Stewart, Janet Dailey before her self-admitted plagiarism, Jayne Ann Krentz, and Nora Roberts.

I choose these writers for three reasons. First, each has substantial individual accomplishments—the quality of her books is high. Analyzing the work of the best romance writers provides the beginnings of a canon for this genre that has been criticized so harshly based on novels chosen in haphazard ways, or for their interchangableness.

Second, each has produced works that have changed the romance novel landscape in important ways: Heyer, Stewart, and Dailey have been particularly influential on writers who have followed, influence being one way to qualify as a member of any literary canon. In her work both fictional and critical, Krentz has systematically explored the hero of the twentieth-century romance, the character who most contributes to the special nature of the form at this point in its history. In a list of books that out-Trollopes Trollope, Roberts has promulgated her mastery of the form, what one of her editors calls "perfect pitch," to a huge audience.

Third, taken together, these writers innovated or perfected one or more of the primary subgenres of romance. Heyer wrote a kind of historical romance known as the "Regency" which is now a popular subgenre. Stewart wrote romantic suspense and many authors have followed in her footsteps. Dailey wrote the first wildly successful Western romances that expanded and deepened the short contemporary form set on the American frontier. Krentz pioneered futuristics, romance novels set in the future. Although Roberts is the only writer who has not been an innovator in this realm, she has written superlatively in most of the subgenres mentioned above, as well as in other subgenres such as the paranormal (in which characters have telepathic abilities) and time-travel romances.

Considered along with the watershed at midcentury marked by the advent of Harlequin and Silhouette books as dominating forces in the market for short contemporary romances, the works of these five writers provide a way to track the romance novel through the century. From the 1920s through the 1960s, Heyer and Stewart produce a series of romance novels successful at the time and even better loved now. At midcentury first Harlequin and then Silhouette established the short romance novel set in the present (the "short contemporary") which gave Dailey, then Krentz, and finally Roberts their first opportunities to publish. I will take them up in roughly chronological order. In analyzing the works of these writers, E. M. Hull's *The Sheik* (1919) shows the way. It was enormously popular. Hull presents the courtship between the heroine and her hero with emotions foregrounded. Her heroine is independent; the hero is dangerous. *The Sheik* embodies the spirit and essence of the romance novel and still inspires imitators.

The twentieth century is the modern romance novel's third century of existence. In the year 2000, 2,289 romances were released. In that same year, 55.9 percent of popular paperback fiction sold in North America was popular romance. In 1999, 41.4 million people (including 3.5 million men), 18 percent of the reading-age population in America, read a romance novel (Romance Writers of America/Statistics). Indeed, it is now a commonplace to say that as the twentieth century progressed the romance novel in its popular form eventually dominated the fiction market. The literary, highbrow romance novel is still written but is no longer a main boulevard for the novel; it is more of a nostalgic byway. As in all periods of Western literature, love stories, which are not necessarily romance novels as I have been defining them here, abound. In contrast to the works that we looked at in Part III—*Pamela* and the rest—which were mass culture when they were published but became literary and canonical as critical assessment of these novels and others wrote the canon into being—the romance novel in the twentieth century has remained a mass cultural phenomenon.

Like the literary forebears in Part III, the best romance novels of the twentieth century were wildly popular. They were fixtures on the best sellers lists. They were collected, purchased, and resold by readers and used book vendors alike; they occupied large percentages of shelf space in bookstores and were available in supermarkets and at airports. They were everywhere. So were their more modest sisters: the short contemporaries that had a shelf life of the average magazine, the Harlequin reprints of Mills and Boon hardbacks with their narrower compass, the writing of which Nora Roberts has likened to performing "*Swan Lake* in a phone booth."

Every one of these romances—from the best sellers to the most obscure—contained the basic elements laid out in Part III: each was a work of prose fiction that told the story of the courtship and betrothal of one or more heroines. Each contained the eight essential narrative elements. Each defined the disordered society in which it was set and which the union of heroine and hero would put right. Each described the meeting, the barrier between the lovers, their attraction, their declaration of love for each other, the point of ritual death when the union looked impossible, the lovers' recognition of the new information that would overcome the barrier, and finally, each included a betrothal. Some of them incorporated the optional elements: some exiled scapegoats, converted the bad characters, or ended with a wedding, dance, or fete. These elements of the "core" romance novel apply to the works in Part IV just as they did to those in Part III. They are all members of the same genre. The long life of this genre attests to the power of the story of courtship and betrothal as both a subject and a narrative structure in the thinking of English-speaking people. And of other people as well: at least since *Pamela,* these books have been translated. Harlequins and Silhouettes are widely translated for a world-wide market. Japan, for example, constitutes a huge market for the romance novel. The books are also sold in China. The romance novel form transcends cultures.

Courtship, as we have seen, is the essence of the romance novel genre. Yet in the twentieth-century popular romance novel it differs markedly from the sort of narrative about wooing that we saw in the canonical works of the eighteenth and nineteenth centuries. There we found three sweeping societal trends—affective individualism (acting for one's own happiness), property rights for women, and companionate marriage (marrying for love)—that informed, propelled, and inspired the courtships in the novels examined in Part III. We saw the heroines Pamela Andrews, Elizabeth Bennet, Jane Eyre, Lucy Roberts, and Lucy Honeychurch struggle against a variety of factors to become an affective individual—to act for her own happiness above all. Each heroine faced her own difficulties with personal property. Pamela had her modest accumulation of money and clothes confiscated. Elizabeth Bennet (before she married one of the richest men in England) was in danger of dropping out of the genteel classes. Jane Eyre was a penniless orphan before she inherited a small fortune late in the novel. Lucy Robarts had a very small dowry, no parental roof (or parent), yet she married a young baron. Lucy Honeychurch had an inheritance but had to decide to act as the independent woman that she was. Each heroine also had to face difficult decisions to make a companionate marriage—one based on love. Pamela had to reject a union that merely promised to keep her safe from unwelcome assault. Elizabeth Bennet and Lucy Honeychurch had to reject unions that merely pleased a parent. Jane Eyre had to reject a marriage whose suitor argued that it would please God. Lucy Robarts had to hold firm to her companionate choice against the objections of her suitor's mother. The heroines in Part III acted as affective individuals through courtship, they gained financial standing (and, in some cases, independence) through courtship, and they made companionate marriages through courtship. But the issues surrounding courtship in the twentieth-century popular romance novel change from the sort that we saw in *Pamela*, *Pride and Prejudice*, *Jane Eyre*, *Framley Parsonage*, and *A Room with a View*.

For the heroines in the popular twentieth-century romance novels examined in Part IV, courtship is no longer the path to the fulfillment of affective individualism, property rights, or even the right to make a companionate marriage. Although the elements of the romance novel—the eight essential elements, the three optional ones—remain firmly in place, writers of the twentieth-century romance novel ordinarily do not use the courtship as a means to achieve, or in some cases, even to express, these three sweeping social trends. Generally, all of these are in place at the novel's outset. True, an occasional heroine is asked to act otherwise than as an affective individual and sacrifice her happiness, the odd penniless orphan is still in evidence, and even the rare prospect of a loveless marriage faces a heroine. Usually, however, the heroine of the twentieth-century popular romance has the freedom she needs to pursue her own ends; the rights she needs to possess her own property, as well as, often enough, the skills requisite to acquire that property herself; and a right to companionate marriage. She has not yet achieved such a marriage—she has not met her love match—but the possibility is firmly in her power.

Courtship, in the twentieth-century popular romance novel, changes in response to this changed heroine. This is the first distinguishing characteristic of the twentieth-century popular romance novel: the heroine is still at the center of the book, and courtship is still the book's reason for being (and its reason for being a romance novel), but the books present portraits of women in command of their lives. When a novel does not have to follow the heroine to maturity, that is, when it does not have to trace her assumption of affective individualism, her acquisition of property or of the rights to it, or even to trace her coming to believe that she should marry the partner she chooses, the hero can (and does) step to the fore to assume a much larger place in the narrative. This is the second distinguishing characteristic of the twentieth-century popular romance novel: the hero is much more in evidence, much more a part of the action. A final distinguishing characteristic lies in the nature of the courtships themselves: they focus much more on the emotional elements of the heroine and hero's relationship. In the twentieth-century popular romance novel the heroine's issues of self-definition and determination fade, the hero steps forward, and the courtship focuses on emotion. For this reason, I shift my analytical focus in Part IV from barrier and ritual death (although I do not leave them entirely behind) to the heroine, the hero, and the courtship itself. This wider scope will provide a more comprehensive account of the writers and works examined here.

Earlier investigations of the twentieth-century romance novel have focused on the sociological significance of books that were written during its boom at midcentury. Four book-length studies are typical of the critical approach which treats romance as a social phenomenon. Carol Thurston, in *The Romance Revolution* (1987) traces the introduction of erotic elements in what had been "sweet" (i.e., kisses only) novels, claiming "the erotic romance novel is, more than anything else, a social phenomenon" (218). In *Fantasy and Reconciliation* (1984), Kay Mussell focuses on six subgenres of the romance novel. Of "serious" romances, the shortest of the short contemporary novels, she claims "readers choose series books in large quantities, seeking out additional experiences of the same type and reading multiple versions of virtually interchangeable stories" (30). In this view, the romance novels are like other products, consumed in quantity, lacking uniqueness. Mariam Darce Frenier in *Good-Bye Heathcliff* (1988) sought a "popular medium" more "consumer selected" than television for her exploration of "obsessive love" and "overt anti-feminism" and the societal values that promoted "traditional" (i.e., 1950s-style) women. She chose romance novels (3). Jan Cohn in *Romance and the Erotics of Property* (1988) reads "contemporary popular romance . . . mass fiction created and marketed for women and exemplified by Harlequin novels" to reach her conclusion that the romance novel is "a story about power deeply encoded within a story about love" (3). This focus on the romance novel as a movement or product that women, often unwittingly, participated in underlies the critical approach of these accounts of the twentieth-century romance novel. It lumps together rather than differentiating the "products"—the novels—and their "consumers"—the readers.

My approach is different. These novels are literature. A canon exists among their readers and writers. Understanding how emphases within this genre shift in the twentieth century maps unexplored literary territory. My approach serves not as a substitute, but as an addition to the work of critics who approach the twentieth-century romance sociologically. It complements these earlier studies with a traditional literary historical approach that includes identifying the beginnings of a canon and analyzing the novels based on the definition of the literary elements of the genre I established in Part II.

In her *Dangerous Men and Adventurous Women: Romance Writers on the Appeal of the Romance* (1992), Jayne Ann Krentz makes the "dangerous hero" a cornerstone of her criticism on the romance novel. As a very successful romance novelist, such heroes feature prominently in her novels as well. Krentz describes the romance novel hero as a "source of emotional and . . . sometimes physical risk. . . . He is an 'alpha male,' not the sensitive, understanding, right-thinking, 'modern' man who is part therapist, part best friend, and thoroughly tamed from the start." Instead he is one of "the tough, hard-edged, tormented heroes that are at the heart of the vast majority of best-selling romance novels. . . . These are the heroes who carry off the heroines in historical romances. These are the heroes feminist critics despise." This hero, Krentz asserts, "is not only the hero, he is also the villain" ("Trying to Tame" 107–9). He is "the most dangerous creature on earth, the human male," and he must be conquered. The heroine must "force him to acknowledge her power as a woman" ("Introduction" 5). As the villain, the hero provides the heroine with the primary source of conflict. She must tame him in order to complete the courtship. In the terms developed in the definition in Part II, this kind of romance hero is himself the barrier.

Krentz's theory of the hero/villain is powerful, and it explains four of the five heroes from the romances examined in Part III. Pamela's Mr. B is an alpha male: wealthy, powerful, and dangerous. In *Pride and Prejudice,* Elizabeth's Darcy is wealthy; his regard can guarantee a subordinate's security or cast him adrift (Wickham). Marriage to him means untold wealth and the security that it brings. Jane Eyre's Rochester is both wealthy and powerful; in his sinful (if not demonic) secretiveness, he is dangerous as well. Lucy Robarts's Lufton, although absent for much of *Framley Parsonage,* is powerful in the most traditional way of heroes: he's an aristocrat in the habit of getting his own way. The heroine's security—the very roof her brother puts over her head—is endangered by Lufton's declaration of his love for her.

Only Lucy Honeychurch's George in *A Room with a View* does not have to be tamed. He poses no possible danger. He knows from his first meeting with Lucy that she is the right woman for him, and he never wavers. George, before Lucy's recognition of her love for him, is in what we would now recognize as a state of depression. His father says of him, "He will live; but he will not think it worth while to live" (194). Krentz's theory of the "alpha male" hero does not account for George. Nonetheless, he is the hero, and *A Room with a View* is a romance novel. Rather than an alpha hero, George is a sentimental hero in a romance novel that is also a sentimental novel.

Sentimental novels focus on emotion. (*Pamela* with its moment-by-moment account of the heroine/narrator's emotional responses to her ordeals is one such novel.) In its purest form, a sentimental novel has a hero who is involved in one episode after another precisely to evoke emotion—both his own and the reader's. G. A. Starr explains that these heroes "focus not on actions, but on reactions" (188). A hero in a sentimental novel that ends in "wedding bells"—that is, a hero in a romance novel— Starr describes as "a lion among men who is a lamb before women" (181, 197). From this merest glimpse into the history of the novel, we can see the forebear of a second kind of romance hero: the sentimental hero. He is still strong, virile, manly ("a lion among men"), but he is wounded physically, psychically, or emotionally. The heroine must heal him. This is George's situation at the point of ritual death in *A Room with a View.* He will not think it "worth while to live." Lucy's recognition, what Forster calls her becoming "unmuddled," heals him, and from his reluctant willingness to remain alive, he moves in the final chapter to a "content absolute" (201). If the alpha hero must be tamed, the sentimental hero is hurt or damaged in some way, often emotionally, and the heroine must heal him.

Julie Tetel Andresen, like Krentz a romance novelist who also writes criticism about the genre, notes that the romance "foregrounds emotionality—makes it its subject matter." This means that the interpersonal elements of courtship—the chemistry of the interactions between heroine and hero—are not only thought over and analyzed by the heroine, they are dramatized—made into scenes—and become the subject of the romance, whatever other incidents and issues might be going on in subplots (178). Andresen's "emotionality . . . foregrounded" is Starr's "reactions." Whether the novel has an alpha hero or a sentimental one (or a combination of the two), whether the heroine is engaged upon taming or healing (or, again, a combination of the two), these reactions, this foregrounded emotionality, is the stuff of the barrier of the book. It is what the heroine and hero have to argue over, discuss, act upon, research, think about, talk to their friends about, avoid, seek out, and otherwise confront each other about. At the book's outset, this emotional involvement between heroine and hero and their reactions to each other are, to deliberately use a word now loaded in my discussion, disordered. By the end, they are orderly.

In other words, twentieth-century popular romance novels are still comedies, but the expression of the societal disorder (with which all comedies begin) is largely within the heroine and hero themselves, and the twentieth-century hero makes the largest new contribution to this kind of disorder and to its being made orderly by the betrothal at the end of the work. Ordering society is now an issue of taming or healing the hero. If he is an alpha male and the heroine does not tame him, he will regard courtship, wrongly, as merely the actions he needs to go through to get a woman into bed. If he is a sentimental hero and the heroine does not heal him, he will regard courtship, wrongly, as something that he is exempt from: he is not good at it, is not ready for it, or it will merely hurt him. Untamed or unhealed, the hero will not truly appreciate the role of the heroine in his life; he will not engage with her emotionally. The most important lack of emotional engagement, of course, will be his failure to fall in love with her. A novel that ends with the hero and heroine not in love, not betrothed, is simply not a romance novel. The novel will not end in anyone's freedom.

E. M. Hull's *The Sheik* (1919) exemplifies the changes to the heroine, the hero, and the courtship at the heart of the twentieth-century popular romance novel. Heroine and hero are ideal, elemental versions of most twentieth-century romance novel protagonists. *The Sheik* is the ur-romance novel of the twentieth century. It falls early in the century. It was wildly, hugely popular, and the character of the sheik has entered public mythology in much the same way as Don Juan, Robin Hood, or the Scarlet Pimpernel.

However, the novel is, as we now say, politically incorrect. Dealing with this issue, which would not have occurred to Hull, can clear the way for a discussion of the heroine, the hero, and their courtship in this ur-romance. To begin, it is racist. The hero is, the reader believes, an Arab, and this is supposed to raise our fears of miscegenation with the heroine, who is an Englishwoman. Nonetheless, his eventual marriage to the heroine is *not* to be read as a bridging of what is apparently racial inequality: we learn very late in the narrative that he is actually the son of the Earl of Glencaryle and a Spanish mother, and hence, exotic in his origins but still European (244). Nonetheless, he hates the English because of his English father's treatment of his Spanish mother. This hatred accounts for his initial disdain for the heroine. The late revelation of the hero's true origins is the same device used by Edgar Rice Burroughs in *Tarzan*, of course, where the ape man turns out to be Lord Greystoke.

The novel involves abduction, assault, and the imprisonment of the heroine. If this were not bad enough, it also involves rape. And not just any rape, but the rape of the heroine by the hero. Rachel Anderson speaks for any number of critics when she condemns the book on this basis: "*The Sheik* is the most immoral of any of the romances . . . because of the distorting view Miss Hull presents of the kind of relationship which leads to perfect love. . . . the novel could be interpreted as a tract in support of the theory that rape is a physical impossibility, and that any woman who claims to have been attacked in this way was really asking for it. If one accepts unlikely human behavior, dishonorable motivation, and the theory that what all women really want is to be crushed by a fierce, hard lover, then *The Sheik* makes a lively and entertaining read" (*Purple* 188–89). Julia Bettinotti and Marie-Francoise Truel read the book quite differently: "What originally appeared to be a story of captivity and enslavement turns out to be a story of resistance and female liberation" (192). Again, the rape needs to be seen in the context of the setting, and the extreme nature of all of the action in this novel: kidnappings (there are three if you count a foiled escape), a near deadly rescue of the heroine from a rival sheik, the rape itself, a stabbing of the hero, and the heroine's attempted suicide. This list leaves unmentioned the everyday physical struggle that the hero and his band had to conduct against the desert and the horses they bred and trained.

Abby Zidle explains the presence of rape in romances written before the 1970s: "romance heroes from the 1970s and earlier [*The Sheik* was published in 1919] were often actors in rape fantasies and other sexual brutalities because the romance industry thought that women would not accept premarital sex unless the heroine was coerced" (25). In Chapter 1 we read that there had "never been a breath of scandal attached" to the heroine's name; that she was "the divinity," the "cruel fair," and "the coldest little fish in the world" (2–6). Her subsequent sexual relationship with the hero was, therefore, her first, not just one more fling. Her initial coercion and her initial virginity made this relationship acceptable to Hull's contemporaries. Jennifer Crusie Smith notes that in some popular romance novels "although the hero initially rapes the heroine through a misunderstanding, her innate strength and courage force him to love her unconditionally, thereby making the heroine the powerful, secure figure at the end of the story" (56). The sheik misunderstood himself: he thought he did not know love and was impervious to it; Diana, at the end of the book, has him crying: "a hard sob," but a sob nonetheless (296). This is her power.

Perhaps the most important observations about the rape in romance comes from Anne Kaler, who, in examining captivity and rape in twenty-five romances of the twentieth century, finds that events in them are presented as fantasies: "the authors must protect the readers from identifying with any realistic aspect of the capture—trauma, stress, or terror" (94). The rape in *The Sheik* takes place "off"—between Chapters 2 and 3. Because the romance genre is based on "fantasy, escape, and entertainment," the "capture and rape" is read through these filters. Romance readers accept them (98); they understand the difference between a fantasy and a goal or life plan.

Despite its political incorrectness (or, perhaps, because of it), *The Sheik* is the ur-romance. E. M. Hull was one of a group of novelists writing at the beginning of the twentieth century who included in their works "lavish romance, exotic background, and high adventure" (McAleer 47). The works of the other novelists, such as Elinor Glyn (*Three Weeks,* 1907) and Ethel M. Dell (*The Way of an Eagle,* 1911) have been largely forgotten, but *The Sheik* not only achieved popularity immediately upon publication but also has influenced the twentieth-century popular romance novel throughout the century. The heroine begins the book with what the heroine in Part

III strove for—affective individualism, property rights, and the ideal of companionate marriage. She foreshadows the heroines of twentieth-century romance. The hero is the ideal alpha male; he likewise foreshadows many of his twentieth-century brethren. Their courtship, the action that makes this novel a romance novel, foregrounds an unusually elemental set of emotions. It is a pure version of the courtship as it comes to be written after the turn of the century.

Like *Pamela* and *A Room with a View*, *The Sheik* was extremely popular. During the first nine months after its release, Small, Maynard and Company reprinted the book thirty-two times (Hull ii). The story escaped the confines of the novel and entered the culture as one of those legends that everyone knows, whether through popular song, a cartoon, playground chants, or various advertising and brand-name images. As a character, the sheik is as recognizable as Frankenstein's monster. The film starring Rudolf Valentino in the title role was made the same year (1921) as the novel's release in the United States. It propelled him to stardom. The story, whether on the screen or the page, impressed itself on the public as a depiction of fascinating sexual passion. It was scandalous. It was exotic. It was wildly popular. Many saw it, or read it, or both. Even those who had never heard of Hull's novel knew who the sheik was and what the story was about.

Romance novelists were no exception. Eileen Fallon notes that the book inspired some directly (such as Barbara Cartland, who published her first romance novel just four years after publication of *The Sheik*) and others indirectly (116). Patricia Raub claims that this book can "be viewed as the precursor of the mass market romances initiated by Harlequin Romance" in the 1950s (123). Carol Thurston names it as one of a handful of models for the romance boom of the 1970s (51).

The novel, in brief, is the story of Diana Mayo, a flapper and independent British aristocrat who is bored with her life in society and who travels the world seeking diversion. She arranges a horseback trek into the desert of Algeria where Sheik Ahmed Ben Hassan kidnaps her and holds her prisoner. Although he rapes her, she refuses to submit her will to him. She fights him with a courage and dignity that win his respect and, finally, his love. At first Diana hates Ahmed, but living in his camp she observes his courage, strength, and dignity. He risks his life for her and almost dies. These are qualities she has not been able to find among her suitors, whom she regards with amusement or contempt. They are the qualities that she has in abundance herself and which win, first, her respect and then her love.

At the book's climax, she is kidnapped again by a rival sheik. Ahmed comes to her rescue, is stabbed, and almost dies. Upon his recovery he regrets his harsh treatment of her and decides that she must be returned to her own people. But Diana has fallen in love with him and would rather die than leave him. She tries to commit suicide. As she fires the revolver that she is aiming at her temple, Ahmed lunges at her, just managing to spoil her aim and save her life. He admits that he has fallen in love with her too. Their betrothal is a warning: "you will have a devil for a husband" (296).

The heroine is utterly unlike those of the canonical literary romances examined in Part III. Diana, as a woman of the early twentieth century, is a flapper, interested in doing exactly as she pleases. Without being spoiled, she is willful. She is exactly like a man in this respect, and Hull makes the point that she had been brought up by her much older brother in the manner of a boy (3). She rides and hunts. She has great physical courage. She is fearless. At the novel's outset she has achieved what the heroines in Part III spend their novels accomplishing, what Beatrice Hofstadter, speaking of this heroine, calls "male liberty"—equality with men on male terms (242). Diana Mayo, at the outset of the novel acts as an affective individual, has property rights, and believes in companionate marriage. She is as unfettered as a person—male or female—can be.

Diana lives for affective individualism. In the novel's first scene, she refuses to dance (shades of *Pride and Prejudice*'s Darcy, not Elizabeth) and rejects a marriage proposal from a young British aristocrat (10). The dance itself is a party to kick off Diana's piece of "unprincipled folly"—her trek into the desert without chaperones (1).

The desert setting of *The Sheik* gives the heroine's affective individualism the widest possible stage. Yes, the desert is exotic. Yes, it is remote. But it is also not Diana's native society—not the society of England, nor even the society of bored English ex-patriots in Biskra, Algeria. It is a place she chose to be rather than one in which she found herself. For all that, she had hoped to visit the desert as what we would now call an adventure tourist; she ends up imprisoned there. In living for her own happiness, she rejects suitors, her brother's advice, the mores of her own culture, and even the culture of the globe-trotting English aristocracy. She is accused by the more conventional (and everyone in the novel except the sheik himself is more conventional) of rejecting the values of her gender as well (3). Diana is extreme in her adherence to affective individualism, and this trait is in place from the novel's first scene.

Diana is financially independent. She and her brother, Aubrey, disagree about the tour into the desert. He would rather she accompany him to

America, but as she tells the suitor whose marriage proposal she turns down, "I came of age a few months ago, and, in future, I can do as I please. Not that I have ever done anything else" (8). Later she reminds her brother that she had "left [him] all that I have in the world"—more evidence of her having control over her own property (19). By the novel's beginning, Diana has attained her majority (i.e., twenty-five years old) and need not answer to her brother either in terms of her actions or expenses. She can go where she wishes; she can finance her own movements.

Diana believes in companionate marriage, and the book is an account of her making one with the sheik. This choice of hers is not so much choosing a companionate marriage over one that is dynastic, based on property, on religious ideals, or on the wishes of a parent (as is the case for the heroines in Part III) as it is the recognition of an appropriate match—in Diana's case, one is tempted to say "mate." Diana had despaired of ever finding such a mate, but at the outset of the book, she believes in its importance—the marriage she refuses in the first scene is dynastic. With these three values in place, Diana is the prototypical twentieth-century popular romance novel heroine.

Her captor, Sheik Ahmed Ben Hassan, is the prototypical alpha male hero. Before he whispers *"Je t'aime, je t'adore"* (295) on the novel's penultimate page, Hull assembles a portrait of the typical alpha male. Like all of the "desert dwellers" Ahmed is a man "inured to hardships, imbued with magnificent courage," a "splendid healthy animal" about whom there was "nothing effete or decadent" (277). He begins his relationship with Diana when he sees her and decides he must have her. Her captivation of him, although this is not the way he thinks of it, motivates him to sing a love song to her in the darkness beyond a garden where she is sitting, to bribe her guide so that the guide's men will not interfere when he abducts her, and to enter her room while she is asleep and replace the bullets in her revolver with blanks. His thought, money, and effort are evidence of Diana's unknowing hold on him.

For her, the courtship begins when he kidnaps her, "riding her down" (overtaking her) in a horseback chase (49). When she asks why, he replies, *"Bon Dieu!* Are you not woman enough to know?" (57). His horse is "possessed of a devil" and he outrides the heroine and everyone else in the novel (70). He inspires "terror" (72). He is "haughty . . . arrogant, dominating," and "authoritative" (72). He is not subject to the laws of others. After he abducts her, when Diana insists that inquiries would be made as to her whereabouts, he replies, "The French Government has no jurisdiction over

me. I am not subject to it. I am an independent chief, my own master. I recognize no government. My tribe obey me and only me" (74). His kisses
are "fierce" (78). So are his "eyes [which] watch[ed] her with a steadiness
that racked her nerves." She likens him to lions she once observed—"savage, snarling brutes" (84). The sheik is tough, courageous, splendid,
healthy, physically skilled, brave, fiercely sexual, haughty, arrogant, dominating, authoritative, a law unto himself, and like a wild animal. She falls in
love with these very features: "He was a brute, but she loved him, loved him
for his very brutality and superb animal strength" (133). The sheik is literally the alpha male: like the head male wolf with a pack subservient to
him, he led a tribe which obeyed only him. He possesses to the extreme the
characteristics typical of alpha male heroes in twentieth-century popular
romance novels.

Like the heroine and hero in *Pamela, Pride and Prejudice, Jane Eyre, Framley
Parsonage,* and *A Room with a View,* Diana and Ahmed enact the eight essential
elements of a romance novel. Unlike the courtship in these novels, here, at
the beginning of the popular romance novel, the eight elements of the
courtship—society defined, meeting and attraction, barrier, point of ritual
death, recognition, and betrothal—concentrate on the emotion in scenes
between the heroine and hero. Emotion is kept very much in the center of
the heroine's, the hero's, and as a result, the reader's consciousness. Hull
foreshadows a narrative technique that would come to dominate the
romance novel in the twentieth century: the focus on emotion, especially in
scenes between heroine and hero.

The society defined at the outset is the group of spoiled English aristo-
crats (Diana is the daughter of a baronet) in Biskra, Algeria. In the first
scene, Diana not only refuses to dance but also turns down a marriage offer.
The rejection of these two forms of union in the society, one symbolic (the
dance) one quite literal (marriage) and Diana's expedition into the desert
mark not so much the disorder of her society as her total rejection of it.
Indeed, from the point of view of this society, she disappears into the
desert never to return. The novel does not incorporate her into it. Her disdain and amusement with her longing "would-be partners . . . ten-deep"
around her, whom she regards as uninteresting, dominates this first scene
of the novel (4).

The meeting between heroine and hero demonstrates how different the
true society of this novel is to be. It is not a dance refused (like Darcy and
Elizabeth), but a kidnapping on horseback: "She clutched her revolver and
fired twice, full in the face of the man who was following her . . . [he]

swung her clear of the saddle and on to his own horse in front of him" (51–52). This meeting ends with Diana's imprisonment at the encampment of Ahmed, the sheik of a tribe of Arabs. Previously Diana has rejected not only marriage, but men: "God made me a woman. Why, only He knows" (11). Ahmed has rejected love: "Love? *Connais pas!* [I don't know it.] Yes, I do . . . I love my horses" (109). The tone of this courtship is set by the initial attitudes of the heroine and hero toward love—jaded disbelief—and by the nature of their first encounter—violent chase and capture. The meeting is a very long scene—it lasts thirteen pages. Its action— Diana's kidnapping and imprisonment—is quite simple. Diana's emotions are foregrounded (emphasized) as are the sheik's. The reader identifies with her "fear . . . terror . . . [and] horror" (57). The reader may also identify with the sheik's "ardor . . . anger . . . [and] amusement" (58–59).

So it is with all of the elements of the romance novel in *The Sheik*. The author reports the emotions of heroine and, often, too, the hero, in detail. The reader identifies with the heroine and, as Laura Kinsale has argued in an essay called "The Androgynous Reader," with the hero as well (32). The eight essential elements of the romance novel represent the major milestones of the courtship; emotion is strong at these moments. Hull and other authors of twentieth-century popular romance novels foreground it in the meeting and in each of the other seven essential elements.

Like Elizabeth's recognition, Diana's is a matter of identifying a shifting attitude toward the hero. Elizabeth's takes place quietly, while she is alone in her room at the inn in Lambton. Diana's takes place after Ahmed foils her attempt at escape by riding her down for the second time in the novel by shooting her horse out from under her when she refuses to stop at his shouted warning. Lying across his saddle, held fast by his arm around her, she feels secure and "quite suddenly she knew—knew that she loved him, that she had loved him for a long time, even when she thought she hated him and when she had fled from him. . . . She did not care if he was an Arab, she did not care what he was, he was the man she loved" (133–34). Here her emotions are "content[ment]" mixed with "giddiness" and "apprehension along with "yearning" (134–35, 138). And in the scene, for the first time, she feels "love" (133). His emotions are "coldness" and "passion, but not yet love (141). Just as the reader follows, breathlessly, the action of the horseback chase, she follows the descriptions of the heroine's and hero's emotions.

Whereas for Elizabeth the barrier was complex and shifting—society itself, her family, her own prejudice—for Diana the barrier has been her hatred of Ahmed; at the point of her recognition, it becomes his rejection of love. In Krentz's terms, he is both hero and villain. Somehow Diana has to overcome this rejection. Hull spends about half the book bringing Diana to a recognition of her love for Ahmed; the second half she spends having Ahmed recognize his love for Diana. Diana has to tame the hero who already loves the heroine but has to be brought to a realization and admission of this love.

Ahmed threatens to send her away: "You must go back to your own country, to your own people, to your own life" (290). This is the society she has rejected in the opening scenes of the book when she turned down the proposal of marriage from another bored aristocrat and rode off into the desert. The barrier, finally, is completely external for her—because it is completely internal for him. He believes, unwaveringly, that she does not belong in the desert. He cannot envision her at home in his culture. This barrier is entirely a matter of his own beliefs, completely internal. Thus for her, it is entirely external. When one partner comprises the barrier for both hero and heroine, that barrier is as elemental, as basic, and as difficult as barriers come. In this case, the hero is the barrier. Of course, a kidnapping rapist as a hero will always be a villain, but in Krentz's terms, even the least alpha hero, if he embodies a portion of the barrier, will also be a villain. As the villain of this book, Ahmed presents Diana with the challenge of taming him. This feeling of challenge is part of the emotional mix of the popular romance novel that is often overlooked. His disdain, lust, anger, passion, and possessiveness comprise the barrier for more than half of the work. When the emotion changes to love, the barrier falls.

The point of ritual death in this book involves near loss of life. One-half of the novel's ritual death is Ahmed's near death from the stabbing he suffers when he rescues Diana from the rival sheik who has kidnapped her. Diana is desperate at the thought of his death, but he recovers. The second half of the novel's ritual death occurs when he announces that he will send her away. Deciding, like the affective individual that she is, that "her life was her own to deal with," she picks up a revolver, aims it at her head, and pulls the trigger (294). Ahmed saves her, this time from suicide, by deflecting her hand that holds the pistol. This marks the end of the low point in their courtship, the end of ritual death—in the case of this novel, not ritual at all. In deciding to take her own life, Diana maintains her independence. The decision to kill one's self is still a decision, and is, as any number of twentieth-century philosophers and artists would point out, the most fundamental decision a person can make. Ritual death in *The Sheik* puts the lives of both heroine and hero at stake, and the escape from ritual death leaves them facing a stark set of possibilities: he would live on in the desert, but she would be sent away. She adds her own set of alternatives: either she will live on in the desert with him, or she will not live. Her courage, finally, trumps his. He asks her to stay, warning, "you will have the devil for a husband" (296). They marry. She risks everything to tame him and wins. Diana feels determination; Ahmed, finally, love. Ritual death is, for him, recognition as well.

The Sheik is the ur-twentieth-century popular romance novel. Its heroine is recklessly independent. The hero is not just symbolically an alpha male—some guy in a business suit who is nonetheless dangerous and must be tamed—he is an actual sheik, leading a band of men loyal only to him. The novel foregrounds emotion. When their confrontations are not physical (chase and capture), Diana and Ahmed have a series of encounters charged with rage, incredulity, fear, desperation, fascination, passion, mockery, coldness, anguish, suffering, and love.

Defining *The Sheik* solely by its exotic setting threatens to obscure its universality as a romance. The desert setting has attracted attention: Mary Cadogan devotes a chapter to "romantic novels," including *The Sheik,* set in the desert and other exotic places (116–50). Bettinotti and Truel examine "desert fabula" as a way to understand romances like *The Sheik.* Yet despite its exotic setting, despite its elemental emotions, *The Sheik* is like any other twentieth-century popular romance novel. The elements I have examined in *The Sheik* operate in other romances as well: in drawing rooms, at dances, in schoolrooms, in the dining rooms of hotels, in the houses of the wealthy, on farms, on frontiers, on different planets, in the past and the future, in dark, mysterious houses, and anywhere else that men and women meet. The possibilities are broad and varied. They flavor the kind of action that the book will depict, the subplots, the kind of behavior that is acceptable between the hero and heroine, which is a function of the kind of society that the setting provides. Consideration of society is not gone in these books, but it is less important in the popular romance of the twentieth century than it was in the canonical romances examined in Part III.

13

CIVIL CONTRACTS

Georgette Heyer

Beginning in 1921, Georgette Heyer (1902–1974) wrote one and sometimes two historical romance novels per year until her death in 1974. A 1984 survey taken in Great Britain of the public libraries reported that between four and six copies of her novels were borrowed on any given day (Glass 283). Copies in public libraries in America have been borrowed and read until their covers fall off. Perhaps the strongest evidence of her continued popularity is that much of her backlist is still in print. This body of work is her legacy to the history of the romance.

Her influence is felt in every historical romance novel written since 1921, particularly in the Regency romance novel. Heyer is the mother of this kind of romance. The Regency is that period in English history between 1811 and 1820 when the Prince of Wales ruled England as regent for his father, the incapacitated George III. A regent rules during a king or queen's inability to fulfill his or her duties. The Regency period ended in 1820 because the old king died and the prince became King George IV. Regencies are among the most popular historical romance novels and are set in this time period. Each novel includes the core elements explained in Part II: the courtship and betrothal of one or more heroines and heroes (in Heyer's case, usually one) as well as a meeting, barrier, the attraction between heroine and hero, a declaration, point of ritual death, and recognition. The society defined is specifically Regency society.

Heyer's main influence was Jane Austen, who lived and published during the Regency period (*Pride and Prejudice*, for instance, in 1813), but who did not write Regencies. Austen set her romances in her own time, contemporaneous with her own life, and thus wrote contemporaries. Heyer set her novels more than a century before her time and thus wrote historicals. As a number of critics have noted, Heyer borrowed plot elements from Austen's novels (Bywaters 493). She emulated (as much as any writer could) the wit of Austen's outlook and language. She could not, however, glean many period details from Austen. Because Austen's works were contemporary romances, she did not need to include such details in nearly the abundance that they are included in historical novels where authors are writing mindful that the reader may know very little about the period she is reading about. (Anyone who has ever tried to teach an Austen text to students unacquainted with the period can attest to how much must be explained even to those readers eager to read *Pride and Prejudice,* to say nothing of *Mansfield Park.*)

Heyer, educated at a seminary school and Westminster College in London, systematically and exhaustively researched the Regency, filling notebooks with the language, dress, geography, politics, war, and personalities of the era (McGrath 317). Heyer's writing process is now famous—even infamous. To many, meticulous research is synonymous with the well-written Regency romance and the main attraction for readers. Florence Stevenson, writing more than sixty years after Heyer began publishing Regencies, offers this view of the sub-genre when she describes these novels as depicting

> a world peopled by handsome noblemen in well-fitting coats, high-starched cravats, muslin shirts, colored vests, skintight pantaloons, gold fobs, Hessian boots polished to a high shine and adorned with sparkling gold tassels. . . . They have fast horses, country estates, townhouses and fortunes. . . . [The heroine] is beautiful, witty, charming, dresses to the nines in see-through, form hugging muslins, bonnets adorned with cock feathers or flowers, shows a well-turned ankle and a tiny foot. (31)

Heyer writes this glittering language of dress and ornament, as well as the activities and cant of cockfighting, driving, buying snuff, dueling, and so forth with historical accuracy. When she did make the rare mistake in her depiction of Regency England, her biographer Jane Aiken Hodge tells us Heyer "minded this very much" (166).

If this were the whole of Heyer's accomplishment—a series of romances with carefully researched Regency settings—she would not merit a place in this survey of the canon of twentieth-century romance writers. Heyer's true legacy lies in her use of this setting. Regency details inform the heroine, the hero, and the core of the romance itself—the courtship. At the same time, however, heroine, hero, and courtship inform the setting. Heroine, hero, and their courtship throw the setting into high relief; characters and their action comment on the setting.

Together, setting and character reassert the importance of the heroine's Diana-Mayo-like independence. Heyer may set her novels in an historically accurate Regency world of glittering surfaces, but the characters she puts there, particularly the heroines, are not the historical norm. First, the typical unmarried Regency girl of good family would have been far more swayed by confining societal strictures on her behavior than the affective individualist. Second, she would not have possessed money or marketable skills or have the opportunity to learn or practice such skills. Finally, unmarried Regency girls of good family would be as likely to follow the advice of their parents in choosing a mate as they would be in assuming the twentieth-century ideal of companionate marriage that Heyer invests them with. Heyer does not write historically accurate heroines. Instead, they have unusual notions about how to behave (as the conventional-minded characters surrounding them are constantly pointing out), and those notions are distinctly twentieth-century.

Her heroes are similarly ahistorical. The Regency is renowned for its fops, dandies, reckless "bucks," profligate gamblers, and imperious guardians. As A. S. Byatt has noted, it may be the English historical period in which the wealthy were the most secure in their wealth, and the most idle (273). Fops, dandies, and other idlers appear in Heyer, but they are never the hero, who has twentieth-century sensibilities. Thus, the "givens" of the twentieth-century heroine (affective individualism, property, and companionate marriage) are present in these novels written in the twentieth century about the nineteenth. Similarly, twentieth-century attitudes define the heroes. The setting spotlights these beliefs and behaviors of heroine and hero, which would seem much less remarkable in a contemporary romance novel set in contemporary times. The heroine's and hero's beliefs, behavior, and values, in turn, act as a critique of the setting, spotlighting it in turn. Heyer's sensible heroes move among a society full of men who spend their money and time gambling, drinking, and keeping mistresses but who are, nonetheless, viewed as respectable. The ordinary sobriety and seriousness of her heroes who engage in some of these activities, but whose serious side is far more in evidence, expose the corruption of Regency values.

The Regency setting, in addition to limning characters and behavior, and vice versa, reinserts older barriers to the heroine's and hero's courtship. In this it functions like most other historical settings for the romance. In Regencies the union of heroine and hero must take place within a society in which dynastic marriage governed by an elaborate set of calculations as to bloodlines and wealth is the norm. Heyer's heroes, and particularly her heroines, must, therefore, struggle to choose and act on the ideal of companionate marriage. Love does not come easy. This is an added source of drama and conflict in the book. This is the achievement of Heyer's romances: novels strong in their core elements, written with wit and humor that inform and are informed by their temporal setting: the setting is not simply a backdrop.

The following analysis focuses on four books written after Heyer had hit her romance-writing stride up until the time of her death. Hodge cites *Regency Buck* (1935) as one of the two books that "had shown [Heyer] where her genius lay"(78). I analyze it here. *Sylvester* (1957) and *A Civil Contract* (1961) come at the height of her powers, and *Lady of Quality* (1972) at the end of her long career. The heroines are various, but all have the independence that we saw in Diana Mayo of *The Sheik*. The hero in *A Civil Contract* must be healed rather than tamed, and the plot of the novel includes a marriage of convenience, a variation that takes on added resonance when it is set in the Regency. For this reason, and because it may very well be Heyer's best book, I consider it last in the survey below.

Despite the Regency setting of her best romances, Heyer situates her heroines as having attained the three elements of freedom that the heroines in Part III had to struggle for. Elizabeth Bennet, a heroine in what we would now call a contemporary romance novel who actually lived during the Regency, had to struggle to maintain even a modest level of affective individualism; she had very little property to assert any rights over, and her determination to make a companionate marriage was threatened by Mr. Collins and her own family's laxity (her father's governance of Lydia) and rashness (Lydia herself). Heyer, creating characters who live in the same period, manages to imbue them with a twentieth-century heroine's possession of the three elements. They are affective individuals at a time when parental authority governed a girl's behavior. Recall that unmarried women in the early nineteenth century did not control their own wealth and well-born girls did not have marketable skills that permitted them to earn their own livings. Heyer's heroines have control of their wealth or a skill that permits them to support themselves. Finally, a Heyer heroine believes that companionate marriage is simply her due, that it goes without saying that a woman marries for love.

In *Regency Buck*, heroine Judith Taverner meets the hero, Julian St. John Audley, Fifth Earl of Worth, on the road to London to meet her guardian, and although he does not know who she is, he cannot resist kissing her. Their meeting is doubled, first on the road, then in Worth's home where it is revealed that in her recently deceased father's will, he has miscounted his earls, and Worth, rather than his father, is named her guardian. He will control her money, approve her courtships (marriage being a contract, and he having the power to approve or deny her contracts), and supervise other legal matters—until she reaches her majority nine months after the beginning of the novel. Throughout the long middle of the book he rejects her various suitors, rescues her from ridicule, has her introduced into society, and curbs her headstrong younger brother, the "Regency buck" of the title. On the day she attains her majority, he proposes.

Judith is a twentieth-century romance heroine in a nineteenth-century setting. She lives for affective individualism. This imperious, willful heroine flaunts the usual dictates of her society. She dares her brother, "I will lay you a level hundred, Perry, that I reach Brighton before you on May 12th, driving a curricle-and-four" (197). Merely driving alone was scandalous for a woman; racing was another matter entirely. It is impossible to imagine Elizabeth Bennet driving herself from Bath to Brighton, which is to say from one fashionable watering hole to another, even assuming that any carriage were available for this purpose. The behavior would be Lydia-like. To the contemporary twentieth-century reader, however, it seems more like driving one's own car, albeit in a road rally.

Judith's independence, both financial (in prospect) and physical, is the attribute of a twentieth-century romance heroine and is in place before the novel begins. The correct analogy here is not to Elizabeth Bennet; it is to Diana Mayo. The Regency setting makes Judith's independence stand out. It would have been far less remarkable in 1935 when *Regency Buck* was published, even in a society as class-bound as England's. Independence helps make the heroine remarkable. It contrasts with the normative values of Regency society: the surface detail that Heyer worked so hard to get right is not carried through to an unquestioning view of the society's beliefs. Instead Judith is "a very wealthy young woman" (which means that she has cash coming to her) and "heiress to as much of [her] brother's property as is unentailed" (which means that she has the prospect of becoming propertied should anything happen to her brother before he produces an heir) (80). Until she attains her majority, Worth controls her money. At the end of the novel she comes into control of her money to the extent that she is free to choose her own "friends" to manage it for her. By contrast, Elizabeth Bennet, who embodies genuine Regency values, was struggling against an entail to retain her place in the landed gentry. She married to achieve the sort of prestige from property and income that Heyer simply invests Judith with, pending her soon-to-be-attained majority. *Regency Buck,* then, is the story of Judith's making a companionate marriage, despite her misgivings about her guardian/suitor, and then with his approval and most essential participation—as the bridegroom.

In *Sylvester, or the Wicked Uncle,* Phoebe Marlow, the heroine, is a romance novelist. She has written a novel in which she bases an unflattering character on Heyer's hero, Sylvester, Duke of Salford. *Sylvester* depicts a chase across England, from Austerby (Phoebe's home, which she fled because she feared being made to marry Sylvester), to an inn where her brother-like friend is laid up with a broken leg, to London, to Dover, to Calais. Sylvester follows her across England and the Channel, alternately marveling at her propensity for getting into scrapes and helping her out of them.

Phoebe is an affective individual. The hero sums this up when he thinks he's lost her:

> "Oh, yes, she's unusual! . . . She blurts out whatever may come into her head; she tumbles from one outrageous escapade into another; she's happier grooming horses and hobnobbing with stable-hands than going to parties; she's impertinent; you daren't catch her eye for fear she should start to giggle; she hasn't any accomplishments; I never saw anyone with less dignity; she's abominable, and damnably hot at hand, frank to a fault. . . ."(296)

This very physical heroine knows horses as well as men do—shades of Diana Mayo. Phoebe Marlow is not quite wealthy, "she won't inherit much from Marlow, but her mother's dowry was tied up in her, so she'll have that" (29). She has another kind of currency in this society, blood: "Marlow's a fool, but his blood's well enough" (29). She also has a salable skill: she writes romance novels. Like Elizabeth Bennet, Phoebe expected money from her mother's dowry; like Elizabeth's creator, Phoebe writes romance novels. Austen's brothers may have helped her with the business of publishing *Pride and Prejudice,* but the income from this book came to her alone. With it she helped support her mother and her sister and left the money to her sister upon her death (Tomalin 269). Phoebe has this prospect of an independent household as an alternative to marriage. Like Judith, Phoebe in *Sylvester* is at odds with her Regency setting, and it with her.

In *Lady of Quality* Annis Wychwood, the heroine, although unmarried, has reached her majority, and journeys to Bath to set up her household. On the road she meets a young woman whom she befriends and offers to introduce to polite society. This hitchhiker turns out to be the niece and ward of Mr. Oliver Charleton, the hero, a self-admitted rake, who objects to Annis's influence on his young relative.

Annis is easily the most modern of the four heroines examined here. She is twenty-six, which means she has attained her majority (at twenty-five years old). She controls her own fortune. She is rich, "possessed of a considerable independence and it was not to be wondered at that she should avail herself of its advantages" (5). Her move to Bath, over her brother's ineffectual objections, is the move of a woman who lives for affective individualism and who desires a life independent of her family. She is mature and unflappable. Unlike Judith and Phoebe, Annis is not an ingenue. She has made her formal entrée into society and threatens to move to Bath without an older female relative to "give the move countenance"—to act as chaperone. The Regency setting makes these ordinary twentieth-century actions seem bold; the bold heroine makes the values of the Romance setting seem empty.

At the outset of *A Civil Contract,* heroine Jenny Chawleigh, the daughter of a very rich merchant, marries Captain Adam Deveril, Viscount Lynton, to obtain a title; he marries her to save his heavily mortgaged country seat. A marriage without a declaration, particularly one early in a romance novel, means that the marriage-of-convenience plot has been invoked. The courtship, which occurs (as in all marriage-of-convenience novels) after the marriage, is conducted in the shadow of Jenny's meddling father.

In marrying the hero before he actually loves her, Jenny acts as an affective individual. She loves him, and, she admits, "I married him because there was nothing else I could do for him!" (251). Although her father has arranged her marriage to the viscount, Jenny notes that he "doesn't *compel* me" (67, italics Heyer's). She is in love with her husband. Jenny is a considerable heiress, the daughter of "one of the richest men in the country," the heir to "his whole fortune" (54). She is unprepossessing: "She was already plump, and would probably become stout in later life" (57). Still, she has, in her father's phrase, "book-learning" (65) and in her husband's, she is a "capital housewife" (203). Given that the viscount had two homes, one in London and one on his ancestral lands, Jenny hires, fires, trains, and directs staff at both of those homes, as well as overseeing of the purchase and manufacture of what is needed to keep herself, the viscount, the staff, and at any given time, some number of sick and needy villagers fed, clothed, properly housed, clean, and healthy. This is a complicated, demanding administrative post which she had been trained for by keeping her wealthy father's house. Jenny's money from trade and her experience in housekeeping contrast with the Regency setting where money comes from the income from inherited land and a woman's experience beyond genteel needlework is thought coarse. The setting throws Jenny's bourgeois values into high relief and contrasts with the empty values of the Regency society represented by the hero's family (which, ironically, he must reject to save his birthright).

These four outspoken, financially independent heroines who act for their own happiness and make marriages as they, rather than their parents, see fit are historical fictions, of course. In reality, many, perhaps most, women of the Regency were *femes covert* when they married; their parents often dictated when and whom they would marry. That the women would act by consulting only their own interests was often beyond the scope of their prospects or, in some cases, their own sincere wishes. Yet Heyer's typical heroine is like Diana Mayo in her situation at the outset of the novel. In drawing this sort of heroine, Heyer reveals the twentieth-century values that underlie her nineteenth-century heroines. Byatt calls her heroines "lively and resourceful" possessed of "unworldly innocence" (275). In their very liveliness and resourcefulness, in their unworldliness, they inhabit a Regency setting without being of it. Heyer's readers both respond to and demand such heroines—participants in the beliefs at the core of the popular romance novel heroine.

As befits his place in a romance novel, the hero in Heyer's Regencies must be tamed or healed. The four men analyzed here are alpha males. They have power within their society—some combination of wealth, title, and land. They are without the obligations of immediate family, although three of the four have serious responsibilities to extended family. As participants in the marriage mart, they are free to range at large. They are dangerous in Krentz's sense.

They are not, however, participants in the sort of reckless, strenuous leisure that Regency society gave rise to as described by Max Beerbohm:

To spend the early morning with his valet, to saunter round to Whites for ale and tittle-tattle and the making of wagers, to attend 'a drunken *déjeuner* in honor of 'la belle Rosalie,' to drive far out into the country in his pretty curricle followed by two well-dressed and well-mounted grooms . . . and stop at every tavern along the road . . . to reach St. James's in time for a random toilet and so off to dinner . . . dinner done, to scamper off the Ranelagh to dance and sup." (quoted in Byatt 274)

Male society in the Regency included fops, dandies, reckless "bucks," profligates of all stripes—gamblers, skirt-chasers, drunks, and other pleasure-seekers—as well as sinister predators upon respectable women—grasping, imprudent, and sometimes criminal "friends," relatives, and guardians. Heyer's heroes are practical, fair, and moral. Their setting in the Regency emphasizes this.

Worth in *Regency Buck* is a "man of fashion" with "a look of self-consequence" who affects a "languor" about much of the world around him, apparently including, at the outset, the heroine (11). He is full of private rules, "I never drive females" (25), and takes a very high hand with his ward, the heroine Judith. He is no wimp, however; he boxes with the best fighters of the day (299). Worth seems to be just another average Regency male—an idle man of fashion who boxes as a hobby. Again and again he refuses all Judith's suitors, apparently for arbitrary reasons (80) but actually to protect her from predators. He rescues her as well from the clutches of the sexually predatory Prince of Wales at the Pavilion at Brighton (256). He foils her cousin's attempt to kidnap her (274). His judgement is sound; his interventions effective. He is right. Acting for her safety is his job as her guardian, but as the book progresses, it becomes an act of love. This reversal, this change from the trend-setting, willful, and high-handed hero to a man who says, in half-earnest, "That *I* should have given you one moment's pain" (297, italics Heyer's) is his taming. He is dangerous (a fighter), he is powerful (his money and title), he is willful (his denial of all of her other suitors), and he turns out to be doing all of this for her because she has simply riveted his attention. The heroine tames him through her inexperience, her danger, and her simple presence. His own dangerousness and power and give way to her greater power.

The eponymous hero of *Sylvester* is imperious in his own way. He goes about searching for a wife with cold efficiency, listing for his mother the qualities he desires, the women in his acquaintance who meet those qualities, and asking her to choose for him (10–11). He professes not to believe in love (13), except perhaps in one's first adventure with the "muslin company,"—with a mistress (13). An accomplished flirt, Sylvester is known for having "more than one mistress in keeping" (9). It is his duty to marry to produce an heir before his nephew, the current heir apparent to Sylvester's dukedom, grows old enough to understand what it is to be denied an estate by his own cousin (10). As the heroine Phoebe leads him across England and then across the Channel in her efforts first to get herself away from him and later to get his nephew away from him, he finds himself constantly at odds with her. In the middle of a quarrel, she claims, "You say I have ill-used *you*: if I did you are wonderfully revenged, for you have ruined *me*!" Sylvester, the "accomplished flirt," replies, "Have I? Well—if that's so, I will make reparation! Will you do me the honour, Miss Marlow, of accepting my hand in marriage?" (285). Phoebe turns him down, flat. Heyer, of course, has taken a leaf out of Austen's book; this proposal is modeled in part on Darcy's first proposal to Elizabeth in *Pride and Prejudice*. To make amends, the Duke's mother must intercede. From assuming authority in every scene, from acting with *noblesse oblige*, Sylvester becomes the helpless supplicant for Phoebe's hand. Despite his cold-blooded approach to "setting up his nursery," Sylvester is a careful guardian to his brother's son—the widow (the boy's mother) has not been left in legal charge of her own son. Sylvester's imperiousness chases Phoebe away. She is not beautiful, she does not have the usual feminine accomplishments (in fact, she is another Heyer heroine quite at home in the stables), and she does not care if she gets married or not. It is he who describes her as "unusual." The power of these attributes tames him. Like Worth, his virtues contrast with Regency mores; Regency mores, in turn, cast his virtues in high relief.

Carleton's path to tameness in *Lady of Quality* is similar but less drastic. He, too, is an accomplished rake with many other women in his past. His bluntness (199) and his unwillingness to apologize for his temper and his past behavior or to promise that he will attempt to curb his temper (202) make him one of Heyer's most unrepentant heroes. He is sorry for very little that he has done. He is also unclear as to why he loves the heroine Annis: "Don't ask me *why* I love you, for I don't know that either!" (201, italics Heyer's). In this, he is the ur-hero. He undergoes almost no change in the book except to come to love the heroine. In her presence, he is changed. Because he has met her, he wants something he has never wanted before: a wife.

In each of the novels examined here Heyer furnishes a ward, a son, niece, or nephew whom the hero must look after to prevent scandal or actual danger. In Carleton's case, he exercises moral and legal power over his niece. This supervision, which he ends up sharing with Annis, is what sets him apart from Regency values. It provides a contrast to his apparent recklessness. Carleton's concern for his niece serves as the commonsensical, clearheaded contrast to corrupt Regency values.

Adam Deveril, Viscount Lynton is not tamed; he is healed. He begins *A Civil Contract* in love with Julia Oversley, the other woman. Adam had assumed he would marry Julia. Instead he contracts a marriage of convenience with Jenny; at the time of their marriage, he does not love her. In terms of the romance novel, he has not yet declared his love for her. Yet, he eventually describes Julia as "only a boy's impractical dream" (346). Adam is the only hero who has to give up a serious attachment. The others flirt or keep mistresses, a situation in which marriage is never a consideration.

Jenny heals Adam. He returns from the peninsular campaign against Napoleon wounded—he would, thereafter, walk with a limp—and in mourning for his dead father, for his financially impossible love for Julia, and for his heavily mortgaged, poorly maintained ancestral estates. Jenny heals him through her careful attention to his needs and wants: she manages his households with determined efficiency, she learns the duties of being the lord's wife. Her motive is love: she has loved him since she met him at Julia's house as a schoolmate guest. Finally, she gives him an heir. Adam begins the novel as a warrior and ends it as a hands-on farmer interested in experimental techniques and in improving—not just collecting rents from—his land. For him, domestication is healing, and Jenny embodies domestic virtues.

The Regency setting is littered with men with too much money, too much free time, and too few morals. Heyer's heroes are not among them. They are, however, dangerous in the Krentzian sense: they are powerful and willful (Worth), they claim they do not believe in love (Sylvester), they are blunt-spoken rakes (Carleton), or, perhaps most threateningly, they are in love with someone else for part of the novel (Adam). The Regency setting contrasts with their fundamental goodness. The romance form sees that goodness embodied in a tamed, healed hero.

The typical courtship in Heyer's Regencies is a clash of wills often represented by verbal wrangling between the heroine and the hero. She is outspoken, even blunt. He is used to being obeyed and is imperious. Her reaction is often exasperation. His is disbelief and, eventually, fascination and amusement.

In *Regency Buck,* Judith and Worth confront each other to argue about the arrangements he makes as guardian for her life in London. The most galling of these is his insistence that he must approve of any suitor for her hand. She protests. He says to her, "Here is some advice for you: keep your sword sheathed" (80). Till the bitter end, they are at apparently cross purposes: "[H]owever glad you may be to be rid of your ward, you cannot be as glad as I am to be rid of my guardian," she fires at him. He replies, "But I *am* very glad to be rid of my ward" (296).

This contentious battle of wills is bookended by two significant pieces of action—Worth takes a kiss from a woman who turns out to be Judith. She has stopped in Grantham with her brother who wishes to see a prize fight taking place nearby. The town is a magnet for all manner of questionable people, a mixture of classes. Worth finds Judith with her shoe off at the side of a road, removing a pebble, and he grabs her bodily and tosses her up into his carriage, for which she roundly slaps him. He kisses her (25). Then he teaches her how to hit properly, with a closed fist. The courtship ends with a kiss as well, after he is no longer her guardian, and when the kiss is a welcome one (297). Behind the banter and the arch assumption of Worth of his own worth and of Judith of her own entitlements is the much more serious issue of dynastic marriage. Worth's insistence on approving Judith's suitors is companionate marriage operating through a dynastic method. When he denies Judith suitors, he exercises the dynastic right of male relatives (or in his case, guardians) to approve the marriages of the young people in their charge. Worth, however, falls in love with Judith: "I am in love with you almost from the first moment of setting eyes on you" (297). So in exercising his dynastic right to approve her marriage, he preserves his companionate choice, an impropriety he could not commit until he was no longer in charge of her finances or her courtship.

The barrier to this marriage is in the guardianship itself—an honorable man could not marry his own ward. Judith's apparent dislike of Worth forms another part of the barrier. The hero's determination to act honorably and the heroine's resentment of his power over her are results of the dynastic basis for marriage in Regency society. Ritual death underscores the danger of this way of pairing off young people. Within thirty pages, Julia faints in the predatory embrace of Prinny (to be rescued by Worth) and is kidnapped by her own cousin who is after her fortune (again, Worth rescues her); her brother is also the target of a kidnapping plot which, again, Worth discovers and foils. Judith mistakes Worth's companionate actions as dynastic prerogatives (i.e., because he is in charge of her, she does not see that he loves). She also mistakes her own companionate feelings—love—for irritation at Worth's dynastic high-handedness. Ritual death in this novel reminds us that leaving the companionate unattended puts the heroine at risk; she may be ravished or kidnapped.

The courtship in *Sylvester* is characterized by outrage, tumult, and breathless chase. The barrier is composed, in part, of his high-handedness, his assumption of privilege toward those around him, including his own servants (92). He finds her wanting in both manners and conduct, too pert, and without beauty (139–40). In addition, she has published her book. It is a *roman à clef,* and his character is instantly identifiable to her readers through her description of him. He finds it insufferable to be made a public laughingstock. At stake is his pride, which masks a long retreat from the world which began with the death of his twin brother. A man who has manufactured a public persona finds another—a caricature—in danger of supplanting it. Barrier issues revolve around him and his public identity and, more deeply, his private identity.

Ritual death takes place at the time of the bungled, Darcy-like proposal. Sylvester has been listing Phoebe's faults: "You have a genius for bringing trouble upon yourself" (284). When she admits these faults, he continues to criticize, growing very angry. "The harsh, angry voice was having its inevitable affect [*sic*] on her: she began to feel sick." He continues in the same vein, and she finds herself "rigid with shock" (285). She blames him for many of her supposed shortcomings, and he interrupts her tirade with "will you do me the honour, Miss Marlow, of accepting my hand in marriage?" (285). When she turns him down—"How *dare* you?"—at stake is Sylvester's identity. He presents himself as a desirable marriage partner, but Phoebe rejects him based on his history of prideful, distant, superior behavior. Her future is much less at stake. Yes, her future with Sylvester is in the balance, but unlike most Regency heroines, she has an independent income and a profession—writing—that she can follow. She and her old governess had made tentative plans to set up housekeeping together. Her refusal of Sylvester simply calls these plans into being.

The Regency setting of *Sylvester* permits the atmosphere of breathless chase and throws into high relief the identity issues suffered by the hero. Phoebe's rejection of him causes him to question himself and his future. Part of his taming is coming to terms with this self-image as it is reflected through her. This courtship takes place only partly in defiance of dynastic goals: Sylvester's godmother, who is also Phoebe's grandmother, suggests that they might suit, and his own mother, to whom he appeals when Phoebe at first rejects his proposal, cements the union. The old women make this match, but the young people grow to wish it. The marriage is companionate. It also satisfies dynastic conditions. In this, Heyer has it both ways.

In *Lady of Quality*, the courtship is simply a matter of Annis Wychwood and Oliver Carleton overcoming their disagreements, about the proper course of supervision for his niece and ward (whom Annis happens to encounter and rescue on the road to Bath) and about their own relationship to each other. Annis Wychwood, is, like Austen's Emma, handsome, clever, and rich. She, like Emma, takes on the guardianship of a young woman—Lucilla. The hero, Oliver Carleton, is, like Knightly, wealthy, older, and unmarried. Unlike Knightly, however, Carleton is blunt to the point of rudeness and a rake in addition. Unlike Emma, Annis can leave home. She is without parents and in possession of her own financial independence; she leaves her ancestral home (occupied by her brother and his family) and sets up her own establishment in Bath. She finds Lucilla stranded on the road to Bath, takes her home with her, and acts as her guardian until her family can decide on a more appropriate situation for the headstrong, flighty, very young woman. One more element survives from Emma: Miss Bates, the chatty bore, is transmogrified into Miss Farlow, a cousin of Annis's who lives with her as her companion, it being impossible for an unmarried woman to live without some older female to "give her countenance." Miss Farlow also acts as a spy for Annis's brother.

The barrier has several elements: her brother, who, along with Miss Farlow, represents society, is opposed to her marriage to the hero. Oliver's affection for Annis is hindered by his thinking her a bad influence on his niece and ward, the wayward young woman whom Annis befriends. Annis's affection for Oliver stumbles on his reputation, and she states simply, "I have no ambition to marry a rake" (200). When he confesses his love and she realizes hers for him, the barrier becomes single: her brother's disapproval, which, by extension, stands for what all of society is liable to think of her match with this blunt-talking womanizer. The barrier at this point is wholly external and largely comic. Society is powerless to prevent this match: its representatives—the blustering brother and the endlessly chattering Miss Farlow—are helpless to block it.

Ritual death is correspondingly lighthearted. Annis contracts influenza (from Miss Farlow, as it turns out). During her convalescence, Oliver visits her in the sitting room adjacent to her bedroom. She wears a dressing gown. He orders some wine to help fortify her, and Miss Farlow discovers them drinking and talking. She calls this behavior "carousing" and, in an effort to protect Annis's virtue, tries to force Oliver to leave. When this fails, she summons Sir Geoffrey. Neither authority figure can convince either Oliver or Annis that anything untoward is occurring, and the two moralizing busybodies are routed, leaving the blunt womanizer and the beautiful heiress alone. This book relies on the charm of a plain spoken man among so many chattering peacocks catching the eye of a bored, beautiful young woman.

The tone is quarrelsome throughout, a clash of wills, which Annis must understand for what it is—a genuine expression of caring. "They were forever coming to cuffs, and surely kindred spirits didn't quarrel" (205) she asks herself, and finds, eventually, that the answer is yes, they do actually quarrel. The barrier, finally, is quite easy to overcome: her family's objections to the rake that Carleton is, and his shock at finding himself genuinely attached to a woman rather than simply in pursuit of a "convenient." Her financial independence and his utter lack of caring what anyone thinks of him make this courtship seem quite modern.

In *Civil Contract* the tone of the courtship is as subdued as possible, with Jenny Chawleigh, in love with her husband, fighting quietly to win his love. In this, as in most marriage-of-convenience novels, the courtship takes place after the marriage. She knows she is "not the wife [he] wished for" (95). At the prospective bride's (and her matchmaking father's) extremely awkward dinner for the prospective bridegroom she says to him, "I'm not romantic. I perfectly understand the—the circumstances, and don't expect——You said yourself that we are barely acquainted." The next line is "He was obliged to master an impulse to retreat" (67). Jenny wages war with the best weapon she has—her skills as a housewife. She promises to make him "comfortable" (68). She restores order and good management to his ancestral home, and he learns to appreciate the "quite ordinary, everyday things" that are the content of married life with Jenny. His first love fades as an object of desire, and he realizes that she "would have discovered [him] to be a dead bore" because he was interested in being closely involved in the running of his estate rather than in an active London social life (346).

A Civil Contract (1961) is a retelling of Jane Austen's *Sense and Sensibility*, with heroine Jenny Chawleigh representing sense, and the other woman, Julia Oversley, representing sensibility. The hero, Adam Deveril, who finds himself the Viscount Lynton on the death of his father, is forced to choose between the two women. Adam is an honorable Willoughby at the start of this novel—full of the pleasures of being in love and a very sensitive lover—and the novel's work is to turn him into Colonel Brandon—responsible, mature, deliberate, a farmer. The barrier, quite simply, is Adam's love for Julia, to whom he was informally engaged. He breaks it off at the insistence of her father, who knows that Adam's father, the recently deceased viscount, has left his estate badly in debt, and that Adam, to avoid selling his birthright, must make a financially rich match.

In addition to Adam's love for Julia, the barrier consists of Jenny's father's too ready interference in the marriage that he brokered to secure his daughter a title. Mr. Chawleigh, a sympathetically drawn doting father, has business savvy and the money that savvy has earned him. He injures Adam's pride over and over by being too ready to pay for whatever the couple might seem to want or need. At stake is Adam's happiness—his financial future is saved by speculating during the panic in the markets following the battle of Waterloo.

Ritual death comes with Jenny's delivery of the next Viscount Lynton. Her pregnancy is difficult and her labor long and exhausting. Mr. Chawleigh accuses Adam of a want of concern for his daughter when, during the two-day ordeal, Adam spends an hour conferring with his bailiff. His father-in-law delivers a threat: "[I]f my Jenny snuffs it, I'll see to it you don't have it [his estate, which Mr. Chawleigh holds the mortgages to]" (318). At stake in Jenny's brush with death is Adam's future. His inherited lands, more important to him than his title, hang briefly in the balance, as does his happiness when he finally realizes that his love for Julia was "only a boy's impractical dream" and that he does love Jenny (392). Their courtship, conducted in the first year of their marriage, has resulted at last in Adam's declaration, the last of the eight essential romance elements. Heyer described *A Civil Contract* as "neither farcical nor adventurous," noting that it required that she "make the hero as charming as [she] believe[d] he was" as well as on making "a quiet story interesting" (Hodge 133). With its domestication of its young hero and the portrait of the contentment of a well-run household, *A Civil Contract* is Heyer's least mannered, most straightforward Regency.

Georgette Heyer's romance novels interrogate values. The hero is moral and sound. The heroine is devoted to the values that all twentieth-century romance novel heroines share: affective individualism, property or the means to get it, and companionate marriage. The courtship, conducted in the glittering Regency setting, ends, as all romance novels do, in freedom. The heroine chooses the hero. The hero chooses the heroine. In the case of the Regency heroine and hero are freed from the setting itself: freed from its artifice, from its corrupt moral values, from its recklessness. The new couple do not change the structure of society or retire from it as Diana and her sheik do, but they create within it an oasis of calm morality, free from its sham and danger. Heyer's novels are, finally, not just baubles, for all that they are diverting. They champion the good and depict matches between men who can act virtuously and women who, through love, can make them want to do so.

14

Courtship and Suspense

Mary Stewart

Mary Stewart (1916–) is the mother of twentieth-century romantic suspense. Between 1955 and 1967 Stewart produced, at the rate of about one per year, ten novels in this subgenre. All have entered the canon of twentieth-century romance. Eight of the ten are still in print, and there is a lively market for used copies of the two that are not (Amazon.com). Kay Mussell praises the "originality of her literary sensibility" and notes that "reviewers consistently praise the quality of her prose." Mussell concludes that Stewart is "a writer of uncommon . . . grace" and that her novels are "inimitable" ("Mary Stewart" 619). One does not usually hear a romance writer praised for her sensibility, high-quality prose, or grace; and romance novels are commonly thought to be quite imitable. Romance writers active during the decades following the midcentury, including Nora Roberts, repeatedly cite Stewart as a "favorite author" (Fallon 173, 182, 206, 211, 262, 269 ff.). Although she may very well be inimitable, Stewart's influence extends to every writer of romantic suspense, for Stewart understood and perfected this hybrid of the romance and the mystery and used it as a structure for books so beautifully written that they have endured to become part of the canon of the twentieth-century romance novel.

In each of these seminal works of romantic suspense Stewart creates a true hybrid. Each is a romance novel and a mystery. Each of these novels contains all eight of the essential elements of the romance novel as delineated in Part III. Many mystery novels contain a love interest or love subplot, but Stewart's novels of romantic suspense are full-blown courtship narratives that take us from the definition of the disordered society, through the meeting, attraction, the barrier, declaration, point of ritual death, and recognition to the betrothal. To these elements of the romance novel she adds a mystery plot—not, it should be stressed, simply a subplot or incidental puzzle, but a complete mystery. Stewart's combination of romance novel and mystery elements is not mechanical, but organic. The two are seamlessly integrated.

The great British mystery writer P. D. James explores the relatedness of the two genres in an address to the Jane Austen Society entitled *"Emma Considered As a Detective Story."* In prefacing the collection of clues in *Emma* that, added up, solves the puzzle of who would marry whom, James describes both this mystery's and *the* mystery's concern "with bringing order out of disorder and restoring peace and tranquillity to a world temporarily disrupted by the intrusion of alien influences" (244). The romance, as we have seen, brings order out of disorder through the betrothal of heroine and hero. In the romance, too, "alien influences"—always the barrier and sometimes a scapegoat—are ejected.

As James's observation of the similarities between romance and mystery imply, the two genres are compatible. An earlier commentator, John Cawelti, tells us that the mystery story has as its "fundamental principle . . . the investigation and discovery of hidden secrets, the discovery usually leading to some benefit for the character(s) with whom the reader identifies. . . . the problem always has a desirable and rational solution." He notes how ubiquitous the mystery is, serving as a "subsidiary principle in adventure stories, romances and melodrama." The mystery's "structure that is predominantly rational" functions "as a sauce to heroic or erotic action" (*Adventure* 42–43). The romance novel is primarily emotional in its appeal; the mystery story is primarily rational in its appeal. A hybrid provides a complete reading experience.

In fiction, secrets are ubiquitous. As we have noted elsewhere, so are love stories of all kinds. Mystery fiction, the form of the novel devoted to the investigation and disclosure of secrets, often has a romantic subplot—and many romance novels, the form of the novel devoted to courtship (and love), often include a secret. Mary Stewart writes the secret or hidden truth as a full-blown mystery and combines it with all of the essential elements of the romance novel. Neither is a subplot of the other. I will analyze four of her works of romantic suspense—*Thunder on the Right* (1957), *Nine Coaches Waiting* (1958), *The Ivy Tree* (1961), and *Airs Above the Ground* (1965). Her subject matter in these four works is diverse, the nature of the mystery and the courtship various. In all of them, however, we can trace the effects of the mystery elements on the romance elements through a look, once again, at the heroines and how they are situated at the start of each work; at the heroes and how they are tamed or healed; and at the courtship itself as the mystery form turns the heroine (and sometimes the hero as well) into a detective, the hero into a suspect, and the courtship into a sequence that emphasizes ritual death, the barrier, and the recognition. As Stewart explores the relationship between the romance novel and the mystery, she writes heroines and heroes who are, Mussell tells us, "people of commitment . . . to . . . truth and justice" ("Mary Stewart" 619).

Like Diana Mayo, our model of the twentieth-century romance heroine, Stewart's female protagonists are ordinarily established as affective individuals, as financially secure, and as believers in companionate marriage at the outset of their narratives. The mystery half of the hybrid turns them into detectives as well. They help solve the crime at the core of the mystery plot. This, in turn, helps them retain their affective individualism, in some cases their property, and in every case, it permits them to make a companionate marriage. Thus, the mystery half of the romantic suspense hybrid turns Diana Mayo–like adventuring for its own sake into more purposeful discovery of a hidden truth and seeking after justice.

In *Thunder on the Right* (1957) Stewart's heroine is an ingenue, a woman poised at the brink of affective individualism, possession of property, and companionate marriage. Stewart expresses heroine Jennifer Silver's potential in terms of the image from folklore of the "sleeping princess." Jennifer, just twenty-two, "had always been a quiet child, with a poised reserve" possessing a "characteristic serenity" (9–10). Stephen, the hero, courts her briefly, then leaves to serve in the Korean War. She goes to Gavernie, France for a vacation and to investigate her cousin's Gillian's disappearance, the core of the mystery plot. In leaving home and her mother, described in folklore terms as a "dragon," Jennifer takes her first step toward affective individualism (10). She is educated, a step toward the acquisition of property. Like all of the twentieth-century heroines we have investigated, she believes in companionate marriage. Back from the war, Stephen follows her to Gavernie, and together they solve the mystery of the cousin's disappearance. They also conduct a courtship. Away from her mother, away from all influences, Jennifer is free to choose Stephen.

In *Nine Coaches Waiting* (1958) Linda Martin, although an orphan, is a governess, and has made her way in the world for a number of years, for all that she is only twenty-three years old. Her recent job furnished her with what she calls "a qualified independence—a travesty of freedom—as general help and dogsbody at a small prep school for boys in Kent" (7). She has applied for a job in France and made it to Gavernie (a favorite setting of Stewart's), where she is to assume responsibility for the education of a very young French count. Although she worries that "wherever you were, you took your little circle of loneliness with you," loneliness does not compromise her affective individualism. A visit to her old home in Paris where she lived with her parents yields a further release: "The past . . . slipped off my shoulders like a burden" (12). Part Jane Eyre (67), part Cinderella (138), this heroine is nonetheless anchored firmly in the practical—intelligent, an affective individual in command of her own life and as free of self-pity as Jane herself learns to be. With her new job comes enough money to support herself: she has the promise of property. She believes in companionate marriage.

Linda Martin, like Jennifer, becomes a detective. The hero, Raoul Valmy, is a chief suspect, both for his possible implication in the crime at the core of the narrative, the attempted murder of Raoul's cousin and Linda's charge, the very young count, and for his possible trifling with her own feelings in courting (or appearing to court) the heroine. Solving the mystery helps to illuminate Raoul's personality. It helps the heroine make a decision about the courtship as well.

In *The Ivy Tree* (1961) Annabel Winslow, twenty-seven, who is masquerading as "Mary Grey," returns to her native neighborhood to pose as her own physical double in order to reestablish herself in her own household under the nose of a cousin who threatens to steal her inheritance and kill her. If he learns that she is really Annabel Winslow, instead of a lookalike named Mary Grey willing to play Annabel Winslow to help defraud her grandfather, he will kill her. She is, in other words, masquerading as herself. She had run away from a doomed love affair with the neighboring squire, the then-married Adam Forrest. Through acting as an affective individual, "Mary Grey" reassumes her identity as Annabel Winslow, foils the dangerous, presumptive heir, and inherits what is rightfully hers. The heroine single-handedly outwits a man who turns out to be ready to commit murder to get what he wants. Of her recent past she says, "I've spent the last few years living with a friend . . . near Montreal, and looking after her" (15). Upon traveling to England, "I work . . . in a café" (13). This work establishes her financial competence, although it leaves unanswered the larger issue of the book—will the rightful heir, which is to say, will she, get the true financial independence that is due her? Annabel acts as detective through her impersonation of herself. She forces her cousin's hand as he tries to steal her inheritance. His are the crimes she uncovers—fraud (which she goes along with for awhile to uncover) and attempted murder. Through the solution to the mystery her belief in companionate marriage is rekindled.

Vanessa March in *Airs Above the Ground* (1965) has made a companionate marriage to a man whom she believes works for a chemical company. Inexplicably, he appears on a newsreel showing a fire at a circus in Austria when he is supposed to be traveling in Sweden. She flies straight to Vienna after she sees her husband in the newsreel, determined to uncover the mystery of his being there; it is the decision of an affective individual. She is not only independent, but educated, a veterinarian. She says, "I qualified just before I was married" (27). She is tough-minded and decisive as all Stewart heroines are. She, like all of them, is fearless in the face of danger. Vanessa also acts as detective, first to find her husband, then to help him capture members of a drug ring he has been trying to hunt down. Learning her husband's secret restores her shaken belief in companionate marriage.

Each of these heroines is situated at the start of the novel with the three elements that pre-twentieth-century heroines sought through courtship: affective individualism, either property or the ability to make a living, and a belief in companionate marriage. This belief was made real through the courtship in each book. What Stewart understood and exploited when she made each of these heroines a detective in the solution of the mystery was the natural affinity between the romance and the mystery. In classic mystery fiction, the hero, acting as detective, often suspects a woman who the reader assumes is a heroine. This often leads to betrayal. In romantic suspense, the heroine, acting as detective, often suspects a man who the reader (and the heroine) assumes is the hero. This leads to betrothal. The romance heroine is empowered by this role as detective: her affective individualism and her ability to make a companionate marriage are enhanced.

The hybrid genre complicates Stewart's heroes. The mystery half of the romantic-suspense hybrid complicates the romance half, and vice versa. Heroes often act as detectives in the mystery plot, often as suspects, too.

Of course, they are also lovers. Meaning becomes ambiguous when a hero acts as both lover and suspect. The reader grants her sympathy in a straightforward way in a nonhybrid, "pure" romance; whereas, in a novel of romantic suspense, this sympathy can be much more problematic. When they function as suspects, Stewart's heroes are dangerous in the Krentzian sense. They often must also be healed. This range of attributes works with, rather than against, the hybrid nature of these novels.

In *Thunder on the Right* hero Stephen Masefield, musician and Korean War veteran, is literally lamed. The heroine, in a scene told from her point of view, describes the hero as "clever, sensitive, gentle . . . and, however much the paper and celluloid supermen strutted in their invincible splendor, it was the men like Stephen, the thinking men . . . who were the true constant." He, however, doubts this, having just failed, in his view, to rescue Jennifer's cousin. The heroine concludes, "she must give him back himself" (114). She heals him through her love. A storm during which they embrace represents this change. He has already begun to act as a detective in the solution to the mystery. Through her belief in him he finds the courage to confront and fight the kidnappers and art smugglers who are the villains in this novel and to save the heroine's life as well. Stephen begins this novel needing to be healed; he ends it a dangerous man, although one whose woman, heroine Jennifer, has shed her ingenue role to become adventurous.

Raoul Valmy in *Nine Coaches Waiting* must be tamed. Raoul is powerful, willful, and unaccustomed to being argued with or contradicted. He is like the noblemen in Heyer, or like Rochester in *Jane Eyre*: at one point, to recall the heroine from reverie, he says, "come out, Jane Eyre" (67). He is a rake, having had "other women . . . quite a few," and he is an "adventurer" (147–48). In addition, he is a suspect in a scheme of attempted murder of his cousin the young duke; the duke's death would put him in line for the title. His courtship of the heroine, the young duke's governess, may be a ploy to deflect suspicion from what may be his attempts on her charge's life. This atmosphere of power, wealth, and intrigue make his dangerousness, a key element in the romance hero who must be tamed, all the more prominent. Without knowing it for certain until the very last page of the novel, the heroine has tamed this hero by the book's midpoint. He has fallen in love with her and she with him, simply by being the one woman who can stop his restless eye. However, all of the suspicion must be cleared before the romance can truly conclude.

If Raoul is Rochester with Jane at Thornfield, Adam Forrest, hero of *The Ivy Tree,* is Rochester before Jane returns from her self-imposed exile to find

Rochester at Ferndean. He is even maimed like Rochester. Adam's hands have been burned trying to save his wife from what proved to be a fatal fire. Unlike Stephen in *Thunder,* Adam does not act as detective. Unlike Raoul in *Nine Coaches,* he is not a suspect. Adam is, as his burned hands indicate, wounded, and must be healed. The heroine accomplishes this by revealing her identity to him. He reassumes his dangerousness—his power—by saving the life of a man trapped by the collapse of a ceiling.

Hero Lewis March in *Airs Above the Ground* must be tamed. Already married to the heroine Vanessa at the novel's beginning, he has disguised himself as Lee Elliott and is working undercover as a British spy. This alone makes him dangerous. Then, when his wife Vanessa happens to see him in a newsreel in a place where he does not belong, with a woman he does not belong with or to, his dangerousness extends from the question of his identity to the threat that he represents to their marriage. In his work as a spy he has left behind his "Lewis March" identity, not just in the public sphere—he does not, as he has claimed, really work for a chemical company—but in the domestic sphere as well—he appears to be unfaithful to the heroine. Vanessa tames Lewis by entering completely into his case—she becomes a detective and an operative and with him hunts down the drug dealers. With this last case solved, he retires as a spy. He will stay home and get conventional work.

In Stewart's masterful hands, the hero's taming or healing becomes, in these novels of romantic suspense, part of both the romance and the mystery half of the hybrid. Northrop Frye reminds us that "the standard escape device of [both of these forms] is that of escape through a shift of identity, the normal basis of the recognition scene" (*Secular* 136). When the hero is healed (Stephen and Adam), he is revealed as a worthy object of the heroine's love. When he is tamed he is shown not to be a suspect (Raoul), or an adulterer (Lewis). Stewart's novels of romantic suspense restore the public element of recognition, prominent in the much earlier comedies that are the antecedents to all of the novels analyzed in this book (Segal 152). Society's interest in the truth about crime and the capture of criminals— its interest in justice—enters through the suspense side of the hybrid to make public once again the romance's recognition of who, exactly, the hero is. Stewart well understood this dovetailing of the two forms.

Not only can danger be a component of both the mystery and the romance in Stewart's romance heroes, it can similarly overlap in the courtship and mystery plots. Particularly important for our purposes here is the death (real or threatened) that suffuses the mystery and its relationship to the ritual death of the courtship plot. Recall that ritual death is that moment in the romance novel when the union between the heroine and hero, the hoped-for resolution, seems absolutely impossible. Frye identifies it as an echo of the Persephone myth: Persephone, kidnapped by Hades, is sought by her mother, Demeter, goddess of agricultural bounty, who leaves the world barren as she searches. When a romance novel merely echoes this myth, the death is ritual. In a mystery, the death is often real or at least threatened. The ritual death required by the romance can be represented by the death present in many if not most mystery stories.

In a mystery, the death can occur very early. As *Room with a View* reminds us, an author can displace ritual death from its usual position towards the end of the novel to a position very near the beginning. Stewart often does this in her novels of romantic suspense, the "body-in-the-first-few-chapters" convention of the murder mystery, for instance, providing the displacement of death that is real in the mystery plot, ritual in the romance plot. Stewart understood that the barrier, too, can be borrowed, in part, from the mystery half of the hybrid. As we have seen, the heroine (in the case of Annabel Winslow) or, more often, the hero, can be suspects in the crime that is at the core of the mystery. This suspicion becomes part of the barrier in the romance half of the hybrid. The revelation of their innocence can become the "shift of identity" that Frye notes, freeing them both from implication in the guilt for the crime and freeing each to enter into a betrothal with the other. That betrothal and the promise of a new society based on better principles (as it is in all romances) is at the same time the promise of a new society that is free of the crime being investigated in the mystery.

Jennifer Silver and Stephen Masefield, in *Thunder on the Right*, arrive in Gavernie to be told that Jennifer's cousin Gillian is dead (28). Ritual death begins at this early point, less than a quarter of the way through the story. Gillian's death, which the heroine and hero believe in for quite some time, is eventually replaced by their discovery that she is alive. She has amnesia and has been forced to marry to an art smuggler. As an amnesiac dead to herself, she represents a second form of ritual death. Ultimately, heroine, hero, and Gillian are at risk in crossing a perilous bridge over a storm-filled river gorge, and the hero saves them all (182). Stewart brilliantly capitalizes on the romance/mystery overlap here. She begins with Gillian's death—one that is supposed to be final. She replaces it with a forced marriage that has been imposed upon a bride suffering from amnesia. This is ritual death of another order, one that involves exactly the sort of marriage that heroine and hero must avoid. In order for them not to make this sort of marriage, the hero must fully awaken the heroine from her sheltered childhood (recall that she was a "sleeping princess")—and the hero must be healed (10). The final element in ritual death accomplishes both of these as Jennifer and Stephen pursue the criminals, free Gillian, and save themselves from certain death at the gorge. For all that, this is a hybrid work, Stewart invests it with a complex barrier: Jennifer's quiet upbringing, her overprotective mother, the intervention of the war, and Stephen's wound. In acting as detectives who can solve the crime, Jennifer and Stephen restore a just society in which Gillian—and they—can marry. Their betrothal is the symbol of this restored society.

Stewart invests this deft exploitation of the possibilities of genre with a beautiful sense of style and pace. In addition, she has a sure sense of dialogue, a satisfying sense of scene. She uses a set of motifs in most of her books to give them added depth. In *Thunder* it is music: the chapters have such names as "Academic Overture," "Danse Macabre," and "Appassionata." The final onset of ritual death occurs in a chapter titled "Death and the Maiden." The musical references reinforce the novel's tone. The chapters devoted to the courtship are quiet with titles like "Interlude" and "Entr'acte: Con Amore" to contrast with chapters like "The Night on the Bare Mountain." The interactions between Jennifer and Stephen can be calm and without a great deal of strife: their problems are not with each other; they are with the criminals. Stewart realizes that the presence of the mystery half of the hybrid makes this romance more pure, a quiet working out, or discarding of, the barriers that once intervened. The presence of the romance makes the solution to the mystery possible. This, rather than a series of tense confrontations between heroine and hero, is the measure of the courtship's strength.

For heroine Linda Martin and hero Raoul Valmy's courtship in *Nine Coaches,* Stewart establishes ritual death through the series of attempts on the young count's life. Whereas in *Thunder,* Stewart's choice of ritual death put the possibility of companionate marriage at risk (Gillian's amnesia/forced marriage), in *Nine Coaches,* Stewart chooses instead to focus ritual death on an innocent child, thus calling into question the possibility of a society in which children are safe and, by implication, the possibility of a society in which the heroine and the hero can continue the next generation. Stewart implicates her hero in the attempted murders and his role as a suspect becomes a large part of the barrier between him and the heroine, outweighing the issue of class (she is, after all, a servant) that also forms part of the barrier. He is recognized as innocent. This recognition that leads to the solution of the mystery story is also the recognition of his identity as a man who is courting her not to deflect suspicion but because he wishes to court her. The young count retains the title; Linda and Raoul begin their life together. Stewart sets this dark tale in Thonon-les-Bains, near Geneva, among an obscure branch of the French aristocracy. She matches this choice of locale and family with a set of chapter-heading quotations from Shakespeare, Milton, Donne, Browning, and Tourneur; Tourneur's *Revenger's Tragedy* is the source of the novel's title: "Nine coaches waiting—hurry, hurry, hurry— / Ay, to the devil" (5). A revenge tragedy is one in which the death of a father must be revenged by the son, or vice versa, and the revenge itself is directed by a ghost. *Nine Coaches* is a novel in which the death of a son is attempted by family members who want his title. Stewart uses the straightforward and ironic allusions to keep the tone of both the mystery and the romance balanced between treachery and trust.

In *Ivy Tree*, Stewart begins her narrative with the impending death of grandfather Winslow, owner of Whitescar. Again, death hangs over the narrative: *Ivy Tree* is a novel in which characters wait for death, or in which the villain tries to kill others. As in many mysteries, the number of bodies or potential bodies mounts. The heroine herself is the subject of ritual death from the beginning of the novel: she has reported herself dead and left her home. This self-exile echoes Persephone's exile into Hades (in the form of Canada in this particular narrative). The familiar dovetailing of mystery and romance occurs again here. Stewart draws a heroine and hero who are implicated in various crimes in *Ivy Tree*. Heroine Annabel Winslow/"Mary Grey" disguises herself as herself, apparently to help defraud Annabel's grandfather, to thwart his wish to leave his considerable property to the heir he designates (Annabel Winslow). Annabel is supposedly dead, but the grandfather does not believe this. Because this novel is told in the first person with this impersonator as narrator, we are some distance into it before we understand that she is, in fact, Annabel Winslow pretending to impersonate herself. The hero, Adam Forrest, is similarly in question: exactly what was his role in the death of his mentally ill wife, which occurred far away in Florence? These questions form important parts of the barrier, accompanied by the memory of the illicit courtship of heroine and hero, carried on while his wife was still living and broken off by the heroine's abrupt departure. When she is recognized as the genuine heiress, when he is recognized as a widower innocent of his wife's death and ready to make amends for his improper courtship years earlier, the way to their betrothal is cleared. She is the legitimate heir to Whitescar. He is a moral force.

Stewart prefaces the chapters in *Ivy Tree* with traditional north-country ballads; she also includes a subplot in which Roman ruins are a feature. The book's first scene takes place in view of Hadrian's Wall. The landscape itself features importantly as well. Stewart's setting thus evokes not only the land but the history that occurred upon it from ancient times. This is fitting in a book in which the heroine returns to her home to recover her own abandoned landscape and history. The tone is menacing and elegiac at the same time, as befits the risk she runs—death—and the reward she wins—a new life with the hero.

In *Airs Above the Ground,* heroine Vanessa and hero Lewis are already married. Their union is at risk because he is a spy, but has not acknowledged this fact to his wife. The barrier, then, is partly Lewis's deceit. When he admits his secret occupation and accepts his wife as a partner in finishing what he promises will be his last mission, his identity shifts. They not only betroth themselves, they consummate the new relationship. Her identity is altered in this courtship as well as she invokes her training as a veterinarian to solve a portion of the cocaine-smuggling plot by identifying a missing character: a Lipizzaner stallion from the Spanish Riding School in Vienna, in ill health, his white coat dyed black. The heroine recognizes him, and, with the hero, returns him to his home. Ritual death is in its accustomed place in this work, even though the hero's partner is killed about a third of the way in. Both heroine and hero are imperiled toward the end of the narrative by the smugglers.

This work is dark—a marriage that is not what it seems in the context of drug smugglers and horse thieves—but it ends with the optional wedding/dance/fete: in this case, a dance, but it is the horse who dances. Earlier in the book, the heroine had seen a badly groomed black horse staked out one moonlit night "dance" to music filtering from a tent of the circus he sometimes performed in. At the end this horse, identified as Neapolitano Petra, his once dyed coat gleaming white, his identity as a stallion in the famed Spanish Riding School restored, performs after his many years of exile and neglect. The director rides the old horse, and their performance includes the "airs above the ground" for which this horse and all Lipizzaners are world famous. The ending is elegiac, a dance and then a quiet return home: the horse leaves the arena, "to where his name was still above his stall, and fresh straw waiting" (255).

Stewart is the mother of romantic suspense, one of the main subgenres of the romance novel. The novel of romantic suspense, which always involves secrecy and often involves death itself, puts more at stake than does the "pure" or "straight" contemporary romance. In romantic suspense, action is heightened. The hero is magnified and so is the heroine. Her affective individualism extends to risking her own life, reciprocating what the heroes of many romances do for their heroine. The mystery spotlights her independent action. The mystery plot also forces into the realm of law the disordering of society that is at the beginning of every romance novel. If the pure twentieth-century romance novel shrinks the society disordered into that of the heroine and hero (Diana Mayo and her sheik form their own society—at first disordered—then placed in uneasy order by their union), then the novel of romantic suspense widens the disordered society by putting society's expression of order, the law, at risk. In *Thunder on the Right*, ownership of priceless art is put at risk; in *Nine Coaches*, legitimate, bloodless dynastic succession is put at risk; in *The Ivy Tree*, lawful inheritance, and in *Airs Above the Ground*, society's freedom from drugs.

In each book, life itself is put at risk as well, usually both the heroine's and the hero's. Ritual death becomes the threat of real death, and the echo of the Persephone myth is louder in these books than in most romance novels. The courtship itself is more straightforward than that in the "pure" contemporary romance where the hero and heroine usually must overcome problems in their own personalities or psyches. In the novels of romantic suspense examined here, heroine and hero often undergo a period where they misunderstand each other's motives (*Airs*) and sometimes even doubt each other's identities (*Ivy Tree*), but these issues are eventually cleared up, and the barrier becomes the external dangers facing the heroine and hero in their roles as detectives. Mary Stewart pioneered these books, and wrote them with a deep understanding of the possibilities of her chosen subgenre.

15

HARLEQUIN, SILHOUETTE, AND THE AMERICANIZATION OF THE POPULAR ROMANCE NOVEL

Janet Dailey

In 1975, when Janet Dailey (1944–) sold her first novel to Harlequin, the center of the popular romance novel began to shift away from Great Britain. There the form had been important to the development of the British novel. There the form had been popularized and distributed widely to an enthusiastic audience. And there the most popular romance writers had lived and written, writers such as those we have examined in Part III, as well as E. M. Hull, Georgette Heyer, and Mary Stewart. Just after the turn of the twentieth century, historian Joseph McAleer tells us, British publishing house Mills and Boon was established (254). Popular romance writers such as Violet Windspear and Roberta Leigh were Mills and Boon authors whose works were far more likely to be known to American audiences as Harlequin reprints of the Mills and Boon originals. Janet Dailey began as a Harlequin writer, but eventually became more famous, more popular, more widely read than most Harlequin authors. Dailey turned the popular romance into an American phenomenon by being the first American to break into the solidly British list at Harlequin and by employing that quin-tessential American setting, the West.

Janet Dailey was there at the beginning of the romance boom—the phe-nomenal increase in titles, readers, and authors of romance that took place in the latter half of the twentieth century. This boom was fueled in large part by three publishers: the aforementioned British house Mills and Boon, established in 1908; the Canadian reprint house Harlequin Books, estab-lished in 1949; and American publishing's first response to Harlequin, Sil-houette Books, established in 1980. Dailey's career, and indeed the career of every romance novelist writing today, has been influenced by these pub-lishers and the many others who followed their lead.

The history of Mills and Boon, Harlequin, and Silhouette are entwined and, taken together, their history takes us from *The Sheik* to the present. In the beginning was Mills and Boon, established in 1908 in Great Britain by Gerald Mills and Charles Boon. At first, the house published "anything it could lay its hands on—fiction, politics, humor, health, child care, cooking, travel" (McAleer 17). In the 1930s, Charles Boon turned the firm toward the romance, and it prospered (McAleer 66). Meanwhile in Canada, Har-lequin Books, founded in 1949 by Richard Bonnycastle, began life as a paperback reprint house. Its list was also varied. Within ten years Richard's wife, Mary, noticed that the Mills and Boon romance titles that they were reprinting sold the best of all of their books. Harlequin, too, turned its list toward romance.

By the late 1950s, Harlequin Books was publishing and distributing a Mills and Boon reprint every few months (McAleer 117). By 1971, Har-lequin's efficient distribution and marketing system, including, by this time, direct mail, was getting the kind of book that readers wanted—romance novels—to them in record numbers. On October 1, 1971 Harle-quin acquired Mills and Boon (McAleer 139). By 1980, Harlequin had grown complaisant; Simon and Schuster seized the opportunity to publish in the lucrative paperback romance market when it formed Silhouette Books. From 1980 through 1984, Silhouette made huge inroads into a market that Harlequin had regarded as its own (Grescoe 157). In 1984, Harlequin bought Silhouette.

Both Harlequin and Silhouette, however, continued publishing, each under its own imprint and with its own editorial staff. Each split, in turn, into different "lines" of paperback romance. Lines vary in length, in the presence and kind of sex, the presence or absence of a suspense plot, in their chronological setting (for example, Regencies) or their geographic setting (for example, Westerns) and other elements that some readers look for in a romance novel. For all their superficial differences, however, each line consists of books that have the eight essential elements of the core romance. They share, in addition, other attributes with other books in the same line. Readers of a given line, therefore, know that they are not only getting a romance novel, they are getting a romance novel of a certain kind. By 1985 Harlequin and Silhouette had been joined by lines from many other publishers: by this time there were eighty romance titles per month in sixteen different lines (Thurston 62–65). This, then, was the romance novel boom.

Janet Dailey noted in 1984 that the opportunities presented by this array of publishers and lines were "a great place for . . . [a] writer to learn her craft. It [took] the place of the magazine fiction market, where so many renowned American writers got their start and perfected their skills" ("View" 54). To publish and distribute eighty titles a month, publishers needed more than nine hundred titles a year. The sheer number of new titles required to fill the publishers' production schedules gave writers like Dailey an opportunity to write steadily, be published, be paid, and learn. In giving writers an excellent chance at being published—assuming that the writer was good enough—the boom did romance writers and readers a huge service and changed the face of the distribution and sale of romance novels. This much is clear.

What is less clear is the claim that these publishers influenced romance *editorially* as much as they are sometimes given credit for. As we have seen, the form is old. As we have seen, the form has enjoyed enormous popularity. Mills and Boon, Harlequin, and Silhouette did not change the essential core elements of the romance—quite the reverse. First Mills and Boon, then Harlequin, excluded other forms from their lists to focus on romance. Silhouette entered the market with their romance focus already in place. Without necessarily being able to articulate it entirely, they were each looking for novels which defined a society, described a meeting, barrier, attraction, declaration, point of ritual death, recognition, and betrothal between heroine and hero.

Editors at Mills and Boon recognized this. They published books in which "heroine meets hero in an interesting setting, falls in love, and marries" (McAleer 6). This is a description of a courtship narrative, a core romance. Mills and Boon also recognized two very popular conventions of romance in the twentieth century: what they called Lubbock's Law and the Alphaman. Lubbock refers to Percy Lubbock, a literary critic *(Craft of Fic-*

tion, 1921), who claimed that the best fiction was written from the heroine's point of view because it intensifies, emotionally, whatever is being told. The Alphaman is Alan Boon's description of what a romance hero ought to be—in accord with the "law of nature," he ought to be the "strongest male of the species" in order to attract females (McAleer 149–50). This, of course, is the forerunner of Jayne Ann Krentz's "dangerous man" who must be tamed.

Given romance's long history and stable form, these recognitions are unremarkable, even predictable, and were not unique to Mills and Boon. In tracing the firm's editorial policies over the years, McAleer fails to find a "formula." True, he can chart in the romances both the concerns that women in British society had as the century unfolded and the concerns that the firm had about the conduct of the heroines, the settings of books, the adaptation of the narrative for serial publication, and other like matters, but none of these goes to the heart of the romance novel. The basic core romance is never tampered with. Changes occur on a more superficial level. It was not that Mills and Boon was the making of romance. How could it be? Romance was at least two centuries older. Instead the venerable but always popular romance form was the making of relative upstart Mills and Boon as soon as their editors had the wit to focus on the romance and leave other forms behind.

Across the ocean at Harlequin we find editorial mistakes and misjudgments. Mary Bonneycastle and her daughter Judy Burgess, both of whom exercised some editorial control over what did and did not get reprinted, had what one colleague describes as a "decency code" which caused them to reject some of the more sexually explicit Mills and Boon titles submitted for reprinting as Harlequins. Eventually Harlequin founder Richard Bonneycastle actually read his first romance novel ever—one of these more explicit Mills and Boon books that had been rejected—and approved a market test of it and one sexually tamer work. The consequence of Harlequin's failure "to keep up with the readers" was brought home when the test title outsold the tamer book (Grescoe 95).

Harlequin made perhaps its most serious editorial mistake in the late 1970s, when American romance novelists, setting their romances in America, were trying to break into print. Nora Roberts, who would eventually be published by Silhouette, explains that her first personalized rejection from Harlequin (she had received two form rejections for earlier submissions) was "a nice little note which said that my work showed promise, and the story had been very entertaining and well done. But that they (Harlequin) already had their American writer. That would have been Janet Dailey" (Mussell, "Interview with Roberts" 155). The implication, of course, is that Harlequin needed only one American writer. The further implication is that readers would not care to read romances set in America. Simon and Schuster recognized this as the editorial myopia that it was and created Silhouette to publish the backlog of rejected manuscripts from American writers. Four years later Harlequin bought Silhouette to absorb the newer company's inroads into Harlequin's formerly undisputed market. Because of Harlequin's editorial decision about "unnecessary" American writers, Silhouette began with an inventory of about 180 titles (Grescoe 14, 159). Aside from its short-sightedness as a business decision (Silhouette simply took this market that could have been Harlequin's), this refusal to consider a romance because of the nationality of its author belies an ignorance of the possibilities of the form. As we have seen, the romance form centers on the courtship and betrothal of a couple. Whether this takes place in America or Great Britain, and whether an American or British cultural sensibility informs the plot, it is the courtship that makes the romance. The lesson, of course, is that editors are not omniscient; even the editors at one of the most successful romance publishing houses make mistakes. Screenwriter William Goldman's comment about the movie industry, "nobody knows anything" might well be applied to romance editing, at least as it was practiced by Harlequin in this instance (39).

Despite their editorial myopia, Harlequin published Janet Dailey who was perfectly positioned to exploit Harlequin's wide distribution, gain practice in writing the core romance, and cultivate a readership. Building on her success at Harlequin, Janet Dailey's career as a romance writer has extended to Silhouette, to single-title paperback releases for Pocket Books, to hardback releases for mainstream houses such as HarperCollins. Her readers respond enthusiastically. Like the other writers in this history, Dailey is extremely popular. There are 300 million copies of her books in print, making her the third best-selling author of all time; her novels have been translated into nineteen languages ("Janet Dailey").

Dailey's Americanness is essential in her work. She provides our first look at heroines, heroes, and courtships that take place in America, with American sensibilities, assumptions, history, and, most of all, settings. Not only was Dailey Harlequin's first American author, she wrote best when writing about the quintessential American setting: the West. Nancy Regan refers to this setting as Dailey's "emotional center of gravity" (160). It is a setting she knows intimately; she was born in a small town in northwest Iowa, still a part of the frontier as late as the 1840s. The Western frontier animates many of her heroines, her heroes, and the kind of courtship they enact.

Dailey wrote short contemporary romances for Harlequin, the novels less accurately called "categories." These novels are set in the present (hence "contemporary") and—at 55,000 words—are the shortest romances published. (Compare *Pamela* at approximately 240,000 words and *Pride and Prejudice* at 127,000). When a novel is that brief, the author must pare the story down to its essentials. Subplots and minor characters are eliminated or relegated to the backstory—that portion of the action that occurs before the novel begins and that is represented, if at all, in flashback. What is left is a distillation of the romance novel, contained primarily in scenes between the heroine and hero. For all that the books are short, however, a reader finds wide variety in them: all eight of the essential elements are present in each book, and their order can be (and is) varied, emphasized, doubled, reported "off," and otherwise manipulated within the limited compass of these works known affectionately as "little books" within the romance community.

The first Harlequin that Janet Dailey read was Nerina Hilliard's *Dark Star* (1969); thereafter she began reading Harlequins steadily and soon decided that she could write better ones (Grescoe 121). In 1976 Harlequin published Dailey's first novel, *No Quarter Asked*, and her career was launched. She has written more than ninety romance novels, most of them short contemporaries. Included among these are novels set in every state of the Union (Grescoe 119). Dailey made the transition to single-title release with *Touch the Wind* (1979) and to hardcover with *Silver Wings, Santiago Blue* (1984). Thus, Dailey's career grew out of the Harlequin-Silhouette boom—writing short categories gave her a chance at publication and a springboard for a leap into single-title releases. She capitalized upon it, becoming the first truly mainstream writer of romance novels. Like Stewart and Heyer, she belongs in the canon of twentieth-century romance.

Something Extra (1975) and *Sonora Sundown* (1978) demonstrate Dailey's accomplishment in the short contemporary. Two of her single-title releases, *Touch the Wind* (1979) and *Ride the Thunder* (1980), both set in the West, were her break-out books—titles that permitted her to leave the training ground of Harlequin behind and reach a wide, mainstream readership. Analysis of these works shows Dailey turning to the sort of heroine, hero and courtship that E. M. Hull established in *The Sheik*, but with a distinctly American flavor. Indeed, Dailey's contribution to the romance novel is her exploration of the quintessential American setting: the West.

A note about the choice of these four works: in 1997 Dailey admitted plagiarizing over ten of Nora Roberts's novels (Baldwin 10). The books analyzed here were all released before Roberts began to publish, and so are likely to be safe from plagiarism as there is no author save Roberts who has proven that Dailey plagiarized her. It would have been preferable to choose books distributed across Dailey's quarter-century career, but it is even more important to analyze only the books that Dailey actually wrote.

In *Something Extra,* published in 1975 by Mills and Boon and reprinted in 1978 by Harlequin, heroine Jolie Antoinette Smith breaks with her long-time boyfriend and travels from her home in South Dakota to Louisiana to take a vacation and think about her future. While she is there, she searches for an old family estate. The owner of that estate, Steve Cameron, is the hero.

Joile is at loose in the world. If she does not possess Diana Mayo's style, she does share Diana's values—the three essential beliefs of the twentieth-century romance heroine. Unlike Diana, she does not possess "any startling beauty," and she has no fortune. Still, she has into "three years . . . crammed a four year college course" that has provided her with the skill necessary to make a living (6, 8). Property, at least in prospect, is hers. The first significant action of the book is her breaking up with her boyfriend whom she does not love: "I care about you more than anyone I've ever met. . . . but I'm not really in love with you" (12). Thus the value of companionate marriage is in place. In the manner of short contemporaries, the description of the heroine's person and situation is a sketch; by page eighteen, she has decided upon the trip. Finally, this is the decision of an affective individual, one who has as much freedom as Diana Mayo, if not quite her financial means.

In this first scene, Jolie rides her horse out to see her soon to be ex-boyfriend. This association of her heroines with horses is characteristic of Dailey. Even in this short early work, when the heroine needs to think, she does it on horseback. This not only anticipates the Western romances to come, it is also a shorthand expression of the heroine's physical abilities, her sympathy, and her tastes: she is the sort of physical woman who rides, she is capable of understanding a fellow creature well enough to ride successfully, and she likes the exercise and activity. In addition, of course, putting her heroine on a horse evokes the fantasy that a sizable percentage of female readers have about befriending, training, and riding horses as attested to by the enduring popularity of works such as *Black Beauty, Misty of Chincoteague,* and *The Red Pony.*

Hero Steve Cameron owns Cameron Hall; his family acquired it from Jolie's family generations ago. Dailey calls him a "pirate" who sees the too high "price for love" as "[t]he most precious thing a man has, his freedom" (76). His strategy is to "stay away from spirited virgins" like the heroine so as not to sink "so low as to be seducing" them (164). He is a libertine. He is, in other words, dangerous, in Krentz's formulation. The heroine must tame him by leading him to see that he is the sort of man who gets married. He believes that he is not. She accomplishes this in the most straightforward way. After a few weeks' visit in the neighborhood, she leaves Louisiana and goes back home to North Dakota. This removal of the heroine from the hero's presence is the most elemental form of ritual death, echoing the removal of Persephone herself from Earth to Hades. It precipitates the rest of the action. He follows her, claiming that he has been a man "protesting too much" that "these last few months without you have been hell," and he admits that he loves her (185–88). She tames him by her absence, making him rethink his image of himself, his own identity.

Despite its kisses-only sexual boundary, making this a "sweet" romance in the parlance of the editors and writers, the courtship between Jolie and Steve is intense. Dailey charges the encounters between heroine and hero with sexual energy, a lesson she might have learned from earlier Harlequin authors such as the very successful Anne Mather. The barrier between heroine and hero is complex. It has external components: both the other man and the other woman complicate matters, the other woman deviously so. The hero's view of himself as the sort of man who does not get married is its one internal component. Yet throughout the book the hero makes his passion for the heroine plain. Characteristic of his statements is "I'm generally the one left with the task of fighting the fires you start, as if you didn't know" (138). The compression of the novel and the intensity of the tension, sexual and otherwise, between the heroine and hero contribute to the power of this romance. Compression is the secret weapon of all short contemporaries.

Sonora Sundown (1978) is Dailey's "Arizona" book in the "Americana" series—her fifty short contemporaries, each set in a different state of the Union. Dailey was the first prominent writer of romance novels to understand the possibilities of a Western setting. After her, the Western romance would become a flourishing subgenre. Dailey's founding contribution to this subgenre is an important component of her accomplishment as a romance writer.

What are the consequences of setting a romance novel in the West, specifically Arizona, the setting for *Sonora Sundown?* Jane Tompkins, in *West of Everything*, defines the West of the Western as "the West of the desert, of mountains and prairies, the West of Arizona, Utah, Nevada, New Mexico, Texas, Colorado, Montana, Wyoming, the Dakotas, and some parts of California" (4). John Cawelti generalizes the setting of the Western when he identifies it as "on or near a frontier" *(Six-Gun* 35). *Sonora Sundown*, set in Arizona, is also a contemporary—so the question arises: how can there be a frontier, the frontier having disappeared many decades before Dailey wrote the book?

The first scene, like the first scene of *Something Extra,* has the heroine on her horse, riding out from her home. Arizonan Brandy Ames rides into the desert, dismounts to watch the sunset, and finds herself on foot when her horse spooks and runs away. Dark descends and she stumbles around until she finds the campfire of Jim Corbett, the hero. Neither of them truly lives on the frontier—Brandy works in an arts and crafts store and Jim is a famous actor who has ridden away from the town where a film he is starring in is being shot. The setting is Tompkins's West, however, and the situation is frontier-like: one horse, two people, and a dangerous natural phenomenon (a sandstorm kicks up) in a remote spot. It takes very little to evoke a Western setting. More important than the physical setting, however, are the characters, ethos, and typical narrative of the form.

Cawelti claims that Western plots emerge from three groups of characters: townspeople, "savages" (including outlaws), and the Western heroes who are "the men in the middle" who "possess many qualities and skills of the savages, but are fundamentally committed to the townspeople" (46). Many plot events are possible, but eventually most situations are "reduced to the terms of flight, capture and pursuit" (66–67).

Tompkins, interested in the ethos of the Western, observes that the setting "functions as a symbol of freedom, and of the opportunity for conquest." It promises a "translation of the self into something purer and more authentic, more intense, more real" (4). She also notes that the Western "struggles and strains to cast out everything feminine" (127). The Western romance novel insists that the feminine—the heroine—not be cast out. It in fact insists that the feminine be incorporated into the Western setting.

Although Brandy mistakes Jim for a cattle rustler, this is not a fantasy—cattle rustlers still exist in today's American West. He turns out to be, of course, an actor. This first recognition—of the actor beneath the apparent cattle rustler, moves the hero from outside the law to inside it. He is no longer part "savage" in Cawelti's terms. He is still, however, "dangerous," to use Krentz's term, which is another form of savagery. Indeed, Krentz identifies the cowboy as one of mythical "dangerous" men, the other two being the pirate and the adventurer. Brandy thinks as she watches Jim, "When he was dressed in Western gear that brought to mind the lawless time of the frontier, the ruthless, dangerous quality about him was heightened" (105).

Brandy is the feminine part of Jim's life that he cannot shake. Like Jolie in *Something Extra*, Brandy is very young, twenty, and even more closely tied to home. She lives with her parents, who are a bit taken aback at their daughter's "lack of ambition" (8). She, however, is a young woman at peace with her decisions. Jim, like Steve in *Something Extra,* finds himself confronted by a "virgin," unwisely kissing her (50). Like Steve, Jim is chased by another woman, LaRaine, who schemes to make Brandy believe that the hero loves her. Eventually Brandy understands LaRaine's treachery, and Jim declares his love for her.

Both Brandy and Jolie are blank slates—very young, at the very beginning of adulthood, but with everything they need to make a satisfactory life. In each novel, there is not much time for character development. Brandy and Jolie learn that the hero loves them and not the other woman. The heroes, Steve and Jim, learn that they must submit to the unlikely woman each has fallen in love with—unlikely because apparently without power. Yet each heroine has the ability to tame the hero, to stop him from thinking of himself as an unsuitable companion for virgins. That is her power.

Touch the Wind, published by Pocket Books in 1979, is Janet Dailey's break-out book, her first, very successful, step away from short contemporaries of the sort we just looked at, and the fulfillment of the promise of her early Western romances. Here I will analyze this earliest of Dailey's single-title Western romances along with *Ride the Thunder* (1980). Although Dailey's best-known Western romances may very well be the Calder series—*This Calder Sky* (1981), *This Calder Range* (1982), *Stands a Calder Man* (1983), *Calder Born, Calder Bred* (1984), *Calder Pride* (2000), and, projected, *Green Calder Grass* (2003)—I reluctantly pass over these books because they overlap dangerously with Nora Roberts's career.

In *Touch the Wind* heroine Sheila Rogers is an heiress—rich, willful—but still living with her parents in Austin, Texas and attending college. She is situated like most of the heroines in twentieth-century romances: she has the means to act as an affective individual (if not quite the maturity), she has property or the promise of it (in her case, a great deal of it), and she expects to make a companionate marriage. She discusses the latter issue in the first scene, arguing with her parents over their disapproval of her planned marriage to her boyfriend, Brad Townsend, before he has finished college. Their elopement to Mexico ends this argument but Sheila regrets her hasty marriage almost immediately. Her reaction to her wedding night is "disgust and rejection" when she realizes that Brad's lovemaking is "a demanding act of [a woman's] subservience to a man's will" (40). Companionate marriage has eluded her, but widowhood releases her from her mistaken union with the wrong man. He is murdered by bandits after getting himself and his bride hopelessly lost in the Sierra Madres. In the first forty pages of this book, the heroine undergoes more change than the heroines of most short contemporaries do in the entire novel.

The leader of the bandits, Ráfaga, whose name means "the wind," kidnaps her and holds her for ransom in his mountain hideout. He is the hero, very much in the mold of the sheik. The heroine, being carried away seated across his saddle, sees "[s]lashing grooves . . . carved on either side of his mouth. . . . patrician fineness in his nose . . . a compelling face, too aggressively male and too bluntly carved." He seems "aloof and hard . . . a man to be feared" (66–67). He is an outlaw who, with his band, stages prison breaks to free people unfairly jailed. Ráfaga rides better than anyone else, rules through a mixture of force and moral suasion, and inhabits a world in his mountain fastness that is largely male. He seems to her a "devil-master" (77). "She knew he was dangerous" (110).

This courtship is long. After her disastrous marriage, Sheila hates men: "None of them could be trusted. They were insensitive, selfish animals, caring only about their own physical needs. Love was a trap, devised by man to enslave woman to his will" (95). Speaking in English, she insults him; he understands but chooses to keep this fact from her until later. In this book a fiery sexual consummation precedes sentiment. This physicality before love mirrors the emotional journey that Sheila is on: she must come to trust men, and this kidnapper is apparently the most untrustworthy of men. She is trapped in his stronghold, which is actually a small community. This imprisonment becomes voluntary by the novel's end. According to the hero, Sheila becomes like a "lioness" and she has "bewitched" him (204). Each struggles against admitting love for the other. Sheila tames Ráfaga partly through resisting him, despite her sexual attraction to him.

Sheila's parents have her rescued by the Mexican authorities, but by then Sheila is pregnant and unwilling to return to Texas. Ráfaga, however, has not been seized, and any return to him would lead the authorities to him as well. His taming is slight, like the sheik's. He remains an outlaw. He does not become reconciled with the larger society around him. His taming is focused: the love of one woman "bewitches" him, and he makes a new family unit with her, but away from the larger, conventional society. The last action of the book underscores this separation as he rescues her from her apparent rescuers: "The rifle at his hip sprayed a cover-fire for Sheila. She ran to him" (296). At this point, the end of the novel, they are both outlaws. Sheila has traveled to the frontier, where she has found a companionate marriage, one she could not find in civilization.

In *Ride the Thunder* heroine Jordanna Smith, a wealthy big game hunter, arranges a hunt on the land of hero Brig McCord, an ex-mercenary, now rancher, fallen on financial difficulties. Jordanna's father, Fletcher, is a trophy hunter who seeks bighorn sheep, which inhabit parts of Brig's Idaho ranch. Once again, we have a Dailey heroine whose character is firmly established at the outset of the novel. The prologue is set when Jordanna is quite young, just twelve. In its first scene, she, under her father's supervision, cleans her rifle as they are sitting in his den decorated with trophy heads from various hunts mounted and hung on the wall (2). In the second scene her brother Christopher has wounded a buck but cannot put it out of its misery. Jordanna does it for him (12).

Brig McCord is a rancher cast in the "dangerous" mold of Dailey's heroes. His profile is "hawk-like," he is as "lean as a winter wolf" and "there was something about his rangy build that suggested coiled readiness" (94). As a young boy he lived alone in the mountains for two months after surviving a plane crash which killed his parents. This feral upbringing mirrors the heroine's elementary education as a trophy hunter.

Usual gender differences are simply absent in this work, creating what Deborah Chappel calls "ungendered space" (176). Chappel argues that Dailey's Western heroines and heroes cannot achieve "ideal love" within "traditional dichotomies . . . such as hard/soft, male/female, public/private." In the "Western landscape, itself androgynous," these are "transgressed" (176). Before they even exchange names, heroine and hero have made love (109). This is the physical sign of their love and the beginning of their courtship.

Jordanna must tame Brig and recognize her father as the treacherous would-be murderer that he actually is. Chappel notes that Dailey often splits her heroes into an inauthentically masculine father figure/false hero who must be vanquished (as Fletcher Smith is in this novel) and the genuinely masculine true hero (represented here by Brig McCord) (173–74). The taming then must also be a disentangling of the heroine's love for the false hero and her coming to love the true one.

By the end of this courtship, Brig cannot get Jordanna out of his mind. "She had made him vulnerable. That made her dangerous, because he wasn't certain he could trust her. Why, he didn't know" (182). Until the novel's final scene, he expects her to double-cross him because he cannot convince her that Fletcher is stalking Brig to kill him, thus eliminating him as a witness to a murder that Fletcher had committed. At various points in the book he is convinced that Fletcher has dangled his beautiful daughter in front of him as a sexual distraction (191) and that Joanna's riding to the rescue when Fletcher actually wounds Brig is a "set up" (314). The "flight and pursuit" that Cawelti observes as characteristic of the Western operates in this book's climax. Fletcher and Brig, false hero and true, father and suitor, enact a chase—Fletcher pursues Brig. Rather than just the two men facing each other down, Fletcher targets a wounded Brig, and *Jordanna* targets her own father, unintentionally killing him when her warning shot starts a rock slide which buries him (374). Jordanna and Brig are purified in each other's eyes by the truth. Brig's taming, which began with sexual immersion in Joanna, is completed by her emerging as a dealer in the truth.

Dailey is the first American author to publish the short contemporaries traditionally issued by Mills and Boon and Harlequin. A raft of other American writers would follow her lead as editors realized that their readership would embrace these writers. Dailey's Americanness and her choice of the West as a setting frees her from the constraints of a more rule-governed and gendered society to write novels that postulate heroine and hero as equals meeting in a place that results in their becoming "purer and more authentic" in the process of completing their courtship. Physical hardship purifies the characters. So does the exercise of an extreme respect for the truth which is part of the fundamental values in all of these books.

Authenticity, physical hardship, purity—these are part of the western side of the Western romance's heritage; their working out in the courtship is the contribution of the romance side. Western authenticity parallels the romance's core elements of recognition and declaration. The heroine and hero recognize their love when they see it, and they act on it or speak it. Western physical hardship parallels the romance's core elements of physical courtship. The West requires physical confrontation of the elements; Western romance requires physical confrontation of lovemaking itself. Western purity parallels the conquest of the barrier and the betrothal. The

West helps purge westerners of dross and denial; Western romance encourages similar honesty concerning intentions.

There is little domestication in the conclusions: the core romance elements are all in place, but the wedding/dance/fete that sometimes ends a romance novel does not appear at the end of either *Ride the Thunder* or *Touch the Wind*. The end of these works is marked by death, by the cessation of violence, and then by an abrupt narrative quiet.

The Western romance is the most primal of any of the subgenres. The setting itself is by definition uncivilized. Human life on the frontier is likely to be lived in a solitary way or in a tribal fashion. Ráfaga in *Touch the Wind* has a tribe, similar to the sheik, rather than a community. The primal nature of the pursuit in the pure Western is echoed in the other sort of pursuit found in all romance novels: the courtship. The confrontation of the heroine and hero in an isolated landscape and setting permit the hero to enact an extreme version of one of the three Krentzian types of hero—the cowboy. In this landscape, the heroine can travel very far indeed from any constraining or defining society. Their courtship is a pure confrontation of two individuals, unconstrained by any society's expectations of what they should do and be. This primal courtship has a physical element. Even in *Sonora Sundown,* a Harlequin written in 1978 when courtships in such works were fairly tame, there is a scene in which heroine and hero are alone together, facing the elements on the frontier. If the community is almost absent, so, too, is its purification by the betrothal of heroine and hero. Heroine and hero are as likely to withdraw from civilization as they are to reenter it and contribute to its remaking. In this way, they remain pure—the compromises of everyday community life will not be a part of their future. Western values favor the individual. Western romance values favor the individual couple.

In Heyer's Regency romances, the courtship must be heard above the chatter and nattering of Regency society. Courtship in Stewart's novels of romantic suspense must be heard above the distracting questions of the mystery plot. Courtship in Dailey's Western romances is played in a quieter place, and it takes on the intensity and loudness of any sound projected into a silence.

16

DANGEROUS MEN

Jayne Ann Krentz

Jayne Ann Krentz (1949–), whose pseudonyms include Jayne Taylor, Jayne Castle, Guinevere Jones, Amanda Glass, Stephanie James, and Amanda Quick, lists more than 130 romance novels in her bibliography. More than seventy are short contemporaries or their somewhat longer cousins, all issued by Harlequin, Silhouette, the now-defunct Candlelight, or other "brand-name" publishers. Like Janet Dailey, Krentz is a beneficiary of the training ground that short contemporaries provide. She too has made the transition from these little books all the way to mainstream, hardback titles. Thirty-one of her titles have appeared on the *New York Times* Best Sellers List (Jayne Ann Krentz Website).

In addition to her fiction, Krentz edited and contributed to *Dangerous Men and Adventurous Women: Romance Writers on the Appeal of the Romance* (1992). In this collection of critical articles on the romance by romance writers themselves, she provides a forum in which writers can respond to feminist arguments against the romance novel and explore the elements that contribute to its enormous appeal. Krentz herself contributes an analysis of the romance hero. Her fictional exploration of the hero dates back to her very first romance novel. In fact, in that book, *Gentle Pirate* (1980), the hero completely embodies the ideas laid out in *Dangerous Men*. Krentz did not discover the romance hero that she analyzes in her nonfiction and represents in her fiction. He is at least as old as Mr. B, Darcy, and Rochester—but she sets about examining his characteristics systematically and places him at the center of her books. The heroine who can tame this man and the courtship that results from this taming yields romance novels of rare energy, heightened pace, and great sensuality. Her heroines are brave women who make these men safe to be around—they are the beauties (although none is ever classically or dramatically beautiful) who tame the beasts. This takes energy, perseverance, and an adventurous spirit.

In three of her Harlequin Temptations, a line of romances somewhat longer than the shortest contemporaries but not as long as the single-title releases, Krentz explores what she calls the "dangerous" romance hero in his mythic guises: *The Pirate* (1990), *The Adventurer* (1990), and *The Cowboy* (1990). Despite the nineteenth-century sounding occupations named in the titles, these are contemporary novels, and the heroes are fully grounded in the contemporary world. In these novels Krentz creates "heroes of mythical proportion" (*Cowboy* 2). These three essential Krentzian fictional explorations reappear, in more elaborate form, in her longer, single-title releases, which also have more elaborated heroines, secondary characters, settings, and plots.

Each of the three Harlequins will be paired with a single-title release whose hero is a Krentzian pirate, adventurer, or cowboy. In addition to showing Krentz's exploration of these mythic romantic heroes, these three single-title releases demonstrate her range in the subgenres of romance: *Deception* (1993), whose hero is a "pirate," is a historical set in England just after the Napoleonic Wars; *Absolutely, Positively* (1996), whose hero is an "adventurer," is a work of romantic suspense; and *Shield's Lady* (1989), whose hero is a "cowboy," is a "futuristic," set on another planet after Earth has accomplished interstellar colonization. Krentz's fictional interests are wide ranging, not a characteristic that the critical community usually associates with romance writers. Within the core romance as described in Part III, Krentz writes in all of the major subgenres.

At the center of her romances is the "dangerous" hero. "He is not only the hero, he is also the villain. . . . the romance heroine must face a man who is a genuine challenge" ("Trying to Tame" 108, 109). "He is a worthy opponent, a mythic beast. . . . He has been variously described as a devil, a demon, a tiger, a hawk, a pirate, a bandit, a potentate, a hunter, a warrior. He is definitely *not* the boy next door" (Barlow 19). This is what Krentz means by "dangerous" heroes. In response, the heroine must be "adventurous." "With courage, intelligence, and gentleness she brings the most dangerous creature on earth, the human male, to his knees. More than that, she forces him to acknowledge her power as a woman" ("Introduction" 7). "Any woman who, as a little girl, indulged herself in books featuring other little girls taming wild stallions knows instinctively what makes a romance novel work" ("Trying to Tame" 109). Krentz read the Walter Farley *Black Stallion* books as a girl (Mussell, "Interview with Krentz" 6). Krentz elaborates: "The thrill and satisfaction of teaching that powerful male creature to respond only to your touch, of linking with him in a bond that transcends the physical, of communicating with him in a manner that goes beyond mere speech—that thrill is deeply satisfying" (109). Although in Krentz's novels the primary change in the hero is becoming "tame," the other tradition of romance novel heroes is present as well: the sentimental, in which heroes must be healed. Each of the six heroes in the novels examined here is damaged and must be made whole; each has an essential character of dangerousness that must be tamed. The injured, dangerous hero who is both healed and tamed by the heroine is doubly powerful at the center of a romance, which is where Krentz puts her heroes.

In *The Pirate* the heroine Kate Inskip is positioned as we have become accustomed to think of twentieth-century romance novel heroines: she is free to do as she likes—she has affective individualism. At the beginning of the novel she is not married, and there is no mention of a family. She lives independently in Seattle and writes. She is successful, too, so much so that her other romance writer friends (who will appear as the heroines in *Adventurer* and *Cowboy*) "kidnap" her, charge a plane ticket to her account, and send her off to a South Sea island to force her to take a much needed vacation. She believes in companionate marriage. Her vacation begins unpromisingly: "You remind me of my ex-husband, you little twerp," she says to the mugger who tries, sadly for him, to steal her wallet (18). The hero witnesses the would-be mugger's scurrying retreat after Kate has kicked him in a very sensitive place.

As a romance novel with a heroine who is a romance novelist and a hero who reads one of her books (208), *The Pirate* is self-referential. This novel points explicitly to its own genre. Krentz uses the romance novels that her character has written to create a perspective—an echo, a mirror, a doubling, an ironic contrast—for the essential romance elements of the actual novel, *The Pirate*, that we, the readers, are holding in our hands. Through mirroring or echoing an element of the core romance novel, Krentz adds a set of meanings to the actual romance novel, intensifying them, commenting ironically on them, but never actually undercutting them. This generic self-referentiality becomes part of the courtship.

The hero is dangerous in the Krentzian sense of the term. Some dangerous romance heroes are like Rochester, veritable devils. Krentz's are not. The hero of *The Pirate*, Jared Hawthorne, is the owner of the South Sea resort where Kate vacations, and he owns the island it is located on as well. Like most Krentz heroes, he is a businessman. In a Krentz romance, business is seen as an admirable profession—her businessmen are often heroes. Jared is "a very large man, a couple of inches over six feet, lean and hard and broad shouldered. Caught in the harsh glare and deep shadows cast by the intense tropical sun, he looked infinitely more dangerous than the man with the knife. The slashing, wicked grin that revealed his teeth did nothing to soften the impression. . . . Two hundred years ago, he would have been a pirate" (19). Krentz's imagery evokes pirates without violating the contemporary setting. Later Kate looks at him and "for a moment she stared at him and saw an island lord who lived just beyond the reach of civilization; a man who could indulge himself by playing by his own rules; a pirate. Frowning she dismisses *the image*" (49, emphasis mine). By elaborating the image, and then labeling it one and having the heroine dismiss it, Krentz can evoke the mythic level of this hero—the pirate—without putting an anachronism in her contemporary setting.

Kate conducts the courtship, although Jared declares his desire for her early on. She must overcome his belief that he is not really attracted to the "type" of woman adept at self-defense against muggers. He believes his late wife was his ideal: "soft-voiced, sweet-tempered, gentle and affectionate . . . old-fashioned . . . devoted to hearth and home." The "bossy, assertive, independent, prickly little broads who neither needed nor welcomed a man's protection" did not appeal to him, and the heroine was one such woman (34). He declares his attraction for her in a sensual kiss that takes place at a costume ball at the resort. He, of course, is dressed as a pirate. The kiss begins as speculation on his part, just the satisfaction of curiosity. It ends as a marker of his more serious attraction to her.

She must also overcome her suspicion of him: the book has a mystery subplot involving the old castle on the island, a secret cove, and a smuggler. Kate suspects Jared of being a smuggler (certainly a piratical occupation). It turns out that Jared is deceived by a "friend" into believing that he is helping the government crack down on smugglers, and the friend has double-crossed him. Jared's behavior is suspicious enough, however, to raise a red flag for Kate. The issue is partly trust. Can Kate trust Jared? More important, the issue is Jared's ability to acknowledge that Kate is the woman for him. To get him to do this, Kate must first declare her love for him. She says, "I think I am in love with you, but I'm afraid of that fact precisely because you are too close to being the living image of the man of my dreams." Then she confronts him: "I think that you could learn to love me, but you're afraid to try because I'm not the image of the woman of your dreams" (209). In the face of this honesty, he admits his own attraction. The heroine and hero enact this courtship in a " haze of passion and laughter" (120). The heroine is "a real spitfire" with "a tongue that can tear a man to shreds from twenty paces" (45). The hero, despite his belief that this sort of woman is not his type, cannot stay away from her, and he acts the part of the assertive, ironic, sexy partner to his intelligent, witty heroine. Krentz's women are headstrong. They win the war of words. Courtship in her books is adult—balanced between the woman and the man.

Kate, in *Pirate*, at the masquerade ball, "imagine[s] herself to be a fine Regency lady who [has] been kidnapped and carried off to the island king-dom of a wealthy, dangerous pirate, who [is] secretly the son of an earl" (67). This is basically the hero and setting in *Deception*, a hardback release with a hero who is also a "pirate." Like Kate, heroine Olympia Wingfield is a literate woman, a scholar of what would now be called ethnology. As a scholar, she is interested in the voyages of discovery and travelers' tales being brought back to England at this time, the early nineteenth century. She reflects Krentz's interest in the history of science and exploration (Mussell, "Interview with Krentz" 51). Olympia is a bluestocking: "There was not a book of pressed flowers or a sewing basket in sight" (39). She supports her household, which includes her three orphaned nephews, on the profits that her uncle makes for her in a small import/export business. Like many Krentz characters, Olympia is an entrepreneur.

The hero, Jared Ryder (Krentz reuses the first name), is a viscount and comes from a long line of practitioners of the "free trade" which is to say, smugglers (52). He represents the legitimate side of his family's business, shipping; he is another entrepreneur. He has even lost an eye and wears an eye patch. He carries a dagger and, in Olympia's opinion, "looks altogether dangerous" (53). He is described, from Olympia's point of view, as a beast: "Jared sprawled in her chair with the relaxed grace of a carnivorous beast" (233).

The courtship is a matter of overcoming a series of deceptions, as the title suggests. Jared has represented himself as a tutor for Olympia's three unruly nephews, when, in fact, he is in search of a diary that he is certain is in a shipment which has recently arrived at Olympia's home. Jared comes intending to buy the diary and go on his way. He decides, impulsively, to present himself as a tutor to stay within the household. His passion for her is instantaneous, and it takes him by surprise: "A mundane business arrangement was the very last thing he wanted to enter into with Olympia. Indeed, he could not bear the thought. He wanted her. *Wanted her*" (34, emphasis Krentz's). His misrepresentation of himself, his family's desire for the diary (which seems to promise the map to hidden treasure), his self-deception that he is cold and dispassionate, her self-deception that she is truly a woman of the world (she is actually a virgin)—all of these must be overcome. Jared is dangerous—he is an accomplished knifefighter, a true pirate, but Olympia tames him. He is wounded—he believes himself incapable of passion, but Olympia heals him by understanding him.

In addition, a series of minor characters present all of the conventional reasons why these two should not marry. These are barrier issues more appropriate to the temporal setting of the novel, such as the heroine's comparative lack of rank and money—Ryder "controls a bloody fortune" (191). The real barrier is in the minds of both heroine and hero. She believes that the hero does not really love her, that he is "driven by passion and honor, not true love," and that she must save him from himself by refusing to marry him (178). He, in turn, worries, after she has married him but before they have declared their love for each other, that she has married him only because of his usefulness. In other words, he worries that he is in a marriage of convenience instead of a union based on love. This regard for each other, this consideration for the other's feelings is an unremarkable modern value. The historical setting throws it into high relief. As we have seen in the earlier discussion of Heyer, during the Regency arranged marriages contracted with little regard for the spouses' feelings for each other were common enough to be unremarkable.

Krentz uses the conventions of the Regency as Heyer established them, both unironically (the marriage of convenience) and ironically (ritual death and the duel, which could be deadly and dangerous in Heyer, Krentz plays primarily for laughs with the challenger swooning at the sight of blood and the challenged, the hero, converting the challenger to the cause of the union between heroine and hero). The strictures on behavior make a fitting backdrop to highlight the bravery, independence, and freedom of the heroine. For engaging in activity that many today would find tame and ordinary, such as scholarship, a Regency heroine receives points for extraordinariness, but at the same time seems approachable and familiar to the contemporary reader. Readers experience this dual perspective in any work of historical fiction, but Krentz has honed it to a fine edge in her Regencies. The arch, ironic stance of much of Regency fiction is also a great source of contrast. It can be invoked at any time, and the sincerity of the heroine and hero contrasted with it. The reader may very well share the sense that the world she inhabits is full of irony, that no meaning lasts much longer than an hour or two, if that long, without an ironic version of it being proffered.

Krentz is a master of the Regency tone. The witty, intelligent, but sexually sheltered heroine in private conversation with the equally intelligent, also witty, sexually experienced and aroused hero create amusing scenes full of sexual tension. Heroine and hero in their, well—intercourse—behave alternately according to Regency decorum and modern mores. Conversations about mating rituals among exotic peoples, delivered in the cadences of the Regency drawing room are characteristic of the ironic hilarity of this novel.

Krentz places her pirate-hero in a characteristic setting—the sea—and gives him a characteristic role to play—making his own laws in defiance of the unjust laws that would inhibit the "free trade." She can invoke these characteristics on a mythic level—dress Jared Hawthorne for a costume ball in pirate's garb and the allusion is made—or she can invoke these characteristics by making a character an actual pirate with ships, with a patch over an eye that he lost in a knife fight, and with the knife, too. The invocation, or the actual manifestation, both work because they touch a fundamental archetype.

The Adventurer (1990), the second in the trilogy of short contemporaries examining three prototypical dangerous men, begins with a reference to Kate Inskip's marriage: "There was nothing like a couple of months on a tropical island and marriage to a pirate to give a woman a shot of energy and the sheen of happiness" (9). *Adventurer* heroine Sarah Fleetwood is a romance writer like each of the heroines of this trilogy and is similarly established in life: she is an affective individual, she has an income from writing, and she believes in companionate marriage, although she has been badly hurt—left, in fact, literally at the altar (51). As she admits this to the hero, she includes this account of the "very embarrassing" situation: "But nothing is ever wasted for a writer. One of these days, I'm going to do a romance that starts out with the heroine being left at the altar. Snappy beginning, don't you think?" Betraying his lack of knowledge of the romance genre, the hero asks, "How's it going to end?" The readers of *The*

Adventurer and the readers of fictional romance writer Sarah Fleetwood all know that there is only one answer: "At the altar, of course. With the right man this time" (51). This is more Krentzian self-reference.

Sarah courts Gideon Trace, a professional treasure hunter who is helping her search for family heirloom jewelry hidden by her aunt. Sarah identifies their relationship as a courtship. Gideon asks her at one point:

> "Why the fancy breakfast?"
> She debated briefly how much to tell him and then decided he might as well know what he was facing. "Because it's the first step in the courtship, if you must know the truth." (100)

She is brandishing a whisk in his direction. She is a Krentzian adventurous woman. A few pages later she is calling him a "beast" (106, 115), which, indeed, has been his tag throughout the book. He has "jungle eyes" (22) and feels himself awkwardly to be, from his own point of view, "a great, rutting, male animal" in comparison to her (130).

Their hunt for her aunt's treasure throws them together. The barrier in the courtship includes not only the romantic past of Sarah (being left at the altar), but of Gideon as well. Like each of the heroes in the trilogy, Gideon has a woman in his past who hurt him. Her betrayal of him with a close friend has wounded him, adding the need to be healed to the need to be tamed. The treasure hunt itself is part of the barrier. Its exact nature is unclear. Is Sarah simply out to exploit Gideon's help? Is he simply leading her along because he wants the jewels? Or, is he simply leading her along because he wants sex?

The book is complex, self-referential, simultaneously ironic and sincere. The tone of the courtship is as well. Wit, Krentz's hallmark, features prominently. Heroine and hero spend a certain amount of time exasperated with each other. Suspicion is also an element of this courtship as each partner fears a double-cross and romantic motives clash with the motives in the quest plot. The mixture is often funny and sometimes frightening, although the real threat in this plot comes from outside the courtship. Heroine and hero unite to face this threat, overcome ritual death, and overcome the fear of a double-cross.

Another adventurer is Harry Trevelyan, hero of *Absolutely, Positively* (1996), historian of science and an independent consultant on matters of scientific fraud. Having come from a carnival family, he is also adept at prestidigitation (and can detect fraud using such so-called "magic"). Like

Gideon, he is an independent agent, an expert in his field, and deeply skeptical. He is hired by heroine Molly Abberwick to review grant applications for her family's foundation which funds research and development for promising inventions. In addition to running the foundation, Molly is another Krentzian entrepreneur—she owns Abberwick Tea and Spice Company. She is an affective individual and believes in companionate marriage. Harry is a beast, as we expect from Krentz heroes: he has "fierce features" and Molly's assistant calls him "T-Rex" for his ruthlessness and seeming coldness with applicants (23, 47). This is tinged with the irony we have come to expect from Krentz.

His wound is like Gideon's in that it involves his fiancé who looked upon their relationship as "hours of boredom broken by moments of stark terror" (68). The "terror" stems from Harry's psychic powers—claiming her right as a romance writer to flirt with nonrealistic elements, Krentz creates a psychic hero in Harry. If he has a close enough relationship with another person, that person can hear Harry's thoughts and Harry can hear his or hers. Instead of bringing him closer to others, this power has proven so profoundly alienating that Harry hides it. In addition to this personal wound, Harry's families—his mother's and his father's—are in a state of perpetual feud, and his father's family feuds within itself as well. Everyone depends upon Harry to mediate all disputes. Harry is a misfit, like Jared Hawthorne in *Deception*.

Harry has no personal relationships, no family, no society, no community, and the courtship which yields his taming and healing is both personal and societal. Lovemaking is equated with illness in a pivotal scene in which Molly seduces Harry in the process reassuring him that his sexuality is not "weird" as his ex-fiancé termed it (137–41). Krentz's metaphor for this lovemaking is a glass bridge which Harry wishes to cross but on which he feels in danger, particularly when he is emotionally involved with his partner (141). Molly helps him cross it, and they achieve intimacy. The self-described "distant . . . remote . . . uncommunicative . . . cold" hero (121) gives the lie to all of these labels. To secure their new-found relationship, to keep it safe, Harry and Molly must solve the suspense plot by identifying the stalker who is threatening Molly.

Molly not only heals Harry via the right kind of sex, she tames him as well, and then she tames his family, providing Harry with the sort of community that treats him as one of its own rather than exploiting him. She lays down two demands: "[I]n honor of his forthcoming marriage [to her], I want a bachelor party for Harry. A real bachelor party. One that will be attended by every able-bodied male on both sides of the family. No excuses will be accepted" (325). The other: "I want everyone on both sides of Harry's family to attend the wedding. Anyone who is not there will find it extremely difficult to get to Harry at any time during the next fifty or sixty years" (325). Krentz capitalizes on the meaning of the celebration/fete/wedding element of the romance when she has her heroine deliver these ultimatums to the hero's family. They must stop treating him as the solution to all their problems as well as the family scapegoat and must begin to treat him as a true relative. This is especially true for the hero's ex-fiancé, who has married another member of the hero's extended family. She must stop psychoanalyzing him, stop treating him as a headcase. The solution to the various problems presented in *Absolutely Positively* is broader than the solution in *The Adventurer.*

The Krentzian archetype of the adventurer has no assigned setting (unlike the pirate or, as we shall see, the cowboy). He is a quester or seeker; thus his archetype works well as a detective, someone who finds out secrets.

In *The Cowboy* (1980) heroine Maggie Lark is the third of the romance writer friends in the trilogy first published by Harlequin. Like Kate and Sarah, Maggie is a self-supporting woman, acting from a belief in affective individualism, in possession of her own property, and believing in companionate marriage. In this case, the heroine has missed making a companionate marriage with the hero Rafe Cassidy himself, a cowboy in the businessman style, "overwhelming, fierce, dangerous" (21). A business competitor calls him an "outlaw" (60). When he returns to look for her, she reminds herself that he was the sort of man who "homed in on weakness the way a predator homed in on prey" (30). He is also "the hero . . . of every book she's ever written" (205). The courtship begins *in medias res,* resuming the broken off courtship that is part of the backstory of the novel. That relationship ended with Rafe accusing Maggie of having betrayed him in business by disclosing key information to her employer, Rafe's competitor, about Rafe's business dealings. Maggie accuses Rafe of withholding from her his being in competition with her employer to begin with. Both feel betrayed. This double-cross is part of the barrier as Rafe renews the courtship. The courtship has a history, the lingering sense of betrayal that both heroine and hero feel, and it has another, residual issue: Rafe works too hard.

Heroine and hero are thrown together by Maggie's father's courtship of Mrs. Cassidy, the heroine's mother. Rafe invites Maggie to his Tucson ranch, where he knows that she must go if she is to understand what her father is up to. There they confront the past and each other. They renew their love affair: "Rafe was the only man who had ever been able to do this to her, the only one who could bring her to arousal with only a look and a kiss and a touch" (88). They fight through all of the other barrier issues. Again, the heroine heals the hero with sex. The year they have been apart he described himself as having been "to hell and back" (67).

Cowboy begins and ends with a wedding, bringing the trilogy full circle. It begins at Sarah Fleetwood Trace's wedding to Gideon. It ends with Maggie's marriage to Rafe. She informs her two romance writer friends in a telegram: "Married a cowboy. Definitely an old-fashioned kind of guy. Code of the West, etc. A little rough around the edges but fantastic in the saddle" (250). The double entendre, the arch reference to the code of the West (which Rafe actually follows), the twice-begun courtship itself, all reflect a layered, complex version of the elements of the romance, Krentz's signature arch but sincere tone and her sophisticated knowledge of the genre are also reflected in this medium-length Harlequin .

Shield's Lady (1989) is set on a lost colony of Earth, inhabited by humans whose social institutions are different from those of a twentieth-century Western society on Earth. Krentz calls this book and others like it that she has written a "futuristic." In classic science-fiction fashion (she cites both Andre Norton and Robert Heinlein as part of her early reading), Krentz invents a new planet, Windarra, and peoples it with a society of humans who are "lost" to their colonial forebears (Mussell, "Interview with Krentz" 6). Whereas science fiction and fantasy writers typically invent new forms of politics, war, alternate mythological systems, or material culture, Krentz invents new forms of courtship and marriage. In so doing, she makes intimacy more intimate than it is on twentieth-century Earth. This is a goal of much of the romance that she writes, but in the futuristics, it takes center stage.

Heroine Sariana Dayne serves as a financial steward/business manager to the Avylyn Clan which resides on the western side of the planet. Her own people are from the east, and excel in business; they, like Sariana, often come west to earn a stake. For all her otherworldliness, however, she is like the earthly twentieth-century heroines we have seen—acting for her own happiness (believers in affective individualism) and possessed of her own property (property rights are intact on Windarra, and women are educated so that they, too, can participate in the economy). She is not a believer, however, in companionate marriage; in her homeland, the east, marriage is "first and foremost a business arrangement" (53).

It is the hero who is truly exotic; he increases exponentially the possibilities for intimacy. Gryph Chassyn is a Shield, a member of a clan of warriors who can make fertile marriages with only very few women. All of the resulting children have always been male, which means that the Shields have always been a male clan whose members must, to perpetuate themselves, seek wives from outside the clan. Lovemaking involves the extraordinary "crossover effect" of the consciousness and physical sensations of one partner being experienced by the other (157). The barrier in *Shield's Lady* is, for a time, Sariana's ignorance of what amounts to a private wedding ceremony that takes place before she experiences the crossover effect for the first time (her first experience of sleeping with the hero). The larger barrier implied by this is the barrier that always remains between lovers in the universe that the readers of this book actually inhabit—the barrier of gender, imposed by the different constitutions of men and women, both physical and emotional. Sariana and Gryph inhabit a world in which this barrier is overcome. Intimacy is the final frontier, and Krentz postulates this means of conquering it.

In becoming a Shield's lady simply through the private ceremony of sleeping with Gryph and experiencing the crossover effect, she tames him with sex. For him, at that point, the barriers fall. For her, however, the important barrier of understanding the significance of having experienced the crossover effect remains. Her ignorance of western customs and laws— the law recognizes their marriage as legal—stands in the way of the married couple going forward together. The novel thus follows a marriage of convenience pattern, in which the hero/husband must win the heroine/wife. In *Shield's Lady* the power of science fiction to postulate alternate kinds of reality is harnessed to the romance novel to create, quite simply, a new kind of love, one in which the final barriers to intimacy are removed, and intimacy itself is made more intimate.

For Krentz the cowboy archetype is in a typical setting—the frontier— and he confronts the elements there: Rafe, who does not so much manifest the archetype as invoke it (even though he lives on a ranch), finds himself in challenging business territory and has a "shootout" with a business rival. Gryph is a member of a western clan that truly acts as hired guns or mercenaries and finds himself, with the heroine, seeking the recovery of stolen property in the wilds of the western part of the planet.

Similarities in the Krentzian hero types are, finally, more important than the differences among them. All of them are individuals—they chart their own course (pirate), quest (adventurer), or drift (cowboy). All of them are unconstrained—by law (pirate), by physical obstacles (adventurer), or by civilization (cowboy). All of them fulfill the code they live under—to foil oppressive laws (pirate), to win the quest (adventurer), to endure against the elements (cowboy). Before the heroine heals them, all of them are injured. Before the heroine tames them, all of them are dangerous.

Healing and taming are the powers that Krentz's women have. In the systematic exploration of men that Krentz conducts in her romance novels, the men are dangerous and women are always very intelligent. They are also headstrong; they do not follow advice very well. The combination of dangerous men and heedless women results in a courtship that is a clash of wills and wit. It has energy, a brisk pace, and a sensuality that often owes a great deal to dramatic irony. In *Deception*, Jared finds himself entranced by Olympia (which the reader realizes); the narration carrying this information, however, is told from his point of view, and his feelings and thoughts are unspoken. Olympia does not hear them. This ignorance of his feelings for her is, paradoxically, her power. Without knowing that she is doing so, she arrests his attention, quickens his breathing, and, this being a rather racy Regency, erects a part of his anatomy. In *Absolutely, Positively,* Harry undergoes similar moments. In *Shield's Lady,* Gryph, inhabiting Krentz's alternate universe where lovemaking with a true mate furnishes twice the physical intensity that ordinary Earth-bound lovemaking does, undergoes this experience with the heroine, and she with him, before she understands what it means.

Krentz concentrates the core romance through her understanding of the genre's hero, her willingness to write heroines every bit as strong as the heroes themselves, and her ability to write witty, intelligent, fast-paced scenes. The result is intense courtships and potent, memorable books.

17

ONE MAN,
ONE WOMAN

Nora Roberts

Since 1981, Nora Roberts (1950–) has published over 150 novels, most of them romance. As J. D. Robb she has written a series of police procedurals set in the New York City of the future with a female homicide detective as a heroine. She wrote at least one early title as Jill March (Fallon 174). Roberts has proven to be prolific, inventive, and extremely flexible. She writes in virtually every romance subgenre. She is also very popular. She is, simply, a master of the romance novel form.

Like Dailey and Krentz, Roberts began her career writing short contemporaries, in her case, for Silhouette. In 1979 and 1980, Roberts first submitted manuscripts to Harlequin. She explains, "I got the standard rejection for the first couple of tries, then my favorite rejection of all time. I received my manuscript back with a nice little note which said that my work showed promise, and the story had been very entertaining and well done. But that they [Harlequin] already had their American writer. That would have been Janet Dailey" (Mussell, "Interview with Roberts" 155). Silhouette, which was formed in 1980, stood ready to exploit this decision by Harlequin's editors whose rejection of Roberts proved to be so amazingly short-sighted. Silhouette saw opportunity where Harlequin did not. Roberts went on to write one hundred short contemporaries for Silhouette. Most are still in print; many have been reissued by Jove. Only the most popular romance novelists have a backlist this active. According to *USA Today*, in 1999, Roberts wrote four of the five best-selling romance titles and was the top romance author of that year based on sales ("The Year In Books"). In 2000, Roberts again wrote four of the top five romance novels (no top romance author was named) (Blais and DeBarrow). Counting both hardback and paperback novels, she has had a remarkable sixty-eight releases on the *New York Times* Best Sellers List over a decade-long period ending in October 2001 (Onorato). (Of course, the *Times* has never reviewed any of those titles.) Arguably, Roberts is the most successful romance writer writing at the turn of the twenty-first century.

She is also one of the best. Roberts has a deep understanding of the genre itself and writes fluently in all of the subgenres of romance. She manipulates the basic elements in a masterful way. She has a keen ear for dialogue, constructs deft scenes, maintains a page-turning pace, and provides compelling characterization. Her early work for Silhouette showed the intensity she would bring to this genre; since then, she has matured into a masterful storyteller. Roberts's heroes and heroines, and the courtships she has them enact reflect the long tradition of the romance, the importance of affective individualism, of financial independence, and of companionate marriage for the heroine, as well as the taming and the healing of the hero. Seven works chosen from her earliest to her most recent will demonstrate Roberts's contribution to the romance. *Irish Thoroughbred* (1981) and *Loving Jack* (1989) will illustrate her work in the short contemporary for Silhouette. *Hidden Riches* (1994) will show her at home in the work of romantic suspense; *Montana Sky* (1996) her mastery of the romance set in the American West; and three recent releases, a trilogy about the same family, *Sea Swept* (1998), *Rising Tides* (1998), and *Inner Harbor* (1999) illustrate her mature work in the pure romance—all of these are books that Roberts has called "one man, one woman love stories" (Mussell, "Interview with Roberts" 157).

In 1981, Silhouette published *Irish Thoroughbred* when Roberts was new to writing and the outcome of Silhouette's challenge to Harlequin was uncertain. Roberts explains the difference between the two publishing houses: "Silhouette took the Harlequin framework, the constants such as the one man/one woman love story, the sexual tension, the emotional commitment, the conflict and happy ending, then let its . . . writers give it all a modern and very American spin. . . . The American market was poised for the change, for stronger heroines, less domineering heroes, for more contemporary themes" (Mussell, "Interview with Roberts" 153).

In this, her first published work, we see the influence of the Harlequin romances Roberts had been reading (Mussell, "Interview with Roberts" 156). Hero Travis is domineering, and heroine Adelia is orphaned, even if she is not helpless. Travis owns the horse farm on which Adelia's aged uncle works as a trainer and where Adelia goes to work as an exercise girl, so the power relationship between hero and heroine is that of boss to employee. This is also an artifact of the Harlequins of the 1970s, where the heroine typically held a job but was not pursuing a career. The barrier in this novel turns the tables a bit on earlier barriers. Whereas in many earlier short contemporaries angry heroes were common, *Irish Thoroughbred* has an angry heroine, who is very quick to take offense and not at all backward about telling off the hero. Eventually, her desire for the hero clashes with her morals, and the heroine resolves to stay away from him.

The heroine, although influenced by the Harlequin "Cinderella" heroine, is very much the product of the literary tradition stretching from Hull through Stewart and Heyer to Dailey. She lost her farm in Ireland when it was "sold for taxes" (6) and had to immigrate to America to live with her one remaining relative, her uncle, but she is an affective individual nonetheless. She muses, "She would manage. Hadn't she always managed? She was determined not to be a burden to her uncle. . . . There would be work for her, she reasoned, perhaps on the horse farm her uncle had written of. . . . She was strong . . . and, she reminded herself with an unconscious squaring of shoulders, she was a Cunnane" (7–8). She has lost her property: the farm in Ireland had been hers, left to her when her parents died. Soon enough, however, she has a job on the horse farm as an exercise girl and stablehand (64). She can ride any horse.

The hero, Travis Grant, owner of the farm, is described, in Adelia's point of view, as "a great, thundering blackguard" (213), an "ill-mannered, bad-tempered brute of a man without a brain working in his empty head" (65), and, like all men, a "beast" (78). These characterizations of the hero in the dangerous man mode take place in the heroine's consciousness and offer a fair example of *her* need for taming, as well as his. She has a hair-trigger temper.

The marriage-of-convenience plot typically places the betrothal and wedding before the declaration, which is to say, before the barrier falls. In fact, the marriage itself often becomes part of the barrier, as the vows that the couple has taken create the appearance of a commitment before heroine and hero actually commit to each other. In this structure, the declaration fells the barrier so that the marriage already contracted stands as a true marriage. *Irish Thoroughbred* follows this structure, and it delays the taming of both heroine and hero. The heroine's temper keeps the hero at arm's length; she is angry because she is convinced that he does not love her. To tell her this, he must keep her from leaving, which he does by restraining her physically (211). He physically demonstrates his dangerousness; she speaks her unwillingness to be tamed right up until the last scene, when the marriage of convenience becomes a companionate one. Each tames the other through love.

The courtship in this work is characterized by Adelia's flights of temper and Travis's authoritative responses. This is the most traditional of the courtships in the works examined here and partakes most fully of the Harlequins Roberts had been reading. The twist is that Adelia's temper is presented as an element of her Irishness, but Travis's authoritative imperiousness is simply his stature as the more powerful of the two characters—he is her employer, he is nine years her senior, he is rich. The marriage of convenience helps to prolong this imbalance. *Irish Thoroughbred*, despite its position at the very beginning of Roberts's long list of novels, demonstrates a command of the romance form and an understanding of the dynamics between heroine, hero, and the nature of their courtship that belies its novice author.

In *Loving Jack* (1989), named for the heroine, Jackie, we have a partial exchange of the usual roles of the hero and heroine of the romance novel. Jack is a rich young woman who has not quite found her career niche and who has decided to try writing romance novels. She sublets a house in Florida from her own cousin, which turns out not to be his to sublet. It is owned by the hero, who comes home and wants it back. Heroine and hero both end up living there for a few months. The barrier between Jack and the hero, Nathan, an architect, includes his work, which keeps him on the road and very busy, and, internally, his carefulness, need to plan, and need to control outcomes—a contrast to her openness, her spontaneity, and her willingness to adapt. She is a person completely at home in her own skin. He is a person who questions everything, especially himself. Her declaration for him comes very early (page 95 of a 221-page novel) but he does not reciprocate until much later (page 220).

Jack (note the male nickname) is an affective individual in a particularly American mode: she is described in the novel's third sentence as "wide-open to emotions—her own and everyone else's (5). She is also the daughter of a rich family who has dabbled in a bit of everything—Harvard, cooking school, architecture—without finishing anything. In the course of the book she writes and sells a romance novel (214). At the book's beginning, she has property; at its end, she has the independence that a career lends a life. Jackie believes in companionate marriage and is completely honest about her quite strong feelings for the hero at an early stage in the book.

Roberts depicts Nathan, the hero, as an alpha male through Jack's comparison of him to the hero she's writing in her romance, which happens to be a Western: "The body lean and hard," a "bony face . . . shadowed by the beard he didn't bother to shave. . . . He wasn't a good man, not through and through. It would be up to the heroine to mine the gold from him" (14–15). Jack is daydreaming at this time, and the hero, dressed not as a cowboy but in a business suit, interrupts her. Thus the mythic hero, the cowboy, underlies Nathan. Like a cowboy, Nathan does not believe he should settle down. His reasons for this are rooted in his own family. His mother told him that had he not been born "her marriage could have been saved. Without the responsibility of a child she could have traveled with [his] father." He claims that marriage for him would be wrong (199). This hero must be healed. The heroine heals him by fighting with him. "Absurd is loving someone and having them love you right back, then refusing to do anything solid about it because maybe, just maybe, it wouldn't work out perfectly" (200). When he claims that he cares "too much to go into this [marriage] with two strikes against" him, she replies in absolute anger: "You care too much. . . . Damn you for that, Nathan. For not having the guts to say you love me, even now" (201).

The courtship in this novel consists of the hero, who desires control, and the heroine, who values spontaneity, enacting this ancient battle within the structure of a marriage-of-convenience novel (with the marriage dispensed with). The couple lives under the same roof, and soon enough, are sleeping in the same bed as well. Her spontaneity transforms into verbal wit, and he finds himself kidnapped both verbally and, once, physically, as she injects as much lightness and warmth into his life as one person can. The book is funny. He responds with a growing appreciation for a person who had seemed at first glance to be a scatterbrain; eventually, he responds with passion.

Ritual death in the book is straightforward: the hero leaves on a business trip and the heroine goes home. Before they separate, Roberts writes a stormy confrontation between heroine and hero in which he reveals that his birth, from his mother's point of view, had been a mistake and had ruined is mother's marriage to his father. The hero's own abortion or non-conception is what is contemplated here; it puts at stake his very existence. Symbolically, this is the point in the romance novel where the heroine's existence is ordinarily hazarded. Roberts's use of the hero at this juncture reinforces the turning of the tables that she has effected between the traditional roles of heroine and hero in the short contemporary romance novel. Jack (again, note the masculine name) is stronger than Nathan: healthier, more certain of her wants and needs, and more honest. Nathan, however, is put at risk, symbolically and emotionally, in this form of ritual death which signals the relationship's apparent impossibility at the same time that it explains why the hero is so independent, remote, and unwilling to commit himself: he believes himself to be a man without a family. The heroine leaves at this point, reinforcing ritual death.

With this statement of the heroine to her father, "It is worse than pitiful for a grown man to cheat at Scrabble" we are introduced in one line of dialogue to a relationship between the heroine and this minor character whom we like instantly (209). Roberts introduces Jack's family; families of heroines and heroes are characteristic inclusions in her more mature work. In the end, the hero changes far more than the heroine, for through their courtship, which she engineers, she shows him where love comes from, where we all learn it. In *Loving Jack* there is no character who approximates the old heroines and heroes of the early 1970s short contemporaries. She is independent and self-directed. So is he. They meet as equals.

Hidden Riches (1994), a hardcover release, is a work of romantic suspense, a subgenre of the romance that Roberts is completely at home in. The crime is art smuggling. The heroine, Dora Conroy, buys what she thinks is a piece of contemporary art for her antique/curio shop. It is really a painted-over Monet. The hero, police captain Jed Skimmerhorn, who has recently resigned from the force, ends up working on this case.

The heroine is an affective individual—she owns her own business as well as the building that houses it. While she is away on a buying trip for her shop, her matchmaking father, scheming to put his daughter in close proximity to a likely single man, rented the second apartment to hero Skimmerhorn. Her response to the final line of her father's note, "I couldn't think of anything nicer to give my adored daughter than an intriguing neighbor," is "Sorry Dad . . . you're in for another disappointment" (32). This rejection of an attempt at dynastic marriage—however much it seems like innocent matchmaking—demonstrates that the heroine's commitment to companionate marriage is firm.

The hero is indeed dangerous. Dora finds him drinking whiskey. He is "tall with a tough, athletic build that made her think of a boxer. . . . His face, shadowed by the high slash of cheekbones and the stubble of a beard, seemed grim" (30). He has quit the police force because his sister, the victim of a blackmailer's bomb, is dead; he believes she died because he could not react in time to save her. He does not need money; his family is wealthy. He does need to be healed from the effects of both his parents' bad marriage and his sister's death (413). At the novel's beginning, his family, both at work and domestically, is in disarray. Dora's is supportive, warm, and intact.

The courtship consists of interactions between Dora and Jake which fairly quickly establish the basics of the barrier—he cannot commit because he has been wounded by his own upbringing, his parents' unhappy marriage. Later, Dora is almost killed by the smugglers seeking the Monet. Jake sees this as a near duplication of his failure to save his sister: Dora almost bleeds to death from gunshot wounds. He gets to her just in time. These serious barriers, however, are enacted throughout in a bantering, witty, funny series of interactions.

> "I know," she said at his shoulder. "You went back on the force, and now you're undercover." She caught his soft oath as he turned. "What is it, an international jewel thief? A ring of insidious paté burglars?"
> "Conroy. Do you have to be everywhere?" (149–51)

They interact similarly in the solution to the crime: the smuggling of the artwork. Dora is involved because the smugglers figure out that she has the painting. She participates in the police investigation, and Jed, having returned to the force, is a part of that investigation.

Her warmth and good nature heal him, let him see that something other than his parents' acrimonious relationship is possible. This hero needs to be tamed as well; the ritual death of the romance plot accomplishes this taming. The smugglers shoot her, and her near death and painful convalescence force him to reexamine his decision to keep her out of his life:

> "You were right. Everything you said was right. I didn't want you to get too close, and I made certain you couldn't. You were one of the

main reasons I went back on the job, but I didn't share it with you because I would have had to admit that it mattered. That what you thought of me mattered. It was deliberate." (449)

The violence of this work is not gratuitous: Roberts makes it part of the romance plot, part of the barrier, the courtship, and the recognition.

In writing romantic suspense, Roberts follows in the footsteps of the writer she calls "the queen," Mary Stewart. Citing Stewart as one of her "earliest influences," Roberts notes the "strong characters, vivid settings, tension and romance" as being a primary reason for adding suspense to her work (Mussell, "Interview with Roberts" 156). Indeed, Roberts manipulates the courtship in similar ways, giving heroine and hero the dual roles of lover/detective, adding true danger to the plot, and making the quest for the missing art parallel the quest for the recognition of the hero's love for the heroine.

Nora Roberts sets *Montana Sky* (1996) on Mercy Ranch, whose patriarch, Jack Mercy, has just died. The ranch is on the edge of the frontier, with the usual divisions of law and civilization represented by human settlement at the ranch, and lawlessness and the wild represented by the surrounding wilderness. Roberts complicates this dichotomy found in many Westerns by disordering the civilization that the ranch represents. Jack leaves his land to his three daughters, half sisters all, who do not know each other at the book's beginning. Jack's habit of marrying a woman, fathering a daughter, and then divorcing has resulted in a set of siblings scattered from California to Montana to Virginia. The half sisters must reassemble to secure their inheritance for their father has stipulated that they cannot inherit unless they all live on the ranch for a year after his death.

The half sisters are the novel's three heroines. Willa, the only daughter who grew up on Mercy, expected to inherit it free and clear. Tess, a Hollywood screenwriter, is unhappy at the prospect of living in the middle of nowhere for a year. Only Lily, a schoolteacher who is the victim of an abusive husband, and is, at the book's opening, the target of this now ex-husband-turned-stalker, is happy to spend a year on the ranch which promises a security that she has not known in recent years. Willa's affective individualism has turned her, essentially, into a cowboy. She is the "operator" of Mercy, making the decisions and taking part in all of the work: driving cows, riding fences, and castrating bulls. Her attachment to it is fierce, composed of equal parts sweat equity and a desire to prove herself able to do what is still very much a man's job. Tess is the affective individualist through her career: she is a self-supporting screenwriter, unattached and ambitious. Only Lily's affective individualism has wavered. She has taught school but has recently been on the run from her stalking husband who is following her as she moves from place to place. Willa regards Tess and Lily as usurpers, undeserving of a portion of the ranch that she has always worked hard to help run. Tess regards Willa and the ranch as unacceptably remote from her concerns, yet representing such a financial interest that walking away from the inheritance was not an option. Lily regards the world as such a threatening place that the security represented by her sisters and the ranch they all will own together outweighs her shyness. Desperate for security, she will accept it even from her sisters who are strangers to her.

Each half sister has property in her inheritance of a part interest in Mercy. This property is conditional, however, in that each needs to live out the year on the ranch in order for any of them to inherit. Overseeing this forced cohabitation (a family of convenience, if you will, rather than a marriage of convenience) are the three heroes: two neighboring ranchers, Ben McKinnon and Nate Torrance who are named as legal guardians for the duration of the year. A third, Willa's half brother Adam Wolfchild, lives on the ranch; he is a spiritual support for Willa, and, eventually, for the other sisters as well.

Companionate marriage is remote from the minds of the women as well as the men with the exception of Adam. Cowboy Willa is as much in need of taming as neighboring cowboy Ben, probably more so. In an early scene where he comes upon her skinning a bear she has had to shoot, he says to her, "You're a pretty thing, Willa. I believe that's the first time I've ever said that over bear guts. . . . We can get this whole thing [the guardianship] over quick. Just get ourselves married and be done with it" (38–39). Willa meets this offer of dynastic marriage with scorn. Willa does not, at this point in the book, consciously believe in companionate marriage, but she certainly rejects the obvious matchmaking of her father, who had always coveted adjacent McKinnon land, and had, she knows, offered her hand to Ben in exchange for 10,000 acres. When she considers her half sisters' one-year stint on the ranch, she also sees it in a dynastic light: "If the daughter who had stood beside him her entire life, had worked beside him, had sweated and bled into the land wasn't lure enough—well, he had two more" (30). Screenwriter Tess is simply anxious to return to her life in Hollywood and intends to do just that when the year elapses. Marriage of any kind is not an option for her. Lily has been so wounded by marriage, literally and figuratively, that it is not an option at the novel's outset either. For all three women, for different reasons, making a companionate marriage at this point seems remote.

The ranch is located on two frontiers: first, the wilderness of Montana lies just across the fences that Willa works so hard to maintain; second, the unsettled disorder of Jack Mercy's fragmented family is a wilderness which family members must negotiate in order to win the ranch and form new families as members of a harmonious new society.

The heroes, suitors for these unmarried women, come in the form of three local cowboys. The two trustees, Ben McKinnon, owner of Three Rocks Ranch, courts Willa, and Nate Torrance, ranch owner and attorney, finds himself drawn to Tess. Adam, Willa's half brother (and thus no blood relation to Jack), is drawn to the wounded Lily. They are, each of them, cowboys, not in the mythic sense that Krentz sometimes applies to a businessman-hero, but in the actual sense. They run, or help run, ranches. They ride horses and punch cows. They do not need to make a long emotional journey in this novel, for here, they are the tamers rather than the tamed. Roberts can stand the usual romance convention on its head in this way because the heroes are, indeed, so literally dangerous—at home with unbroken horses, knives, and guns—and because death itself threatens everyone in the novel in the form of a murderer on the loose.

Three distinctive courtships take place. Ben courts Willa, without either of them quite knowing it at first, in scenes such as the bear-skinning skirmish recounted above. They "butt heads" as he calls it, over his supervision of her operation of Mercy Ranch. Emotions intensify as the murderer threatens. Lily is almost killed, and when Ben and Willa return from rescuing her, a scene typical of their courtship ensues. He insists that, immediately, she rest, and that for the near future she "stop riding out alone" (364). She refuses. He threatens to enlist Nate, the other guardian and adds, "You butt against me on this, you risk losing Mercy." He wrestles her to the ground, then lets her up.

> He could have forced her down again. It would have been easier than saying what he had to say. "I care about you, Willa. I've got feelings for you, and they go pretty deep." It was harder yet when she turned and stared at him. "Maybe I don't know what the hell to do with them, but they're there. . . ."
>
> "Threatening me is sure a damn fool way of showing them." (365)

Later in the same scene she says, "Maybe I've got feelings too. . . . I don't want to punch you every time I see you these days, so maybe I do" (365). This physical courtship between a dangerous man, and, in this case, a dangerous woman is by turns amusing and alarming. The betrothal scene is especially so: Ben finds Willa mending a fence, and he proposes to her with one eye on the hammer that "she'd picked up to hit him with" (466). This hero and heroine live an elemental, violent life. They court through confrontation—there is even a wrestling scene that recalls childhood play. Yet there is another tone to their courtship as well. Midway through the novel, at a New Year's party planned by Lily, the domestic half sister staying out her year at the ranch, Ben kisses Willa "so all the men eyeing you know whose brand you're wearing these days" (195). Later in the same scene, Ben, spinning a fantasy, says "I always think of that last minute between years as untime"—a time of unreality between last year and next year. He asks Willa to kiss him. When she does, and the New Year ticks into being, she says, "It is real . . . it is" (198). He has tamed her as much as she has tamed him.

The courtships of the other two heroines are more straightforward. Lily, who arrives at Mercy Ranch literally bruised from her battering ex-husband, is healed by Adam's patience and understanding. "Adam was so patient," she thought. "And he was gentle as a mother with the horses. With her as well." (197). Adam and Lily also share a midnight kiss at the New Year's party. We see it from Willa's point of view. Ben says, "That's a pretty sight," and Willa thinks, "Even through her own confusion, she had to admit it was. Adam, with his hands cupped on Lily's face, and Lily's fingers holding his wrists" (198). Adam himself needs to be tamed as he confronts the limits of his ability to save and help Lily. Kidnapped and imprisoned in a cave by the murderer, Lily makes it through the hideous ordeal of his threatening her, then is rescued not from the killer (who is no longer a threat at this point) but from the elements—the cold—a far less threatening force. Adam unwillingly accepts the limits of his ability to protect Lily and of her need to be protected. Adam says to her,

> "I let him take you."
> "No."
> "I thought he would kill you."
> "Adam."
> "I thought if I touched you it would make you think of it, of him."
> "No, no Adam. . . . I won't break."
> But he might. (379)

Like Persephone, Lily emerges from the clutches of the evil ruler of the dark world she has been taken to and marries her protector/rescuer. Adam is healer and tamed. Lily is healed and tamer. Their courtship has an elegiac tone, punctuated by the violence that stalks Lily.

Tess's courtship is even more straightforward than Lily's. Nate Torrance simply outwaits her. Between Tess the screenwriter and Nate, the barrier is her belief that she cannot live and work in an area as remote as Montana. Driving them together is sex—Roberts writes the steamiest sex scene in the novel for these two characters. Tess shows up at Nate's house and simply seduces him, much to his amused and somewhat stunned satisfaction. She explains, "I've been thinking about this since the first time I saw you" to which he replies, "[W]ell that makes two of us" (180). This charged atmosphere, if not this level of actual arousal, distinguishes this courtship. On her way into his house to seduce him, Tess must walk by a dead wildcat draped over the rail of the front porch. Nate is a lawyer and a cowboy, but this emblem of a more elemental dangerousness frightens Tess. She does not, however, associate it with him, at least not immediately. Instead, Roberts lets Tess characterize him differently:

> "And there he was, all gangling and sexy and Jimmy Stewart-ish in a high-backed leather chair behind a big oak desk. The desk lamp slanted light over his hands as he made notations on a yellow legal pad. His brow was knotted, his tie loose, his hair, all that thick gold of it, mussed. From his own hands, she noted, as he raked his fingers through it." (176)

Her thoughts conclude, "Well, well . . . just feel my heart go pitty-pat" (176). She underestimates him, a miscalculation that Roberts takes the rest of the novel to remedy. Yet at the same time, she manages to ensnare him. Like the relationship between Willa and Ben, this is a mutual taming.

Montana Sky demonstrates one of Roberts's strengths as a writer: the control of tone. This novel offers representations of three areas of behavior: first, the psychopathic acts of the threat to this Montana community from the murderer; much less seriously, the broadly drawn near caricature of Tess's mother (a former stripper) and the plans for Lily's wedding; finally, the serious, hard work of ranch life, the difficult legal issues besetting the Mercy Ranch, and the courting couples who inhabit this scene. The tone is regret, rage, and disgust in the murder scenes; warmth and laughter in the scenes with Tess's mother; and, the most "realistic" tone, objective and serious juxtaposed with wit in the scenes with the courting couples. Roberts manipulates tone across this range of events without false notes and without jarring shifts.

Roberts exploits the Western setting to juxtapose lawlessness and the danger that it visits upon those who must live there with the order of civilization and family. The marriages, particularly Lily's and Willa's, represent life in the face of death and civilization on the edge of the wilderness. Unlike Dailey, who has her heroines marry their kidnappers, Roberts finds in the West the boundary of the civilized and the wild, of the lawless and the law-abiding. Her courting characters restore peace to the wilderness through upholding the law. They hunt down and kill the "savages"—the murderers—then marry and found an ordered society in spite of the chaotic legacy of the patriarch.

Sea Swept (1998), *Rising Tides* (1998), and *Inner Harbor* (1999) constitute Roberts's Chesapeake Bay trilogy. In contrast to *Montana Sky*, where she concentrates on the women, in this trilogy, Roberts concentrates on the men—and on the boy who joins them. The Quinn family, whose members are patriarch Ray and adopted sons Cameron, Ethan, Phillip, and young Seth, is the focus of this work. All of the sons were street kids—"lost boys"—before Ray (and his wife, Stella) adopted them. In each book, one of three adult Quinn brothers chooses a wife, and the youngest would-be brother, Seth (his adoption is incomplete at the trilogy's beginning) moves a step away from his abusive birth mother and a step closer to a permanent place in the Quinn family.

Rumors fly in St. Christopher, a small waterman's town, that young Seth, who looks like the now-dead Ray, is actually Ray's illegitimate son by a former student at the college where Ray taught. The Quinn family's society is in disarray: Ray's reputation is in serious question; his adult sons must learn the secret of Seth's paternity; the boy must be made a part of the Quinn family. Roberts's theme is family-building, the stalwart heart of comedy and the core of the romance form: the result of the courtship, after all, is the continuation of the new society in the form of the next generation.

Ray's ghost is a character in all of the novels. He is the only paranormal character, and he appears only to the adult heroes of the novels, to Cameron, Ethan, and Phillip Quinn. Ray punctuates each romance with guidance from beyond the grave, the sort of cryptic, partial guidance that has been associated with the spirit world at least since Delphi. In *Sea Swept*, just before Cameron declares his love for the heroine Anna, Ray's ghost appears to him on the dock at the family home. In a brief conversation, he answers Cameron's "I want answers. I need answers" with "'You'll find them . . . when you slow down" (262). This does not solve the mystery of young Seth's paternity, but it proves to be the way for Cameron to recognize his love for Anna. A major part of the barrier has been Cameron's fast, unsettled lifestyle. In a cryptic way, Ray helps his son recognize this.

Heroine Anna Spinelli, social worker, is pursuing her career when she comes into the hero's life. Roberts introduces her with details that establish this heroine's affective individualism. Anna is driving, "deliriously thrilled with her spanking-new car. She'd worked her butt off, budgeted and juggled funds to afford the down payment. . . . as far as she was concerned, it would be worth every carton of yogurt she ate rather than a real meal." This heroine, like every Roberts heroine we have examined, is "devoted to her work" (42). She also believes in companionate marriage, although she is extremely wary of men, having once been raped. She needs to be healed, just a bit. She possesses the three characteristics of a twentieth-century romance heroine.

The hero, Cameron, is dangerous in at least two ways. He shares his brothers' past—as "lost boys"—a dangerous adolescence of abusive parents and living on the streets. Rescue and adoption by Ray and Stella Quinn saved him from early death. Cameron is also dangerous because he is in a risky profession. He is a hydrofoil racer with "working man's hands" and a "toughness about his face, a hardness that had to do with more than tanned skin tight over bones" (3). In an early scene his escort, a swimsuit-model arm-candy bimbo, has just enough insight to say to him, "You're a bad boy, Cameron," and he replies, "So I've always been told" (3). Later she calls him "animal, beast" (4).

The barrier between Anna and Cameron is, in part, the peripatetic playboy lifestyle of a champion hydrofoil racer featuring "champagne, generous casinos, [and] mindless, no-strings sex" (2). Anna hopes for a home, for stability, for permanence. Her profession, social work, forms another part of the barrier. Assigned to Seth's case, she is the official who must agree that the older brothers are fit guardians for the not-yet-adopted newcomer to the family.

Patriarch Ray Quinn's traditional role in comedy as the philandering *senex* is fulfilled, despite his death. The rumor that he has an illegitimate child forms a barrier between Cameron and Anna. If the rumor is true, it means that Ray betrayed the family and its reputation in the community is a sham. Anna sits in judgment as the social worker assigned to the case; she is the community's official voice.

Their courtship consists of wary circling interrupted by lustful attraction. Anna has a professional, and at first adversarial, relationship to Cameron. She sees herself as young Seth's advocate, and Cameron and his brothers as offering a less than desirable home for Seth. Cameron sees her as commitment and permanence. He admits that he does not "usually care one way or the other" about knowing women, quite aside from his desire to sleep with them (98). He believes, even as Anna seems to have abandoned him, that "he never worried about women" (309). Cameron's conversion to permanence has to take place so that he can keep Seth and win Anna. Their attraction is elemental, often against her better judgment, and it intensifies throughout the book. The betrothal scene takes place after ritual death (Anna unexpectedly leaves town), and after she has decided that she and Cam are not right for each other: "We don't want the same things. We were going nowhere, and I'm not going to keep heading there, no matter how I feel about you." He asks:

> "How do you feel about me?"
> "Tired of you!" she shouted. "Tired of me, tired of us. Sick and tired of telling myself fun and games could be enough. Well, it's not. Not nearly, and I want you out!" (326)

The scene reverts from anger to the mixture of slapstick, danger, and passion that Roberts manages so well. In response to his "You're in love with me, aren't you?" Anna says, "You arrogant, conceited, cold-blooded son of a bitch," and she throws a vase at him. The fruit in a fruit bowl follows, then the bowl itself. He threatens to kidnap her and fly with her to Vegas, and it is only when he utters the word "married" that her temper is "pierced" enough to realize what is happening: he has proposed.

In changing his mind about the sort of relationship he desires with Anna, Cameron makes not one, but two declarations of his commitment: first to Seth, whom he had been treating as a duty, and then to Anna. In male-speak he declares to the boy, "There's that crappy attitude of yours, and you're ugly, but you kind of grow on a guy" (321). And to Anna, more conventionally, "I love you. It feels so damn perfect loving you. I can't believe I wasted so much time" (330).

The humor in this witty novel comes from the interaction of the three grown brothers with each other and with their sibling-to-be. Seth's adoption is left incomplete, and the mystery of Ray's past unsolved. Emotion and the family form the engine of this novel, the romance plot and the Seth-Cameron plot providing parallel challenges of commitment to the hero.

In *Rising Tides* the threat to the Quinn family (i.e., to the eventual adoption of Seth) is a life insurance company that threatens to withhold payment on Ray's policy, claiming that Ray has killed himself. A second threat is Seth's biological mother, who accepted a large payment from Ray to leave the boy with him, but who is capable of showing up in St. Christopher's and demanding her parental rights.

The heroine of this novel is Grace Monroe, a hometown girl and single mother, divorced from a man who "a month before Aubrey was born" had "taken her savings, her car, and most of her self-respect" when he left her (15). Despite this setback, she acts as an affective individual. In defiant response to hero Ethan's protest that she works too hard, she says,

> "That's right. I clean houses, I serve drinks, and now and then I pick crabs. That's how amazingly skilled and versatile I am. I also pay rent, insurance, medical bills, utilities, and a baby-sitter. I buy food, I buy clothes, gas. I take care of myself and my daughter. I don't need you coming around here telling me it's not right." (37)

She does not own much property—her car is her most valuable possession—but she aspires to the American dream in her desire to own her own home. Despite her failed first marriage, she still believes in companionate marriage. Grace demonstrates the range of Roberts's heroines. She has all of the characteristics of a twentieth-century heroine, but she is a woman in extremely modest circumstances. She is getting by, but just barely. She is a single parent. She has few illusions but has not lost hope.

The hero is an alpha male. Grace sees Ethan as having "the lean and rangy body that moves as easily as a dancer. . . . Innate grace . . . and still so blatantly male. He always looked as though he was walking the deck of a ship." His face was "bony and rugged and somewhere just at the edges of handsome" (35). The animality that the romance alpha male carries within himself is usually double edged, and in Ethan's case he feels that he cannot marry Grace, whom he has always loved, precisely because of that animality. "Lost boy" Ethan fears the "beast inside him" (100), a result of a childhood so damaged, so full of abuse, that he is convinced he will pass these tendencies on to any children he might have and that he will hurt Grace if he allows himself to be around her. Ray and his wife rescued Ethan from a mother who sold her son to male johns for drug money, and Ethan is convinced that this background, right down to his genes, will doom any family life he hopes to have.

Roberts understands that the worst danger the hero poses is to the heroine herself. Linking that danger with the healing that the hero must undergo yields a complex character, the form doing the work, rather than an elaborate delineation of the hero's character. Indeed, Ethan is, on the surface, the most straightforward, the "simplest" of the three adult Quinn brothers. This manipulation of form is part of the book's power and evidence of Roberts's skill.

Their courtship takes place in two sorts of scenes. In one sort Aubrey, Grace's two-year-old, is always present and is a unifying and mediating force. In one masterful scene, Ethan has come to Grace's house to apologize for telling her how to live her life the night before when he saw her, dressed provocatively, serving drinks in the bar in which she worked. Grace is outside ready to mow the lawn, and daughter Aubrey is in the sandbox with a phalanx of stuffed animals. Ethan bobbles his apology: "Look, Grace, I'm sorry if I was out of line last night." She replies, "If?" Throughout this failed conversation, tiny Aubrey runs to her friend Ethan to be kissed herself, then to have each of her stuffed animals kissed as well (43). Eventually, she demands that Ethan kiss her mother, which he does, he thinks, chastely, touching "his lips lightly to hers" (45). The reaction of heroine and hero to this slightest of contacts and to the subsequent conversation over a lawn mower defies the extreme domestic setting of this scene. "She didn't have a clue, he decided, what it had done to his usually well-disciplined hormones to have her trim little butt snugged back against him. What it did to the usually moderate temperature of his blood to have all that long, bare leg brushing against his" (47).

A second sort of courtship scene involves seduction. Grace stages a seduction of Ethan. This scene is enacted slowly. Roberts plans it right down to the wardrobe: Grace has put on a dress that she wore to a wedding, with tiny buttons down the front. She begins by unbuttoning one. Ethan says, "Stop Grace. . . . Don't do that." She assumes that he means not to make love to him. He, however, says, "Let me do it," and he unbuttons the dress (164). This languid pace and detailed description continues, unrelenting, until both partners are satisfied. Roberts has an unusual ability to describe the varieties of sexual interaction in such a way that it contributes to the character development of each heroine and hero. Grace put away her own desires when her very young husband left her and Aubrey was born. Ethan is deliberate. The love scene reflects this without losing any of its passion.

Ray's ghost appears to Ethan at the point of ritual death, at the point where Ethan has explained to an uncomprehending and increasingly angry Grace that he cannot marry her because he is so tainted by his past that he dares not risk harming her. Ethan's habit, at times like this, is to think his way slowly through a problem. Ray says, "Got it all figured out yet?" Ethan replies, "Not exactly. I can't seem to think it through so it gets clear." And Ray then recommends that Ethan not follow his usual pattern: "Sometimes you have to go with the gut instead of the head. You've got good instincts, Ethan" (323). Ray's appearance is the death (he is, after all, a ghost) that marks this prolonged ritual death, one in which no character, main or secondary, is actually threatened with bodily harm. *Rising Tides* is a book in which the characters carry such a weight of family-shredding history—Ethan was an unwilling child prostitute, Grace was abandoned as a young, pregnant wife—that Ray as the marker of ritual death signals the formal element without adding bodily harm, either threatened or actual, to the load of misery in this domestic society. The languid love scenes, the courtship itself, heals Ethan as it gives him time to realize that he can make a marriage and that he should not let his horrible childhood rob him of the chance to have a happy adulthood.

Sybill, the heroine of *Inner Harbor,* is the most accomplished of the trilogy's three heroines. She is an urban anthropologist with several best-selling nonfiction books to her credit. The most independent of these affective individualist heroines, she can "write her own ticket" (35). She has property too, in the form of an independent income. What she does not have (at the beginning of the book) is much of a belief in companionate marriage. She admits at a difficult moment that she is "not good with emotions. Reactions and behavioral patterns are more my forte" (154). She needs to be healed.

Hero Philip Quinn, the third brother, is in advertising in Baltimore, the scene of his own scarred childhood. As a child he was the victim of a drive-by gang shooting and had been a gang member himself: Stella and Ray Quinn took him from the hospital room where his life had narrowly been saved after two bullets just missed his heart. As an adult he prefers "the single life and all its benefits" (13). The heroine sees him first as he helps his brother hang a sign at their boatbuilding business:

She caught herself goggling. This, she thought, was a prime example of sheer male beauty.

Then he was bellying over the edge again, grabbing for the chain, hauling it into place. And swearing ripely. When he rose, he scowled at the long tear down the front of his shirt where she supposed it had caught on something on the roof.

"I just bought this sucker."

"It was real pretty, too," Cam called up.

"Kiss my ass," Phillip suggested, and tugged the shirt off to use it to mop sweat off his face.

Oh, well, now, she thought, appreciating the view on a purely personal level. The young American god, she decided. Designed to make females drool. (32–33)

At the point of ritual death in the courtship, he wishes to see her, to apologize for insulting her, but she will not open the door to her hotel room. Phillip leaves the basketful of champagne, caviar, and roses on the floor in front of her door, walks down the fire stairs, climbs up the side of the building, and enters her hotel room through her balcony door. This act of a former second-story man (part of his misspent youth) makes him dangerous—"bold and foolish"—in his behavior toward her (295).

Their courtship consists of a series of encounters that put them at odds over Seth's biological mother (Sybill's half sister). These are resolved by mid-novel, however, when Sybill becomes convinced that her sister really was as abusive a mother as the Quinns, including Seth, claim her to be. The attraction between heroine and hero, and the conclusion of their courtship, circles around the problem both of them have with commitment and the corresponding problem that the heroine has with intimacy. Philip's cheerful response to her hesitation is to "shanghai" her for a sail.

In their first lovemaking scene, in the sailboat, Phillip observes, using Sybill's behaviorist-speak, "As an objective observation, I have to conclude that you've never been ravished before" (195). At the end of this scene, after they've made love not once but twice, She says,

"We—this—can't continue."

"Not right this minute," he agreed. "Even I have my limitations."

"I didn't mean. . . . This was just a diversion, as you said. Something we both apparently needed on a physical level. And now—"

"Shut up, Sybill." He said it mildly, but she caught the edge of annoyance. "It was a hell of a lot more than a diversion, and we'll discuss it to pieces later." (196)

Then, realizing that she "was just beginning to feel awkward . . . uneasy with being naked, and with the situation," he threw her overboard and dove in after her (196–97).

Roberts's manipulation of the tone of this scene (despite its depiction of one steamy act of intercourse and the prelude to another), her ability to make it more than just a sex scene, to depict the strength and dangerousness of the hero (he, after all, kidnaps and ravages the heroine) as well as the passion and doubt of the heroine, and to do so with humor and wit— all of these features are characteristic of her mastery of the form, including one of its most reviled elements, the sex scene.

A second scene later in the novel demonstrates this mastery as well and is emblematic of the conclusion to the courtship. At Seth's eleventh birthday party the boy remembers details of the single time he had met his Aunt Sybill when he was a very young child. Sybill, overcome with emotion, rushes out of the party, and Phillip follows her. She cries, he drives her back to her hotel and promises not to leave her alone that night. He draws her a bath then extracts the entire story of her time with Seth eight years earlier. Later she awakens to find him beside her, and she makes love to him. Demonstrating her command of character, Roberts has Sybill initiating this lovemaking:

> "When you wake up in the middle of the night in bed with a woman, and she wants to seduce you, do you mind?"
> "Hardly ever."
> "Well, if you wouldn't mind. . . ."
> "I'll let you know when I start to mind. . . ."
> It was dark. She could be anything she wanted to be in the dark.
> "Maybe I won't stop if you do."
> "Threats?" He was every bit as surprised, and aroused, by the teasing purr of her voice as he was by the deliberate, circling trail of her fingertips down his body. "You don't scare me."
> "I can. . . . I will."
> "Give it your best shot. Jesus." His eyes all but crossed. "Bull's eye." (270–71)

This scene ends unhappily, as the hero, frightened by his realization that he loves the heroine, picks a fight with her on the morning after and leaves.

The ghost of Ray says of the heroine, "Lady up there, she's got you worried, though, because it's not just about sex. It's about love." Phillip denies this, "I'm not in love with her. Exactly. I'm just . . . involved." Ray points out, "Love was always a tough one for you" (291). Cameron needed to slow down, Ethan needed to trust his instinct, and Phillip needs to recognize love when he is in it. Ritual death in this case is once again marked by Ray's presence, although the heroine is convinced that she is about to lose contact with her nephew, again, and for good. Her loss is echoed in Ray's final appearance to Phillip. The scene ends with Ray giving Phillip a boost up to the first row of balconies of the hotel, the act a physical echo of the advice that he's given his son. The hero and heroine do not declare until the last page of the novel when they make parallel declarations. He says, "All my life I said I would never do this because there would never be a woman who would make me need to or want to. I was wrong. I found one. I found mine. Marry me, Sybill." She says, "All my life I said I would never do this because there would never be a man who'd need me or want me, or matter enough to make me want. I was wrong. I found you. Marry me, Phillip, and soon" (324). Phillip has healed Sybill, and each of them has tamed the other through passion and a willingness to break through the temptation to overanalyze their relationship.

Ray's character is the center of the mystery in this trilogy. His sons miss his guidance, but they question his motives in adopting Seth, wondering if Seth is the result of an affair Ray is said to have had while married to their beloved mother. Ray as *senex* is ironic. On the one hand, he blocks the young men from pairing off because his apparent betrayal of his marriage vows argues against marriage itself. On the other hand, the very fact of his dying brings each of the heroines into the lives of the heroes, and in this sense he serves as an enabler.

The marriages made in the trilogy create the new society we come to expect at the end of the romance novel. Roberts reaches beyond this core to the bonds that men and boys make with each other as they fight and argue, work side by side, ridicule one another, and close ranks against a common enemy. The ties in the extended Quinn family are made not only by the women marrying the men, but by the men pulling closer to each other as well. In addition, there is a new son/brother: Seth is adopted.

The Chesapeake Bay trilogy contains the paranormal element of Ray's ghost. *Hidden Riches* is a novel of romantic suspense. *Montana Sky* is about the women, set in that most western of Western settings, a ranch and the wilderness beyond it. Paranormal, romantic suspense, the Western— Roberts's facility with the subgenres of romance is masterful. She has an understanding of the possibilities of comedy that permit her to explore the grimmer side of human life—abuse, murder, mutilation, child abuse— while putting these in the context of characters who overcome these hardships and courting couples who find not just a resolution to the troubles that beset them, but joy and love.

There is more to Roberts, however; she is not just a writer of romance, although an extraordinary romance writer. Roberts writes comedy in both senses: in the sense of the romance novel and the novel that elicits laughter (the broader meaning of comedy). In her work, courtship is a matter of wills and wit. She writes of willful heroines and heroes acting wittily in a context of serious issues. Roberts has very finely calibrated control of the tone of her scenes. In *Montana Sky*, perhaps of the novels examined here the one with the widest range of tones, she employs regret, anger and rage in the scenes about the heroines' father; almost clownlike flippancy in the scenes about the heroines' mothers; verbal wit in the courtship scenes; and, finally, straightforward, sober reporting in the scenes about the murders. This facility marks Roberts as a master, not only of form, but of tone. Roberts is a consummate comedienne: she can play all the notes on the romance novel scale, as well as evoking, at will, the laughter of comedy more broadly understood.

CONCLUSION

The romance novel is old. The form is stable. Since the birth of the novel in English, the romance novel as I have defined it here—the story of the courtship and betrothal of one or more heroines—has provided a form for novels. What is more, the form has attracted writers of acknowledged genius—Richardson, Austen, Brontë, Trollope, and Forster to name just the ones examined here. Using the eight essential elements of the romance novel form as identified—society defined, the meeting, the barrier, the attraction, the declaration, the point of ritual death, the recognition, and the betrothal—doubled, amplified, diminished, echoed, made as comic or as serious as context required—these and other canonical romance writers have employed this form to free their heroines from the barrier and free them to choose the hero. Joy and happiness, both for the heroine and hero, and for the reader, follow. Trollope, Forster, Richardson, Brontë, and Austen are in the literary canon and on required reading lists; the romance novels they wrote were best sellers in their day.

The romance novel, as we have seen, is a species of comedy with the heroine displacing the hero as the central character. The great societal shifts toward affective individualism, property rights, and companionate marriage coincide with the rise of the novel in English. When Pamela, Elizabeth, Jane, Trollope's Lucy, and Forster's Lucy enact their courtships, they strive for, and win, affective individualism, property rights, and, above all, companionate marriage. The courtship novel, up to the twentieth century, is the story of the heroine's struggle for one or more of these great goals. The heroines are varied: a lady's maid (Pamela), the daughter of a gentleman of the landed gentry (Elizabeth), a governess (Jane), the penniless sister of a clergyman of extremely modest means (Trollope's Lucy), and the "muddled" young woman who comes into her inheritance mid-novel (Forster's Lucy). The courtships are complicated: there are two proposals in *Pamela*—B asks Pamela to be his mistress, then his wife. In *Pride and Prejudice*, Darcy proposes twice, the first time in a painful tone-deaf fashion to heroine Elizabeth who has a headache. There are three courtships and three proposals in *Jane Eyre*. In *Framley Parsonage*, there are two proposals; the second one from the hero's mother. In *Room with a View* the heroine is betrothed to the wrong man, whom she has trouble breaking up with, and whose name, appropriately enough, is Vyse; the second betrothal comes as a result of the hero's father's proposal on behalf of his son. The heroine's and hero's struggles in each these novels are not trivial yet the tone in these novels is often lighthearted. When the outcome is freedom and joy, and in the romance novel these are the outcome, the tone can be light, even if the issues are serious.

In the twentieth century the romance novel becomes the most popular form of the novel in North America. Rather than achieving affective individualism, property rights, and companionate marriage through courtship as the earlier heroines did, the twentieth-century heroine begins the novel with these in place. The book still focuses on her, but the hero steps forward to take an equal place with her. The novel chronicles the heroine's taming of the dangerous hero or her healing of the injured hero, or both. Taming and healing can work the other way as well. Heroines can need taming and healing, too.

Consider the heroes: Hull's sheik, Heyer's Worth, Stewart's Raoul, Dailey's Ráfaga, Krentz's Jared (either one of them), and Roberts's Ben. All of these men are dangerous. Each has a mythic component: sheik, earl, count, Robin Hood–like bandit, pirate, cowboy. They are Krentzian dangerous men and must be tamed. They are also very intelligent. Heroes are not stupidly dangerous.

Consider the corresponding heroines: Diana, Judith, Linda, Sheila, Olympia, and Willa. They are, respectively, an independently wealthy globe-trotting adventuress, a soon-to-be independently wealthy heiress, a governess, a college student, an entrepreneur/scholar, and a ranch manager. They do not have mythic components. If they are characters in a historical romance, they have independent means of support. If they are in a contemporary romance, they usually have jobs. Heroines in twentieth-century romance novels are not wispy, ephemeral girls sitting around waiting for the hero so that their lives can begin. They are intelligent and strong. They have to be. They have to tame the hero. They have to heal him. Or they have to do both.

In chronicling the courtship through the eight essential elements of the romance novel, the twentieth-century romance focuses on emotion. Literature that focuses on emotion and that ends happily veers towards the sentimental. Romance novels are, therefore, profoundly out of step with the prevailing contemporary high culture simply because of this emotional sensibility. My litany throughout this book has been that, despite their quality, popular romance novels of the twentieth century might appear on the *New York Times* Best Sellers List, but they are never reviewed in the newspaper itself. Other popular forms—mystery, science fiction, and horror—are. Romance novels are excluded, I suspect, because of an ignorance of the form itself and of the sensibility—the reliance on emotion—that suffuses the form. Emotion is suspect. Emotion is especially suspect when it is joyful, and every romance novel ends in joy. The practical critics of prevailing high culture ignore romances.

Academic critics, as we have seen, also condemn romances. I have already offered a defense of the romance, but would like to add one more observation here. The story of the courtship and betrothal of one or more heroines, is, finally, about freedom and joy. In the twentieth century, for the most part, romances are stories written by women and read by women. They feature women who have achieved the ends fostered by affective individualism, control over their own property, and companionate marriage. In other words, romance heroines make their own decisions, make their own livings, and choose their own husbands. I admit, unapologetically, that these values are profoundly bourgeois. I assert that they are the impossible dream of millions of women in many parts of the world today. To attack this very old genre, so stable in its form, so joyful in its celebration of freedom, is to discount, and perhaps even to deny, the most personal hopes of millions of women around the world.

WORKS CITED

NOVELS

Austen, Jane. *Pride and Prejudice*. 1813. Ed. R. W. Chapman. Oxford: Oxford University Press, 1932.

Brontë, Charlotte. *Jane Eyre*. 1847. Ed. Richard J. Dunn. New York: W. W. Norton, 1987.

Congreve, William. *Incognita: Or, Love and Duty Reconcil'd*. 1692. New York: Houghton Mifflin, 1922.

Dailey, Janet. *Ride the Thunder*. New York: Pocket, 1980.

———. *Something Extra*. 1975. Toronto: Harlequin, 1978.

———. *Sonora Sundown*. 1978. Toronto: Harlequin, 1993.

———. *Touch the Wind*. New York: Pocket, 1979.

Fielding, Henry. *An Apology for the Life of Mrs. Shamela Andrews*. 1741. Berkeley: University of California Press, 1953.

Forster, E. M. *A Room with a View*. 1908. New York: Bantam, 1988.

Heyer, Georgette. *A Civil Contract*. 1961. New York: G. P. Putnam's Sons, 1971.

———. *Lady of Quality*. 1972. New York: Bantam, 1973.

———. *Regency Buck*. 1935. New York: Bantam, 1967.

———. *Sylvester: or The Wicked Uncle*. 1957. New York: Jove, 1980.

Hull, E. M. *The Sheik*. 1919. Boston: Small, Maynard and Company, 1921.

Krentz, Jayne Ann. *Absolutely, Positively*. 1996. New York: Pocket, 1997.

———. *The Adventurer*. 1990. Don Mills, Canada: Mira, 1998.

———. *The Cowboy*. 1990. Don Mills, Canada: Mira, 1999.

———. [Amanda Quick]. *Deception*. New York: Bantam, 1993.

———. [Jayne Castle]. *Gentle Pirate*. New York: Dell, 1980.

———. *The Pirate*. 1990. Don Mills, Canada: Mira, 1998.

———. [Amanda Glass]. *Shield's Lady*. 1989. New York: Warner Books, 1996.

Mitchell, Margaret. *Gone with the Wind*. 1936. New York: Warner Books, 1993.

Richardson, Samuel. *Pamela; or, Virtue Rewarded*. 1740. Ed. Peter Sabor. London: Penguin, 1980.

Roberts, Nora. *Hidden Riches*. 1994. New York: Jove, 1995.

———. *Inner Harbor.* New York: Jove, 1999.

———. *Irish Thoroughbred.* 1981. New York: Silhouette, 1992.

———. *Loving Jack.* 1989. New York: Silhouette, 1989.

———. *Montana Sky.* 1996. New York: Jove, 1997.

———. *Rising Tides.* New York: Jove, 1998.

———. *Sea Swept.* New York: Jove, 1998.

Seidel, Kathleen Gilles. *Again.* New York: NAL/Onyx, 1994.

Stewart, Mary. *Airs Above the Ground.* 1965. New York: Fawcett, 1966.

———. *The Ivy Tree.* 1961. New York: William Morrow, 1961.

———. *My Brother Michael.* 1959. New York: William Morrow, 1966.

———. *Nine Coaches Waiting.* 1958. New York: William Morrow, 1959.

———. *Thunder on the Right.* 1957. New York: William Morrow, 1958.

Trollope, Anthony. *Framley Parsonage.* 1861. New York: Oxford University Press, 1980.

SECONDARY WORKS

Allott, Miriam J. *The Brontës: The Critical Heritage.* London: Routledge and Kegan Paul, 1974.

Andresen, Julie Tetel. "Postmodern Identity (Crisis): Confessions of a Linguistic Historiographer and Romance Writer." Kaler and Johnson-Kurek 173–86.

Anderson, Rachel. "E. M. Hull." Henderson 340–41.

———. *The Purple Heart Throbs: The Sub-literature of Love.* London: Hodder and Stoughton, 1974.

Baldwin, Kristen. "Stolen Kisses." *Entertainment Weekly* 15 August 1997: 10.

Barickman, Richard, Susan MacDonald, and Myra Stark. *Corrupt Relations: Dickens, Thackeray, Trollope, Collins, and the Victorian Sexual System.* New York: Columbia University Press, 1982.

Barlow, Linda and Jayne Ann Krentz. "Beneath the Surface: The Hidden Codes of Romance." Krentz, *Dangerous Men* 15–29.

Bettinotti, Julia and Pascale Noizet, eds. *Guimauves et fleurs d'oranger.* Quebec: Nuit Blanche (Études paralittéraires) 1995.

Bettinotti, Julia and Marie-Françoise Truel. "Lust and Dust." Mussell, *Paradoxa* 184–94.

Biddle, Wayne. *A Field Guide to Germs.* New York: Henry Holt, 1995.

Blais, Jacqueline and Anthony DeBarros. "Which Books Reached the Top?" *USA Today on the Web.* 19 December 2000. 9 January 2002. <http://www.usatoday.com/life/enter/books/book997.html>.

Bloom, Harold, ed. *The Brontës.* New York: Chelsea House, 1987.

Boone, Joseph Allen. *Tradition Counter Tradition: Love and the Form of Fiction.* Chicago: University of Chicago Press, 1987.

Booth, Wayne. *The Company We Keep: An Ethics of Fiction.* Berkeley: University of California Press, 1988.

————. *The Rhetoric of Fiction.* Chicago: University of Chicago Press, 1961.

Bowers, Toni O'Shaughnessy. "Sex, Lies, and Invisibility: Amatory Fiction from the Restoration to Mid-Century." Richetti 50–72.

Brown, Julia Prewitt. *Jane Austen's Novels: Social Change and Literary Form.* Cambridge, Mass.: Harvard University Press, 1979.

Byatt, A. S. "Georgette Heyer Is a Beter Novelist Than You Think." Fahnestock-Thomas 270–78.

Bywaters, Barbara. "Decentering the Romance: Jane Austen, Georgette Heyer, and Popular Romance Fiction." Fahnestock-Thomas 493–508.

Cadogan, Mary. *And Then Their Hearts Stood Still: An Exuberant Look at Romantic Fiction Past and Present.* London: Macmillan, 1994.

Carlton-Ford, Cynthia. "Intimacy Without Immolation: Fire in *Jane Eyre.*" McNees 342–51. (*Women's Studies* 15 (1988): 375–86.)

Cawelti, John G. *Adventure, Mystery, and Romance: Formula Stories as Art and Popular Culture.* Chicago: University of Chicago Press, 1976.

————. *The Six-Gun Mystique.* Bowling Green, Ohio: Bowling Green University Popular Press, n.d.

Caywood, Cynthia L. "*Pride and Prejudice* and the Belief in Choice: Jane Austen's Fantastical Vision." *Portraits of Marriage in Literature.* Ed. Anne C. Hargrove and Maurine Magliocco. Macomb: Western Illinois University Press, 1984. 31–54.

Chappel, Deborah Kaye. *American Romances: Narratives of Culture and Identity.* Ph.D. diss., Duke University, 1991. Ann Arbor: UMI, 1995. 9202485.

Cohn, Jan. *Romance and the Erotics of Property: Mass-Market Fiction for Women.* Durham, N.C.: Duke University Press, 1988.

Colmer, John. "Marriage and Personal Relations in Forster's Fiction." *E. M. Forster: Centenary Revaluations.* Ed. Judith Scherer Herz and Robert K. Martin. Toronto: University of Toronto Press, 1982. 113–23.

Cranny-Francis, Anne. *Feminist Fiction: Feminist Uses of Generic Fiction.* New York: St. Martin's Press, 1990.

Dailey, Janet. "The View from Janet Dailey." *Publisher's Weekly* 17 August 1984: 54.

Doody, Margaret Anne. *The True Story of the Novel.* New Brunswick, N.J.: Rutgers University Press, 1996.

Dubino, Jeanne. "The Cinderella Complex: Romance Fiction, Patriarchy, and Capitalism." *Journal of Popular Culture* 27 (1989): 103–18.

DuPlessis, Rachael Blau. *Writing Beyond the Ending: Narrative Strategies of Twentieth-Century Women Writers.* Bloomington: Indiana University Press, 1985.

Eagleton, Terry. *The Myths of Power: A Marxist Study of the Brontës.* New York: Barnes and Noble, 1975.

————. *The Rape of* Clarissa: *Writing, Sexuality, and Class Struggle in Samuel Richardson.* Minneapolis: University of Minnesota Press, 1982.

Eaves, T. C. Duncan and Ben D. Kimpel. *Samuel Richardson: A Biography.* Oxford: Clarendon, 1971.

Ellrich, Robert J. "Prolegomenon, or, Preliminary Musings to Make the Gentle Reader Think, or Fume, or Snort. In Which We Modestly Propose to Deal with the Origin, History, Nature, and Meaning of the Romance." Mussell, *Paradoxa* 269–85.

Fahnestock-Thomas, Mary. *Georgette Heyer: A Critical Retrospective.* Saraland, Ala.: PrinnyWorld Press, 2001.

Fallon, Eileen. *Words of Love: A Complete Guide to Romance Fiction.* New York: Garland, 1984.

Finkelstein, Bonnie Blumenthal. *Forster's Women: Eternal Differences.* New York: Columbia, 1975.

Folsom, Marcia McClintock. *Approaches to Teaching Austen's* Pride and Prejudice. New York: Modern Language Association of America, 1993.

Forster, E. M. *Aspects of the Novel.* New York: Harcourt Brace, 1927.

————. "Pessimism in Literature." *Albergo Empedocle and Other Writings.* Ed. George H. Thomson. New York: Liveright, 1971.

Foster, Shirley. "Female Januses: Ambiguity and Ambivalence Towards Marriage in Mid-Victorian Women's Fiction." *International Journal of Women's Studies* 6 (1983): 216–29.

Frenier, Mariam Darce. *Good-Bye Heathcliff: Changing Heroes, Heroines, Roles, and Values in Women's Category Romances.* New York: Greenwood Press, 1988.

Friedman, Alan Warren. "Forster and Death." *The Modernists.* Ed. Lawrence B. Gamache and Ian S. MacNiven. Rutherford, N.J.: Fairleigh Dickinson University Press, 1987. 103–13.

Frith, Gill. "Women, Writing, and Language: Making the Silences Speak." *Thinking Feminist: Key Concepts in Women's Studies.* Ed. Diane Richardson and Victoria Robinson. New York: Guilford Press, 1993.

Frye, Northrop. *Anatomy of Criticism.* 1957. New York: Atheneum, 1969.

————. *The Secular Scripture: A Study of the Structure of Romance.* Cambridge, Mass.: Harvard University Press, 1976.

Furbank, F. N. "The Personality of E. M. Forster." *Critical Essays on E. M. Forster.* Wilde 21–30. (*Encounter* 35 (1970): 61–68.)

Ganguly, Keya. "Alien[ated] Readers: Harlequin Romances and the Politics of Popular Culture." *Communication* 12 (1991): 129–50.

Garrett, Peter K. *The Victorian Multiplot Novel: Studies in Dialogical Form.* New Haven, Conn.: Yale University Press, 1980.

Gérin, Winifred. *Charlotte Brontë: The Evolution of Genius.* London: Oxford University Press, 1967.

Gilbert, Sandra and Susan Gubar. "A Dialogue of Self and Soul: Plain Jane's Progress." McNees 254–83. (*The Madwoman in the Attic: The Woman Writer and the Nineteenth-Century Literary Imagination.* New Haven, Conn.: Yale University Press, 1979. 336–71, 678–81.)

Glass, E. R. and A. Mineo. "Georgette Heyer and the Uses of Regency." *La Performance Del Testo.* Siena: Libreria Ticci, 1986. 283–92.

Goldman, William. *Adventures in the Screen Trade.* New York: Warner, 1983.

Greer, Germaine. *The Female Eunuch.* New York: McGraw-Hill, 1970.

Grescoe, Paul. *The Merchants of Venus: Inside Harlequin and the Empire of Romance.* Vancouver: Raincoast, 1996.

Guntrum, Suzanne Simmons. "Happily Ever After: The Ending as Beginning." Krentz 151–54.

Hagan, John. "Enemies of Freedom in *Jane Eyre.*" McNees 187–209. (*Criticism* 13 (1971): 351–76.)

Hall, N. John. *Trollope: A Biography.* Oxford: Oxford University Press, 1991.

Halperin, John. *The Life of Jane Austen.* Baltimore: Johns Hopkins University Press, 1984.

Harris, Jocelyn. "The Influence of Richardson on *Pride and Prejudice.*" Folsom 94–99.

———. *Samuel Richardson.* Cambridge: Cambridge University Press, 1987.

Hayes, Elizabeth T., ed. *Images of Persephone: Feminist Readings in Western Literature.* Gainesville: University Press of Florida, 1994.

Heath, Jeffrey. "Kissing and Telling: Turning Round in *A Room with a View.*" *Twentieth-Century Literature* 40 (1994): 393–433.

Henderson, Lesley, ed. *Twentieth-Century Romance and Historical Writers.* 2nd ed. Chicago: St. James Press, 1990.

Herz, Judith Scherer. "The Double Nature of Forster's Fiction: *A Room with a View* and *The Longest Journey.*" Wilde 84–94. (*English Literature in Transition* 21 (1978): 254–65.)

Hodge, Jane Aiken. *The Private World of Georgette Heyer.* London: Bodley Head, 1984.

Hofstadter, Beatrice K. "Popular Culture and the Romantic Heroine." *Literary Taste, Culture, and Mass Communication.* Vol. 7, *Content and Taste, Religion and Myth.* Ed. Peter Davison, Rolf Meyersoh, and Edward Shils. Cambridge: Chadwyck-Healey, 1978. 235–44.

Holcombe, Lee. *Wives and Property: Reform of the Married Women's Property Law in Nineteenth-Century England.* Toronto: University of Toronto Press, 1983.

Horwitz, Barbara. *"Pride and Prejudice* and *Framley Parsonage:* A Structural Resemblance." *Persuasions* 15 (1993) 32–36.

Hufton, Olwen. "Women, Work, and Family." *A History of Women in the West.* 5 vols. Ed. Georges Duby and Michelle Perrot. Vol. 3, *Renaissance and Enlightenment Paradoxes.* Ed. Natalie Zemon Davis and Arlette Farge. Cambridge, Mass.: Harvard University Press, 1993. 15–45.

Hughes, R. E. *"Jane Eyre:* The Unbaptized Dionysos." McNees 115–30. (*Nineteenth-Century Fiction* 18 (1964): 347–64.).

James, Henry. "Anthony Trollope." *The Trollope Critics.* Ed. N. John Hall. Totowa, N.J.: Barnes and Noble, 1981. (*Partial Portraits.* London: Macmillan, 1888. 97–133.).

James, P. D. "Emma Considered As a Detective Story." Jane Austen Society Annual General Meeting. Chawton, England, 18 July 1998. Appendix. *Time to Be in Earnest.* By P. D. James. New York: Knopf, 2000.

Janet Dailey Official Website. 2000. Janet Dailey. 27 July 2001. <http://janetdailey.com/>.

Jayne Ann Krentz/Amanda Quick—Official Website. 2002. 16 July 2002. <http://www.jayneannkrentz.com/>.

Kaler, Anne K. "Conventions of Captivity in Romance Novels." Kaler and Johnson-Kurek 86–99.

Kaler, Anne K. and Rosemary Johnson-Kurek, eds. *Romantic Conventions.* Bowling Green, Ohio: Bowling Green State University Popular Press, 1999.

Kincaid, James R. *The Novels of Anthony Trollope.* Oxford: Oxford University Press, 1977.

Kinkead-Weekes, Mark. *Samuel Richardson: Dramatic Novelist.* Ithaca, N.Y.: Cornell University Press, 1973.

Kinsale, Laura. "The Androgynous Reader." Krentz 31–44.

Krentz, Jayne Ann, ed. *Dangerous Men and Adventurous Women: Romance Writers on the Appeal of the Romance.* Philadelphia: University of Pennsylvania Press, 1992.

———. "Introduction." Krentz 1–9.

————. "Trying To Tame the Romance: Critics and Correctness." Krentz 107–14.

Linke, Gabriele. "Contemporary Mass Market Romances as National and International Culture." Mussell, *Paradoxa* 193–212.

Locke, John. *Two Treatises of Government.* Ed. Peter Laslett. Cambridge: Cambridge University Press, 1970.

McAleer, Joseph. *Passion's Fortune: The Story of Mills and Boon.* Oxford: Oxford University Press, 1999.

Macfarlane, Alan. *Marriage and Love in England: Modes of Reproduction 1300–1840.* Oxford: Blackwell, 1986.

McGrath, Joan. "Georgette Heyer." Henderson 316–17.

McKillop, Alan Dugald. *Samuel Richardson: Printer and Novelist.* Chapel Hill: University of North Carolina Press, 1936.

————. "Wedding Bells for Pamela." *Philological Quarterly* 29 (April 1949): 323–25.

McNees, Eleanor, ed. *The Brontë Sisters: Critical Assessments.* Vol. 3. The Banks, East Sussex: Helm Information, 1996.

Modleski, Tania. *Loving with a Vengeance: Mass-Produced Fantasies for Women.* Hamden, Conn.: Archon, 1982. Chapter 2, "The Disappearing Act: Harlequin Romances," reprinted in *Gender Language and Myth: Essays on Popular Narrative.* Ed. Glenwood Irons. Toronto: University of Toronto Press, 1992.

Moglen, Helene. *Charlotte Brontë: The Self Conceived.* New York: W. W. Norton, 1976.

Morgan, Susan. "Intelligence in *Pride and Prejudice.*" *Jane Austen's* Pride and Prejudice. Ed. Harold Bloom. New York: Chelsea House, 1987. 85–105.

Mudrick, Marvin. "Irony as Discrimination: *Pride and Prejudice.*" *Jane Austen: A Collection of Critical Essays.* Ed. Ian Watt. Englewood Cliffs, N.J.: Prentice-Hall, 1963. 76–97.

Mussell, Kay. *Fantasy and Reconciliation: Contemporary Formulas of Women's Romance Fiction.* Westport, Conn.: Greenwood Press, 1984.

————. "Mary Stewart." Henderson 618–19.

————. "*Paradoxa* Interview with Jayne Ann Krentz." Mussell, *Paradoxa* 46–57.

————. "*Paradoxa* Interview with Nora Roberts." Mussell, *Paradoxa* 154–63.

————, ed. *Paradoxa* 3 (1997): 3–309.

————.*Women's Gothic and Romantic Fiction: A Reference Guide.* Westport, Conn.: Greenwood Press, 1981.

Nestor, Pauline. *Charlotte Brontë's Jane Eyre.* New York: St. Martin's Press, 1992.

Newman, Karen. "Can This Marriage Be Saved: Jane Austen Makes Sense of an Ending." *ELH* 50 (1983): 693–710.

Onorato, Kathy. Fax to the author. Ridgewood, N.J.: Creative Promotions. 31 October 2001.

Perkins, David. *Is Literary History Possible?* Baltimore: Johns Hopkins University Press, 1992.

Rabine, Leslie W. *Reading the Romantic Heroine: Text, History, Ideology.* Ann Arbor: University of Michigan Press, 1985.

Radford, Jean, ed. *The Progress of Romance: The Politics of Popular Fiction.* New York: Routledge and Kegan Paul, 1986.

Radway, Janice A. *Reading the Romance: Women, Patriarchy, and Popular Literature.* 2nd ed. Chapel Hill: University of North Carolina Press, 1991

Raub, Patricia. "Issues of Passion and Power in E. M. Hull's *The Sheik.*" *Women's Studies* 21 (1992): 119–28.

Reed, Joseph W., Jr. "A New Samuel Richardson Manuscript." *Yale University Library Gazette* 42 (1968): 215–31.

Reeve, Clara. *The Progress of Romance.* 1785. New York: Facsimile Text Society, 1930.

Regan, Nancy. "Janet Dailey." Henderson 158–60.

Richetti, John, ed. *The Columbia History of the British Novel.* New York: Columbia University Press, 1994.

Romance Writers of America. *Website of the Romance Writers of America.* 1997. <http://www.rwanational.com/> (15 January 1998).

————. *Welcome to Romance Writers of America.* 2002. <http://www.rwanational.com/> (15 July 2002).

Rosecrance, Barbara. *Forster's Narrative Vision.* Ithaca, N.Y.: Cornell University Press, 1982.

Ross, Deborah. *The Excellence of Falsehood: Romance, Realism, and Women's Contribution to the Novel.* Lexington: University of Kentucky Press, 1991.

Segal, Erich. *The Death of Comedy.* Cambridge, Mass.: Harvard University Press, 2001.

Seidel, Kathleen Gilles. "Judge Me by the Joy I Bring." Krentz 159–77.

Shaffer, Julie. *Confronting Conventions of the Marraige Plot: The Dialogic Discourse of Jane Austen's Novels.* Ph.D. diss., University of Washington, 1989. Ann Arbor: UMI, 1995. 9006995.

————. "Not Subordinate: Empowering Women in the Marriage Plot." *Criticism* 34 (1992): 51–73.

Silhouette Publishers. "Editorial Guidelines." <http://www.author-link.com/> (5 June 1997).

Smith, Jennifer Crusie. "Postmodern Identity (Crisis): Confessions of a Linguistic Historiographer and Romance Writer." Kaler and Johnson-Kurek 173–86.

Snitow, Ann Barr. "Mass Market Romance: Pornography for Women Is Different." *Radical History Review* 20 (1979): 141–61.

Starr, G. A. "Sentimental Novels of the Later Eighteenth Century. Richetti. 181–98.

Staves, Susan. *Married Women's Separate Property in England, 1660–1833.* Cambridge, Mass.: Harvard University Press, 1990.

Stevenson, Florence. "The Regency Romance." Fallon 31–50.

Stevenson, John Allen. "'A Geometry of His Own': Richardson and the Marriage-Ending." *Studies in English Literature* 26 (1986): 469–83.

Stone, Lawrence. *The Family, Sex, and Marriage in England 1500–1800.* New York: Harper and Row, 1977.

Tennyson, Alfred. "Ulysses." *The Norton Anthology of English Literature.* Vol. 2. Ed. M. H. Abrams. New York: Norton, 1974. 1024–25.

Thurston, Carol. *The Romance Revolution: Erotic Novels for Women and the Quest for a New Sexual Identity.* Urbana: University of Illinois Press, 1987.

Tomalin, Claire. *Jane Austen: A Life.* New York: Knopf, 1997.

Tompkins, Jane. *West of Everything: The Inner Life of Westerns.* London: Oxford, 1992.

Trollope, Anthony. *An Autobiography.* London: Oxford University Press, 1950.

Utter, Robert Palfrey and Gwendolyn Bridges Needham. *Pamela's Daughters.* New York: Macmillan, 1936.

Wagner, Philip C., Jr. "Phaethon, Persephone, and *A Room with a View.*" *Comparative Literature Studies* 27 (1990): 275–84.

Watt, Ian. *The Rise of the Novel: Studies in Defoe, Richardson, and Fielding.* Berkeley: University of California Press, 1964.

Weisser, Susan Ostrov. "The Wonderful-Terrible Bitch Figure in Harlequin Novels." *Feminist Nightmares: Women at Odds.* Ed. Susan Ostrov Weisser and Jennifer Fleischner. New York: New York University Press, 1994.

White, Laura Mooneyham. "Jane Austen and the Marriage Plot: Questions of Persistence." *Jane Austen and Discourses of Feminism.* Ed. Devoney Looser. New York: St. Martin's Press, 1995. 71–86.

Wiesenfarth, Joseph. "The Case of *Pride and Prejudice.*" *Studies in the Novel* 16 (1984): 261–73.

Wilde, Alan, ed. *Critical Essays on E. M. Forster.* Boston: G. K. Hall, 1985.

Wright, John W. *The Universal Almanac 1996.* Kansas City: Andrews and McMeel, 1995.

"The Year in Books." *USA Today on the Web* 20. December 1999. 9 January 2002 <http://www.usatoday.com/life/enter/books/book662.htm>.

Zidle, Abby. "From Bodice-Ripper to Baby-Sitter: The New Hero in Mass-Market Romance." Kaler and Johnson-Kurek 23–34.

INDEX

ACKNOWLEDGMENTS

My husband, Ed Regis, listened to me talk about romance, helped me find my arguments, read portions of the manuscript, and compiled the index. He cleaned the house and kept my car running. He walked the dog and put up with a distracted spouse. I thank him for his support and dedicate this book to him.

A number of people at McDaniel College helped in various ways: LeRoy Panek suggested the project and Hope Jordan did extensive bibliographical research financed by the Faculty Development Committee. Ginny Story and Bobby Anderson kept me organized when the manuscript distracted me from my on-campus duties. Without a sabbatical leave, Part IV would still be unwritten. The interlibrary loan staff at Hoover Library zealously tracked down hard-to-find materials. I am lucky to be part of this academic community.

Patricia Smith of the University of Pennsylvania Press sought me out to encourage my writing a history of the romance, and Kay Mussell of American University generously read the manuscript. Both of these women strengthened this book by permitting me to tap their extensive knowledge of the twentieth-century romance novel. I thank them both.

Washington Romance Writers, a local chapter of Romance Writers of America, graciously permitted a literary critic to address several of their annual retreats. I am especially indebted to the late Nancy Richards Akers for inviting me to West Virginia to the first such gathering, which she helped organize. Many of the ideas in this book were tried out in the talks that I gave at Harpers Ferry.

Kathleen Gilles Seidel helped in the formulation of many of this book's ideas, and her understanding of the romance from the inside out, as a romance writer, as well as from the outside in, as a literary critic, has been a rich resource, generously shared. The term "barrier" is hers. Her comments on an early draft strengthened the manuscript. Her support and friendship have been invaluable, indeed, indispensable.